Current English Grammar

Sylvia Chalker

Akna Rugg

MACMILLAN

First published 1984
Reprinted 1986, 1987, 1989, 1990

Published by MACMILLAN EDUCATION LTD
London and Basingstoke
*Associated companies and representatives in Accra,
Auckland, Delhi, Dublin, Gaborone, Hamburg, Harare,
Hong Kong, Kuala Lumpur, Lagos, Manzini, Melbourne,
Mexico City, Nairobi, New York, Singapore, Tokyo.*

ISBN 0–333–35025–1

Printed in Hong Kong

Contents

(References following each item are to section numbers.)

Abbreviations

A	adverbial		**lex**	lexical verb
act	active		**mass**	mass noun
adj	adjective *or* adjectival		**n**	noun
ADV	advanced grammar		**neg**	negative
adv	adverb		**nom**	nominal
Am Eng	American English		**non assr**	non-assertive
appo	apposition		**non defg**	non-defining
assr	assertive		**non fin**	non-finite
attrib	attributive		**NP**	noun phrase
aux	auxiliary			
			O *or* **obj**	object
Br Eng	British English		**OC**	complement of object
			op	operator
C	complement			
comp	comparative		**P**	past
condit	conditional		**pasv**	passive
conj	conjunction		**perf**	perfect
co-ord	co-ordination *or* co-ordinating		**pers**	person *or* personal
count	countable (noun)		**pl**	plural
			PP	prepositional phrase
def	definite		**pred**	predicative
defg	defining		**predet**	predeterminer
det	determiner		**prep**	preposition(al)
DO	direct object		**pres**	present
dir sp	direct speech		**pro**	pronoun
			prog	progressive
ed	past simple			
ellip	ellipsis		**qu**	question
en	past participle			
			reg	regular
fin	finite		**rel**	relative
fml	formal (formal language contrasted with informal)		**rep sp**	reported speech
fut	future		**S**	subject
			SC	complement of subject
gen	genitive		**simp**	simple
			sing	singular
imp	imperative		**subjc**	subjunctive
imperf	imperfect		**subord**	subordinate
indef	indefinite		**superl**	superlative
infin	infinitive			
infml	informal		**trans**	transitive
interj	interjection			
intrans	intransitive		**V** *or* **v**	verb
IO	indirect object		**VP**	verb phrase
irreg	irregular		**vs**	versus, as opposed to
			wh-word	*who, whoever* etc (including *how*)

& symbols

< >	example sentences or phrases
( )	around a letter or letters — add as appropriate; eg <the keen(er) boys>. Around a word — the whole word is optional; eg <He says (that) he understands.>
/ /	phonetic symbols; eg *says* /sez/
/	the words on either side are — alternatives as appropriate; eg *a/an, he/they, was/were* or optional; eg <She *says/said* she is coming.>
[ ]	follows an example — to explain grammar; eg [manner adverbial] *or* to explain meaning; eg <We are *just leaving.*> [at this moment]
—	omission — ZERO; eg <__ Furniture like this is expensive.> *or* ellipsis; eg <the man __ you met>
←→	the words on either side should be read as linked together (see introduction)
*	the word(s) or sentence following is unacceptable; eg <* ten clothes>
?	dubious; eg <. . . when he arrived> (? had arrived)
WRITE	any verb printed in CAPITAL letters means that verb in any of its parts (eg *write, writes, wrote, writing, written*) as appropriate
DO DID DONE	parts of the verb *do* only are used to indicate that the corresponding tense of any verb may be used as appropriate; eg I would DO if you DID

6

INTRODUCTION

1. What grammar is and is not

There are two popular misconceptions about grammar. One is that the 'rules' are somehow there in the language more or less ready formulated, waiting to be dug up. According to this view there can only be one 'correct' solution to any grammatical problem. Unfortunately it is not like this. There are many different ways of interpreting and organising the data. Of course, some explanations are more satisfactory than others, but not even word classes are clear-cut or self-evident, while what is grammatically possible and what is grammatically unacceptable often converge in an uncertain grey area.

A second misconception is that the rules of grammar — wherever they come from — are arbitrary. Grammar, it is supposed, consists of meaningless rules and equally inexplicable exceptions.

The current emphasis on teaching English as communication is good. But the danger of such a method is that the grammar may be presented as a collection of fragments. Just as too prescriptive an approach may emphasise rules for their own sake, so an extreme communicative approach may conceal the real nature of these rules. Both approaches can fail to show that the grammar itself, though not perhaps logical in the strict sense, is nonetheless both systematic and meaningful.

2. The purpose of CEG

The main aim of *Current English Grammar* is to show that although many features of English can be variously interpreted, and the language cannot all be neatly pigeon-holed, nevertheless the grammar is an interlocking system in which the grammatical choices themselves contribute to the communicative meaning.

Current English Grammar (CEG) is therefore concerned primarily with syntax — what most people consider to be the core of grammar. But meaning is discussed throughout — both grammatical meaning and the meaning of many individual words. For example, chapter 6 seeks to show how the many apparently unconnected communicative uses of modals relate in each case to one basic meaning. Prepositions are similarly analysed. At a discourse level *CEG* illustrates connecters in context; it also shows how ellipsis and substitution work across sentences. Phonology and intonation are discussed when this is particularly relevant to the grammar. For example, usage of *a* or *an* in both speech and writing depends on phonological criteria.

The language described in *CEG* is standard modern British English, with an occasional note on American English. The examples are fairly neutral in style, though particularly *formal*, *informal*, or *rare* usage is indicated. Authentic examples from contemporary written and spoken English have been used where possible.

3. Terminology

CEG is based on current mainstream grammar and uses terminology that is widely used in course books for foreign learners. A special feature of *CEG* however is that it defines its terms and also indicates the other main meanings that are sometimes attached to the same terms. (See for example 10.20 where the different meanings of the term *phrasal verb* are discussed).

A number of labels not adopted by *CEG*, but still used in textbooks, will be found in the index. For example, *continuous* in the index has a reference to 4.3. If readers refer to this they will see why *CEG* prefers the term *progressive*, and if they check the index at that point they will find further references. Other labels not used in the text at all may also be found in the index — for example a reader looking for *contracted forms* is referred immediately to *short forms*. But inevitably some readers are going to look for some terms in vain, while others may wonder if all the terms used are essential. The question of terminology is not an easy one. I have tried not to burden the text with difficult linguistic jargon; on the other hand, a concept like *noun phrase* needs to be distinguished from *noun* — and *noun phrase* is a well-established term which many readers will be familiar with. Substituting some other wording or avoiding the term altogether would probably be more confusing.

4. Organisation

CEG is arranged so that it can be used for easy reference by anyone with an elementary knowledge of a few traditional labels.

Chapter 1 outlines the basics of the English language; the structure and word order of simple sentences, and the classification of words into word classes (parts of speech). It also explains such important concepts connected with sentence structure as *theme, comment and focus.*

Chapters 2-10 deal with the different word classes one by one. The familiar classification and names are largely retained, but the widely accepted term *determiner* is used to cover the articles and those pronoun-related words that more old-fashioned grammars describe as adjectives. Four whole chapters are devoted to verbs — their forms, the meaning of these forms, and the relationship of different kinds of verbs to different sentence patterns. The now orthodox abandonment of the idea of an English 'future tense' will not, I hope, worry any readers. There is little justification for singling out *will* and *shall* for this role, and a lot of confusion has resulted from doing so. Once one accepts that the English tense system is binary, and that *will* and *shall* are just two of the modals, the whole verbal system and its meaning appears much neater and more understandable.

Chapter 11 deals with conjunctions, which lead on naturally to compound and complex sentences.

Chapter 12 deals briefly with ellipsis and substitution. The terms may be unfamiliar to some readers, but the concepts will not be. Once again, I hope that, if readers see for instance that question-tags <Couldn't he?> or short responses like <So does Susan> are examples of a much more generalised feature of English grammar, they will gain a deeper appreciation of the English language.

5. Cross-references

Every section of *CEG* is meant to be self-explanatory, but since grammatical items are mutually interdependent, the text is extensively cross-referenced to particularly relevant sections. Readers who wish however to pursue an item more fully should check for further references in the index.

6. The tables

A special feature of *CEG* are the many tables. These are of various kinds but all are meant to be read initially in conjunction with the explanations that usually follow them. Once these are understood, the tables constitute a quick summary at a glance of the grammatical usage under discussion. For example, the chart at 2.5 summarises the main rules about mass and count nouns. Other tables contain example sentences illustrating particular words or grammatical items in context. Readers should notice that only some tables are substitution tables — that is, tables where any item in a particular section of the first column can be followed by any item from the corresponding section of the second column and so on. For example in 3.3. the second section of the first column overlaps both A and B in the second column. Thus one can say <this dollar, that story, this money>, but not <*less dollar>, since 3 and A do not overlap. More conventional substitution tables with complete sentences are exemplified at 3.10 where one can say <What is that? Who are those people?> but not <*What are that?> or <*These are my mother and father.>

Other tables use a linking symbol (←→) to show that although all the items in each column have something in common, they are not full substitution tables and meaningful sentences are only to be obtained by following the links. In 7.27 for example, the first column is for subject and verb, the second for object, and the third for bare infinitive. But the linking sign prevents the production of <*Please help me snow there in the summer.>

7. Two important concepts

Two very general concepts in modern linguistics (form and function, and markedness) are explained here, since they underlie much of *CEG*.

1) **Form and function.** At its simplest, the concept of form and function is straightforward, as can be illustrated with a simple sentence:
     <People in glass houses shouldn't throw stones.>
In form, *people, glass, houses* and *stones* are nouns (even though these particular nouns are not uniquely noun-like — see 2.2). In function, three of them also have typically noun-like functions. *People* functions as the subject of the sentence, *stones* functions as object, and *houses* fills a typically noun-like position after a preposition. But with *glass* there is a mismatch between its noun form (contrast adjectives *glassy* or *glazed*) and its descriptive function before the noun, which is more like the role of an adjective. So we see that the same class of words (eg nouns) may have more than one function, and that the same function (eg adjectival) may be carried out by more than one word class.

Similar distinctions between form and function can be made at other levels. For example, *in glass houses* is a prepositional phrase in form. Its function here is adjectival (post-modifying *people*). But elsewhere it could be an adverbial of place <People shouldn't live in glass houses.>

The term function is also widely used today with the meaning of communicative function. Thus <Isn't that easy> (a question in form) might function communicatively as persuasion, disapproval and so forth.

Notice that the word formal may be used in contrast to functional. But in *CEG* the label *formal* is used with its formality meaning — that is *formal* versus *informal*.

2) **Marked and unmarked.** The term *unmarked* is used of the base or neutral term in a group of related items:

a) Grammatically we can say that the word *house* is unmarked by inflection and *houses* is marked. This means that the noun *house* is neutral as to number. It often is singular, of course, but it is not marked for singular or plural for example in *house-agents,* whereas *houses* is always plural and therefore marked. Similarly the verbal form *throw* is unmarked while *throws, threw, thrown, throwing* are marked for person, time and so on. Verbs may be further marked for voice and aspect (see 4.3.).

b) The term *marked* is also applied to word order when an unusual order is used for special effect <Stones, people in glass houses shouldn't throw.> (1.4 and 1.9.)

c) Semantically the concept of markedness applies to certain sets of words. For example *horse* is unmarked as to sex, but *mare* is marked for feminine and *stallion* for masculine.

8. Postscript

No one can write a grammar book today without an extensive debt to some of our leading modern grammarians, and in my own case I have been particularly influenced by the work of Quirk, Greenbaum, Leech & Svartvik, M.A.K. Halliday and F.R. Palmer. My analysis of prepositions in chapter 10 leans heavily on the work of D.C. Bennett, while elsewhere in *CEG* readers will doubtless find many unacknowledged borrowings.

I hope however that I have shed some light myself on a number of vexing problems that have long puzzled teachers and students. But — to echo R.W. Zandvoort — 'a handbook is only a point of departure'.

Grammar is both fascinating and challenging. I would like to think that the users of *CEG* will set out on their own paths of discovery.

S.C.

1. BASICS

What is a sentence?

1.1   Traditionally the basic unit of language for the purpose of analysing its grammar is the sentence. But this immediately presents a problem: what is a sentence? There is no easy definition but, roughly speaking, an English sentence must have
(a) a subject (often a noun) that 'governs' the verb
(b) a finite verb (that is, a verb with tense).
The apparent exception to this is the imperative, where usually the subject is implied rather than stated (1.3).

It is important to distinguish between a sentence and an utterance. In connected speech or writing, there are plenty of utterances which fail conditions (a) and (b) above but which are grammatically acceptable. They are clearly signalled as complete in spoken English by intonation, and in written language by punctuation:
    <Oh dear! Not at all. Thanks. O.K. Coming!   Meaning what?
    In London. What a pity! But now to more serious matters.
    To be honest, no!>

1.2 Simple, compound and complex sentences

One important way of analysing sentences is by the number of clauses they contain:

A **Simple sentences.** As defined above, a simple sentence contains one subject and one finite verb. This definition is also the traditional definition of a clause, but modern grammar has widened the term 'clause' to include structures with non-finite verbs and also some verbless structures (11.7). Nevertheless, the traditional relationship between a simple sentence and a clause remains, if we qualify it: a simple sentence is a finite clause that stands alone.

B **Compound sentences.** In a sentence containing more than one clause, if the clauses are of equal importance (joined by *and, or, but,* etc) they are said to be co-ordinated and the sentence is called *compound* (11.5).

C **Complex sentences.** Alternatively, a sentence may contain a main clause and one or more subordinate clauses (introduced by *if, when, although,* etc). These sentences are called *complex* (11.5).

Compound-complex sentences also occur. This chapter deals with simple sentences — ie finite clause structure.

1.3 Statements, questions, commands, exclamations

A	**Statements** (Declarative) usually with the word-order *subject + verb* = **S + V**	*I saw a flying saucer.* *He has seen a flying saucer.* *He could have seen one.*
B	**Questions** (Interrogative) normally with inversion of the first auxiliary or modal — called the *operator* or **op** — and the subject (4.8).	*Has he seen a flying saucer?* *Could he have seen one?* *Why are you waving your arms?* *Who are you waving to?*

DO is used if there is no other operator: **(wh-word) + op + S + V** etc.	*Did you see a flying saucer?* *What do you believe?*
There is no inversion when a *wh-* word is the subject: **wh- word + V.**	*Who saw a flying saucer?* *What has happened?*
C **Commands** (Imperative) normally without subject unless it is needed for emphasis or to avoid ambiguity.	*Look!* *Wait a minute!* *You look!* *Everybody look!*
D **Exclamations** **What (+ adj) + noun** } **+ S + V** **How + adj./adv.**	*What a (strange) story he told us!* *How strange it all is!* *How oddly he behaved!*

Simple sentences are of three main types: statements, questions and commands formed as shown in A-C. Structurally we also have a fourth distinct type, exclamations. These are introduced by *What* + (optional adj) + noun or by *How* + an adjective or adverb (D). Not themselves a very important class, exclamations are not to be confused with
(a) the minor class of interjections, which are also usually signalled in writing by exclamation marks:
      <Alas!> <Ouch!>
(b) other exclamatory utterances and semi-fixed expressions that do not qualify as complete sentences (1.1 above):
      <Oh dear!>
Verbless utterances with initial *What* or *How* may however be regarded as ellipted versions of exclamations (D):
      <*What a strange story* (it was)!>

1.4 Communicative functions of sentence types

If we think of the social role of language, we can say that language is broadly concerned with giving and requiring information, and with offering and requiring 'things' or actions. Unfortunately, there is only a partial correspondence between the four principal sentence types (1.3) and these four major communicative functions.

Statements and questions in general correspond to the first pair, while commands often require some non-verbal response:
      <Look at this.> <Please pass the salt.>
But 'non-verbal' giving or offering, the fourth communicative role in this kind of analysis, has no specific sentence type and is often realised by commands or by questions:
      <Have another!> <Would you like another?>

Mismatch between sentence form and function		
Form	*Function*	
Statements	Interrogative	You don't ´like it?
	Imperative	You will ˋdo as you're told.
	Exclamatory	She ˋis a lovely girl.
Questions	Declarative	What's the ˎpoint! [= There is no point.]
	Imperative	ˋWill you be ˎquiet!
	Exclamatory	ˋIsn't it a marvellous day!
Commands	Interrogative	Everybody ´look? [Do you mean that?]
	Exclamatory	Everybody ˇlook! [You can't mean that!]
Exclamations	Interrogative	How oddly he be´haved? [Is that what you said?]

In practice there is a much greater discrepancy between sentence forms and functions than the analysis above the table suggests. The table indicates a few other possibilities: statement forms are often used to ask questions or give commands; question forms are frequently used to make statements or comments or give commands. And any sentence form can have an interrogative or exclamatory function if the speaker repeats what someone else has said.

1.5 Negative sentences

A	**Negative statements** *not* (usually abbreviated to *n't*) is placed after the operator. As with the interrogative, DO is used if there is no other operator: **S + op + n't + V**	*He didn't see a flying saucer.* *He has not seen one.* *He couldn't have seen one.*
B	**Negative questions** Negative *n't* is combined with interrogative inversion: **(wh- word) + op + n't + S + V**	*Didn't he see one?* *Hasn't he seen one?* *Couldn't he have seen one?* *Why couldn't he have seen one?* *Didn't he really see one after all?* *Didn't someone prove their existence a few years ago?*
C	**Negative commands**	*Don't look! Do not look!* *Don't you look!* *Nobody look!*

The three main sentence types of 1.3 (but not exclamations) are negated as shown. (For a formal alternative to B, see 4.8). Negative questions imply that either (a) the speaker now tends to believe that something he previously thought true is/was not in fact so, or (b) he is still clinging to the belief that something is/was so, despite contrary evidence (ie — he is hoping for a positive answer.)

Context and/or intonation usually makes the meaning clear.

Negative commands (C) normally require the operator DO + *not* (*n't*). Notice the word order when subject *you* is present. (See also 4.9).

Instead of using *not* in the verb phrase (VP), negation can also be marked by

(a) adverbs: *never* and *nowhere* and semi-negatives: *hardly, rarely, scarcely*

(b) determiner: *no*

(c) pronouns: *none, nothing, nobody* etc.

In general, everything after the negative word is negated, so position affects the scope of the negation. Hence the difference (9.38) between:

<*I haven't still got the keys.*> [I haven't got them now, though I had them once.] and

<*I still haven't got the keys.*> [I have never had them.]

1.6 Questions

A	**Yes/No questions**	Is Mark listening? Is Mark listening carefully? Does Mark ever listen?

B	**Tag questions**	
	1 positive statement + negative tag	He usually listens, *doesn't he?*
		You are listening, *aren't you?*
	2 negative statement + positive tag	He isn't listening, *is he?*
		He can't hear me, *can he?*
	3 positive statement + positive tag	You're listening, *are you?*
		He can, *can he?*
C	**Alternative questions**	Is he listening or talking?
D	*Wh-* **questions**	Who is listening?
		What is Mark doing?
		Why isn't he listening?

Question types can be considered in relation both to form and meaning.

A **Yes/No questions** These are so called because they can be answered by a simple 'Yes' or 'No'. They begin with an operator. They are also called 'truth questions' or 'open questions'. They ask for confirmation or denial of the statement they contain:

<Is Mark listening?> [Mark is listening. True or not true?]

The speaker has an open mind about the answer.

With a longer sentence there can be some uncertainty as to whether the truth being questioned is the whole statement or only a part of it, such as the final adverbial:

<Is Mark listening carefully?> [I know Mark is listening, but is he listening *carefully*?]

In spoken English, different words may be stressed to show that one particular word is being queried.

B **Tag questions** These are questions added on to statements, and in form they consist of operator only (not the whole verb phrase) + the subject, which must be a pronoun. Thus, as with ordinary questions and negatives, DO may be needed. The normal patterns are (1) and (2) in the table above.

In spoken English, the tags are commonly spoken on a falling tone (like a statement rather than an open question). This indicates that the speaker assumes his listener agrees with the main statement and he is just seeking confirmation:

<That's `true, `isn't it?>

A tag on a rising tone is more like an open question; the speaker is doubtful and seeks information (Appendix 2):

<That's `true, ,isn't it?>

Notice the irregular *am/aren't* and *let's/shall*:

<I *am* silly, *aren't I?*>

<*Let's* go, *shall we?*>

Positive statements plus positive tags (3 above) are possible, but they often express disbelief, sarcasm, surprise etc. Negative plus negative tag is *rare*.

Tags can also appear with what are structurally commands:

<Come early, won't you?> [invitation]

<Hold this for me, can't you?> [command]

The tags here show that *you* is the unexpressed subject of a command.

C **Alternative questions** These imply that one of the two (or more) possibilities suggested must be true. They are normally spoken on a final fall. They expect one and only one of the suggested answers.

14

<'Is he listening or talking?' 'He's talking'.>

Spoken with a final rising tone, such a structure could be an open question, to which 'Yes' or 'No' could be a possible answer.

<'Would you like a cup of tea or´coffee?' 'No thanks'.> [I don't want a drink.]

D **Wh- questions** The term 'wh- questions' covers all questions beginning with *Why, When, Where,* etc and *How.* They are sometimes called 'content questions' because they require some substance or content in the reply. They do not query the truth of the statement, but they ask for details about a part of it. *Why* questions are possibly the most common type of negative *wh-* question.

Assertion and non-assertion

1.7

Assertive forms	
Statements	I have *some* news for you.
	It's *a long way.*
	He's got *a lot of* money.
Questions	Is there *some* news? [Expecting the answer 'Yes']
(neg)	Isn't there *some* news by now? [Surely there is.]

Non-assertive forms	
Statements	*Any* news would be better than this waiting.
Questions	Is there *any* news?
	How *far* is it?
	Has he got *much* money?
Negatives	There isn't *any* news.
	I don't know *any* of the other students.
	It isn't *far.*
	He hasn't *much.*
	Isn't there *any* news? [I hoped there would be.]

Negative forms	
Statements	There is *no* news.
	He has *none.*
	I know *none* of them.
Questions	Is there *no* news? [I'm surprised.]

Old course books often state that the *some* series of words are used in positive [affirmative] statements, and the *any* series in negative statements and in questions. This kind of explanation means that the common use of *some* in questions and other *some/any* usages have to be described as exceptions. A better explanation of the *some/any* distinction is in terms of assertion and non-assertion. Positive declarative statements usually make assertions and therefore use the *some* series, so *not* <*I have any news for you> although *any* forms meaning identity rather than quantity (3.13) are possible in some kinds of statement. Questions may be non-assertive (ie open) or assertive (ie expecting a positive answer) — hence both *any* and *some* are common.

It is important to distinguish between non-assertive and negative forms. Negative statements either use *not* plus a non-assertive form:
    <There isn't *any* news.>
or a negative form (without negating the verb):
    <There is *no* news.>

The so-called double negative (*not* plus a negative form) occurs in dialect, but is ungrammatical in standard English. <*There isn't no news.> <*Nobody knows nothing.>

Unusually, a verb plus *not* may be followed by an assertive form. The meaning is either a contradiction of a previous remark, or only part of the predicate is negated:
    <I`don't know some of the students in my class.> [It is *not* true to say I know some of them.]
    <I don't knowˇsome of the students in my class:> [I don't know *some*, but I do know others.]

In addition to the three-fold *some/any/no* series, there are several pairs of words which tend to follow similar patterns of assertive/non-assertive usage. Common words that are mainly non-assertive include *far*, *much* and modal *need*. (See index entry for NON-ASSERTIVE.)

Subject and predicate

1.8   According to the definition in 1.1, a sentence contains a subject and a finite verb. Another common analysis is to say that a sentence must have:
(a) a subject (about which something is said) and
(b) a predicate (something that is said or predicated about the subject).

Notice that we have now changed the definition of the word 'subject'. It still refers to a grammatical function, but there is a suggestion that it is also the 'subject-matter' of the sentence. A third common use of the word 'subject' is to mean the doer (or actor) of the verb — the 'logical' subject. In many sentences the three uses of the word 'subject' coincide. Thus if we say:
    <The expatriates teach the students English.>
the expatriates is:
1 the grammatical subject of the verb *teach*
2 the subject matter or 'psychological subject' that serves as the starting point for the predication (*teach the students English*)
3 the actor or doer of the action (the 'logical subject').

ADV **1.9 Topic and comment**

On the other hand, if we are distinguishing between the languages taught by different people (eg Spanish is taught by the local staff) and we say <English, the students are taught by expatriates.>, then the starting-point is *English*, the grammatical subject is *the students* and the actor or doer is *expatriates*.

The term 'subject' is usually kept now for the grammatical subject and 'doer' is used for the logical subject when this is different (eg for the agent in passives). The term *topic* is used for the starting-point of the subject matter, for what the sentence is psychologically 'about'. What is said about the topic (in the predicate) is called the *comment*.

A slightly different distinction that is sometimes made is between 'theme' and 'rheme'. 'Theme' roughly corresponds to *topic* as defined here, but 'rheme' includes everything else, so 'rheme' could include the grammatical subject.

For example, in the sentence above, the theme = *English*; the rheme = *the students are taught by expatriates*.

Sentences where all three uses of subject coincide, and where the predicate and comment similarly coincide, are unmarked. Where they do not, the sentence is marked in some way. In this sense even simple questions and commands are obligatorily marked. The word order, or the lack of a subject, marks the sentence, indicating that the underlying topic is 'this is a question' or 'this is a command'.

A Unmarked sentences	
Subject = doer = topic	*Predicate = comment*
Grammar	←→ is fascinating.
Some people	←→ would hardly agree.
The expatriates	←→ teach the students English.

B Marked sentences			
	Topic	*Grammatical subject*	*Comment*
It's raining.	Impersonal (*It*)	*It*	*is raining.*
Please wait for me.	Request (*Please*)	(*you*)	*wait for me.*
What did he say?	Question (*What . . .*)	*he*	*say.*
Does he mean it?	Yes/No question (*Does . . .*)	*he*	*mean it.*
English the students are taught by expatriates.	*English*	*the students*	*are taught by expatriates.*

ADV **1.10 Focus**

The topic or theme is not usually the most important part of the sentence. It is often something already referred to or 'given'. Perhaps we have heard about the expatriates — note *the* (3.5) — but what are they doing here? That is what we want to focus on.

<Oh, the expatriates . . . teach the students English.>
[given information]   [focus]

Even when the topic is new, it usually sets the scene for the more important information that is to follow:

<English is *taught here by expatriates.*>
<English, *the students are taught by expatriates.*>

In both these sentences, the focus of the sentence is on *expatriates*. In two-clause complex sentences (chapter 11) this principle is clearly seen in the ordering of clauses. The final clause, whether main or subordinate, normally carries the greater focus.

Marked word order

1.11   In a sentence with unmarked word order, the grammatical subject is the unmarked topic, and the predicate receives the focus. Various different principles may be involved in changing the emphasis by changing the unmarked word order: subject + verb + (object) + (complement).

An obvious way of marking the topic is to *front* (place first) some element other than the grammatical subject. Similarly, an obvious way of increasing or shifting the focus is to postpone some particular element to the end. Such changes could conflict but often they coincide. Some common ways of marking word order are given below.

ADV **1.12 Fronting — marking the topic**

A **with subject/operator inversion** Fronting of:	
● negatives or semi-negatives (9.39)	*Never have I seen* such marvellous food. *Nor had Alan.* *Little did I expect* that to happen.
● **so** — with a 'me too' meaning (12.3). But *so* meaning 'I agree' takes **S + V** word order (12.3).	'She likes spinach.' '*So do I.*' ('It's raining.' '*So it is.*')
S + V + so/such . . . that [result] (11.19) becomes: ● **So + adj/adv** ⎫ ● **Such (NP)** ⎭ + **op + S(+V)** *that*	*So brilliant was he* ⎫ *So brilliantly did he paint* ⎬ that he became *Such originality did he show* ⎪ very wealthy. *Such was his talent* ⎭
B **Subject/verb inversion (without DO)** Fronting of:	
● Complement of subject (**SC**) ● Adverbial of place (with some verbs of movement and position)	*Just as important* is the question of money. *Here* is the menu. *Here* comes the manager. *There outside the restaurant* were the police. *On the pavement* lay a young man.
● Direct speech (as object) with some reporting verbs	'*I wonder,*' observed my aunt.
C **Fronting without inversion** Fronting of:	
● Complement of subject (**SC**) ● Complement of object (**OC**) ● Direct object ● Verb phrase (part) ● Object of preposition ● Adverbial	*Pleased* I was not. *Disgraceful,* I call it. *Rumours of that sort* I cannot bear. *Interfere* he will. *That sort of advice* I could do without. *Everywhere* there was confusion.

A Fronting involves inversion of subject and operator, and the use of DO if there is no other operator, when the elements fronted are negatives, semi-negatives and sometimes *so*. This is exactly like inversion for questions.

B Fronting of the elements in this section involves inversion of the subject and verb, but notice that DO is not used: <*Here does come the manager.>

C Here various elements are fronted, but there is no inversion of subject and verb.

1.13 Introductory *it* — marking the focus

<It was thought *that he would throw it away.*>
<It's a pity *to throw that old bucket away.*>
<It's useless *asking her not to.*>
<It doesn't matter *what I say.*>

Introductory *it* is commonly used when the subject is a clause (whether finite or non-finite). The device not only shifts the focus to the end, but also is in line with another principle of English, namely the tendency for lengthier phrases or word groups to be placed towards the end of the sentence.

This type of sentence with initial *it* must not be confused with
(a) 'empty it', where the *it* does not stand for a later clause:
<It's raining.> (see 3.30).
(b) *it* as pronoun in initial position: <It's got a hole in it.> [The bucket's got a hole in it.]

1.14 Introductory *there* — marking the focus

<There's *a hole in my bucket.*>
<There's *a dog lying on the bed.*>
<There could be *problems if you do that.*>
<We don't want there to be *any more mistakes.*>

Sentences beginning with unstressed *there* similarly shift the focus to the end. These sentences, in which *there* is followed by BE, are sometimes called 'existential sentences', because they are concerned with the idea of existence. In general these sentences can only be derived from a sentence with an indefinite subject as in <A hole is in my bucket.> which is grammatically possible though odd, or: <A dog is lying on the bed.>

The semantic effect of this construction is to emphasise the indefinite noun phrase by shifting it from the initial topic position (which implies given, and therefore less interesting information) to nearer the end of the sentence, which is the position for new information.

Some grammarians analyse *there* sentences as [*There* + verb + subject] ie as an example of inversion. Others regard *there* itself as a sort of dummy subject, and they point out that *there* behaves like a subject in some ways:
(a) *There* and verb are inverted for questions, including tags:
<Is there a hole in your bucket?>
<There appears to be no point in waiting, *does there?*>
(b) In informal English, *there's* can be followed by a plural noun phrase (replacing *there are*):
<There's so many things to do.>

1.15 Other kinds of marked word order

For other ways of shifting either the topic or the focus of a sentence, see:
(a) *Passive* A device that specifically separates the grammatical subject from the doer, and can change both topic and focus (4.19).

19

(b) *Cleft and pseudo-cleft* A device that makes it possible to mark any sentence element as the focus (11.49).

(c) *Sentence adverbials* Initial position is normal for sentence adverbials, because in effect these adverbials announce the underlying topic: <Frankly . . .> <In my opinion . . .> (9.34).

ADV **1.16** **Verb + direct object**

In the normal unmarked word-order of a sentence (1.11), nothing comes between the verb and its direct object: <*They speak well English.> But this rule may be broken when there is a long object that would otherwise separate the verb from some sort of closely linked complement. In any case a long object may well be the focus of the sentence:

<She *found* peculiarly irritating *his habit of apologising regularly for the boat, the food, the company and most of all for himself.*>

<They want the board to *postpone* by a month *the closure, due to take effect on Friday next week.*>

<If we were determined to yield no more . . . to *bequeath* to our children *a West defensible and worth defending*, we could do so.>

Word classes (parts of speech)

1.17

A Major word classes		**B Minor word classes**	
Lexical verbs:	know, decide, want	Auxiliary verbs:	be, have, must
Nouns:	knowledge, difficulty, window	Pronouns:	he, it, us, this
Adjectives:	difficult, interesting, pretty	Determiners:	the, this
Adverbs:	here, very, interestingly, prettily	Prepositions:	to, by
		Conjunctions:	and, although
		Interjections:	ah, alas, ouch

Traditional grammar attempts to give semantic or 'notional' definitions to the different parts of speech (or word classes). It describes a noun, for example, as 'the name of a person, place or thing' or a verb as a 'doing word'. Though there is some correlation between word classes and meaning, all such definitions fall down. (Is *knowledge* a thing, but *to know* a form of doing?) In fact, whether we realise it or not, we classify words very largely by the positional and functional slots they occupy in a sentence. Secondly, we may be guided by form — some word classes have characteristic endings or inflections. Meaning as a basis of classification comes a poor third.

Using these three criteria, we can establish ten word classes, divided into two broad categories, as in the table:

A **Major (or open) word classes** These are defined as 'major' because they carry most of the content or meaning of a sentence; 'open', because it is to these classes that new words can be added. (Also called 'content' or 'lexical' words.)

B **Minor (or closed) word classes** These are defined as 'minor' because their structural role is often more important than their meaning; 'closed', because normally no new words can be added and the total membership of the class could be listed.

 (Also called 'structure' words or — somewhat confusingly — 'function' words).

This classification is not, however, the only one possible, and it is not in fact as neat and tidy as the table suggests. For example, though adverbs are listed as open class, it is mainly manner adverbs ending in -*ly* that are open; other adverb categories are as closed as the minor word classes. On the other hand, interjections, though minor, could doubtless be added to! Another awkward problem is that, although in general only major word classes have inflectional or derivational endings, pronouns (a minor closed class) have inflection. But in any case it is a mistake to think of word classes as totally distinct and separate. Many words have functions and characteristics that make them belong partly to one class and partly to another. (Eg *few* functions like a determiner and a pronoun, but formally it inflects like an adjective.)

Secondly, whole classes have forms that regularly function as another part of speech. (Eg. verbal *to*-infinitives can function like nouns:

 <To travel hopefully is a better thing than to arrive.>

Occasionally almost any word can shift class. *That* is an informal adverb in: <It was *that* bad!>

Another common feature of English may be mentioned here — the fact that many words belong completely to more than one class, eg: *book* [n, v], *far* [adj, adv], *neither* [adv, conj, det, pro], *orange* [n, adj], *since* [adv, conj, prep].

Sentence elements and verb types

1.18 The grammatical subject of the sentence may be long and analysable into various parts (noun phrases 2.35) but it is not further broken down at the subject/predicate level. The predicate, however, is divided into:

- verb phrase (VP) — essential
- object (O)
- complement (C) } — essential in many verb patterns
- adverbial (A) — usually optional.

It is noticeable that the verb, or at any rate verb phrase, features here, as well as in word classes. This shows the central importance of the verb in sentence structure.

The primacy of the verb is also shown by the fact that it is the verb that dictates the basic patterns of the simple sentence or clause. Modern grammar has reduced the patterns underlying all simple sentences to as few as five. Notice that object (*O*) normally means direct object (*DO*) unless indirect object (*IO*) is specifically mentioned. Notice too that *adverbial* is largely optional and is not included in these basic sentence patterns on the following page.

Five basic sentence patterns

S + VP + C [linking verb]	These biscuits have kept fresh.
S + VP [intransitive verb]	Tom has left. This bread won't keep.
S + VP + O [transitive verb]	He has left the house. She kept the money.
S + VP + IO + DO [transitive]	Her father left her £10,000. Please keep me a packet.
S + VP + O + C [transitive]	He left her alone/happy/crying. She kept the money safe.

ADV **1.19 Realisation of sentence elements**

The four main sentence elements (subject, verb phrase, object and complement) plus the optional adverbial are realised by the parts of speech (ie, words). But these parts of speech may be used and grouped in different ways, so we can think of intermediate levels (see below).

	Main function in sentence	realised by	

A	**Subjects (S)
	and objects (O)**
		1 Noun phrases (**NP**) . . .
		
		In a complex sentence **S** and **O** may be realised by:
		2 *to*-infinitive or *-ing* clauses (7.19-7.20)
		3 finite nominal clauses (11.36-11.37).
			NP consists of
			(a) noun or (b) pronoun
			  — alone, or expanded
			  with determiners,
			  adjectives, etc (2.35).
			(c) In a complex
			  sentence, the **NP** may
			  itself include a
			  relative clause (11.27).

B	**Verb phrases (VP)**	Verbs only . . .	verbs may be
			(a) lexical verbs, or
			(b) auxiliaries/modals
			  [usually finite, but
			  non-finite possible in
			  clauses]

C	**Complements (C) SC = complement of subject OC = complement of object**	**1** Noun phrases (as above) **2** Adjectival phrases In a complex sentence, complement may be: **3** a non-finite clause (7.20) **4** a finite nominal clause (11.36-11.37)	Eg <She became *Prime Minister*.> (**SC**) <She made him *Chancellor*.> (**OC**) (a) adj alone: <The news made him *happy*.> (**OC**) (b) adjectival phrase: <He is *much more determined*.> (**SC**) In a complex sentence an adjective may be followed by a clause: <He was *sure it would work*.>

D Adverbials (A)	**1** adverbs	<He spoke *convincingly*.>
	2 prepositional phrases	<He spoke *with feeling*.>
	3 NP (or **NP** + *ago*)	<He spoke *last night*.> <He spoke *two hours ago*.>
	In a complex sentence adverbial may be: **4** a verbless clause **5** a non-finite clause **6** a finite clause (all in chapter 11).	

1.20   More about sentence elements

A **Subject** For discussion of subject see 1.8-12.

Object There is a well-established distinction between direct object and indirect object.

1 *Direct object (DO)* Noun phrases immediately following transitive verbs that are only capable of taking one object are usually direct objects. <Pamela likes *chocolates*.>

2 *Indirect object (IO)* Indirect objects are also noun phrases. In formal grammatical terms they can only exist with verbs capable of taking two objects, and they then come immediately after the verb and before the direct object: <We sent *Pamela* chocolates.> Direct objects can be realised by the same structures as subjects can, but indirect objects are mainly realised by noun phrases (including pronouns) and never by *that*-clauses (11.37).

Traditional grammar, using a more semantic definition, often glosses indirect object as 'recipient' and therefore includes within indirect object phrases of similar meaning with the pattern [*to/for* + NP] (7.6-8).

B **Verb phrase** *Verb phrase* in the sense in which it is used here means a verb group only: <*may have been trying/won't have been told*.>. This is different from the term 'verb phrase' in transformational grammar, where it often means the whole predicate, including objects and complements and adverbials.

C **Complement** 'Complement' is a rather general term, meaning something that completes something. At this sentence level, complements are divided according to the type of basic verb they pattern with:

1 *Subject complement* A complement in pattern 1 [S + VP + C] (1.18). This type of complement follows a linking verb and therefore refers back to the subject: <She became Prime *Minister*.>

2 *Object complement* A complement in pattern 5 [S + VP + O + C]. It complements the object: <The news made *him happy*.>

Complement in the sense in which it is used here, symbolised by (C) in sentence structure, should not be confused with

(a) complementation at a lower level:
  ● adjective complements — ways of completing adjectives (8.16 and 8.17)
  ● prepositional complements, alternatively called 'objects of prepositions' (10.7) — words added to a preposition to form a prepositional phrase.

(b) the broader use of the term — meaning anything (including nouns as direct objects) that completes a predicate.

D Adverbial Adverbials differ from the other constituents of sentence structure in several ways:

1 Many verbs must have an object or complement, and to this extent these elements may often be regarded as obligatory. But adverbials are usually optional — except with a very few verbs like *put* (7.6).

2 A clause or simple sentence can only have one subject and one verb phrase, but several adverbials are possible in the same clause.

3 The position of adverbials in the sentence is much freer than that of (S) or (VP), with their largely fixed positions.

2. NOUNS

What are nouns?

2.1   Nouns used to be defined as the 'names' of people, places and things. But this kind of definition by meaning does not explain, for example, why *laughter* is a noun but *laughing, laugh* and *laughs* may be nouns or verbs. Instead of using notional definitions, therefore, we establish nouns by applying tests of position and function, and to some extent tests of form.

2.2 Form

There are a number of word endings that formally indicate that a word is a noun: abi*lity*, disappoint*ment*, happi*ness*, organi*sation*, child*hood*. But endings are not an infallible guide, as many noun endings are found with other parts of speech: arri*val* (compare adjective cultu*ral*), bur*den* (but verb rip*en*), mouth*ful* (but adjective help*ful*). A more important formal characteristic of nouns is that they have inflection for plural and genitive (-*s*, -*es*, etc), although not all nouns are inflected.

2.3 Position and function

The most reliable indication of nouns is position and function. Nouns are frequently preceded by determiners <his ability> <a disappointment> <such happiness> and they can fit into certain functional slots in a sentence.

The main functions of nouns (and noun phrases, 2.35) are:

Subject of verb	*The children* are writing.
	Henry is writing.
Object of verb	They are writing *letters/a note*.
Subject complement	The letter is *an invitation*.
Object complement	He made the letter *an invitation*.
Indirect object	Who sent *Mrs Smith* this letter?
Apposition to another noun (or noun phrase)	The letter is for Mrs Smith, *his mother*.
After prepositions	The letter is for *his mother*.
Vocative	*Henry*, what are you doing?

2.4 Types of nouns

Traditional grammar recognised that there were nouns of different kinds, and defined them — as it did nouns as a whole — on notional grounds. A typical classification was into common nouns (subdivided into abstract and concrete), proper nouns (ie names) and collective nouns. But the abstract-concrete distinction can be difficult to apply (Which is *laughter* or *a laugh*?) and the classification as a whole is not a reliable guide to grammatical usage. Modern grammar therefore makes formal distinctions. Two of the labels (proper and collective) are retained, but redefined in strictly formal terms, while the major division is into count and mass.

25

A   Count (countable) nouns

As noted in 2.2, some, but not all, English nouns can take plural. Those that can are called 'count nouns': *a laugh, laughs.*

B   Mass nouns

Nouns that cannot take plural are called 'mass nouns': *laughter.* The term 'mass' is preferred to 'uncountable', because the latter word is used ambiguously. Sometimes it is used as a synonym for 'mass' and sometimes it includes words which are plural only, though some of these are countable: <three *people*>.

Another confusing label is 'unit noun'. Some grammarians use the term as a synonym for count nouns. Others restrict its use to nouns that denote units of mass: <a *blade* of grass> <a *bit* of string>.

C   Proper nouns

This is obviously a notional label, but many names for people and places do behave differently from other nouns in grammatical ways. They therefore constitute a formal category. But notice that on strictly formal grounds, while we include words like *America,* we should exclude *American,* which behaves like a common countable noun: <He is *an American.* They are *Americans.*> or like an adjective: <He is/They are *American.*>

D   Collective nouns

This is also a useful label for a small group of common nouns, eg *army, committee* which grammatically behave differently from other nouns. But since we are using the term formally, we must exclude words that are only notionally collective, eg *people,* (2.12). Some proper nouns, eg *Arsenal,* may also function like collectives.

So even these four redefined formal categories are not mutually exclusive, as some words overlap. In addition, many nouns, whatever their primary category, have potential for switching categories and being used in another way.

Mass nouns and count nouns

2.5   Usage

	Is zero article possible?	Which determiners?	Verb concord
Singular count nouns	**NO:** In the absence of any other determiner (eg *this*), *a/an* must be used.	*one* *each, every* [etc] *this, that*	Singular
	I want *a* chair,	but *this* chair	*is* broken.
Plural count nouns	**YES!**	*many, several* *these, those*	Plural
	Chairs should not break,	but *these* chairs	*were* old.
Mass nouns	**YES!** *a/an* is impossible	*much, little* *this, that*	Singular
	Furniture	like *this* furniture	*is* expensive.

The division into mass and count nouns is the most important division of English nouns. It affects:

(a) usage of articles and other determiners (for more details see chapter 3)

(b) verb concord (4.29).

Notice that article and determiner usage with singular count nouns and with mass nouns is different. It is misleading to describe mass nouns as singular.

2.6 Meaning

Count nouns include many so-called concrete nouns, ie
- names for people and things which can be seen as individual, separate units: *boy, leader, chair*
- units of measurement: *day, dollar, metre*
- individual parts of a mass: *bit, piece, portion*

But notice that many abstract nouns: *arrival, discovery, failure, hour, joke, mind, quarrel, solution* etc, are also countable:

<What we need are better *solutions!*>

Mass nouns include:
- many abstract nouns: *happiness, importance, patience*
- substances, gases: *gold, hydrogen, wheat*
- many verbal nouns: *clothing, jogging, shopping, training*
- most diseases: *chicken-pox, malaria*

But notice *wedding(s), saving(s)* = count nouns, and *belongings,* etc = plural only (2.12).

2.7 Some common mass nouns

advice, ammunition, anger, assistance, behaviour, bread, chaos, china, conduct, courage, dirt, education, employment, evidence, fun, furniture, harm, housework, information, knowledge, laughter, legislation, leisure, lightning, luck, luggage, machinery, money, moonlight, news, permission, photography, poetry, produce, progress, rubbish, safety, scenery, shopping, sunlight, thunder, transport, underwear, violence, weather

The terms 'mass' and 'count' are strictly grammatical in reference. The word *money* is mass, so <*a money> <*two moneys> are not acceptable even though you can count the thing referred to: <*one dollar> <*two pounds>.

Listed above are some common mass nouns which often have countable equivalents in other languages.

Occasionally some mass nouns are used with a preceding *a* when the meaning is modified in some way:

<His parents gave him *a good education.*>

<*A knowledge of mathematics* is useful.>

But these words are not count nouns in any full sense: <*each education> <*two knowledges> do not occur, and even this usage with *a* is not possible with all mass nouns:

<*More detailed information* is needed.> and not <*a more detailed information . . .*>.

2.8 Nouns with both mass and count usage

Many nouns are used as both count and mass nouns, with various distinctions of usage. Examples are given in (2.8-2.11).

A General vs. individual meaning

Mass (more general sense)	Count — separate units or different types
This hotel only does bed and breakfast.	The beds were hard, but that was a good breakfast.
This bad weather is affecting business.	You can't start a business without money.
Let's have cheese for lunch.	That shop sells fifty different cheeses.
Come to dinner on Tuesday.	His friends held a dinner for fifty people when Henry retired.
This sauce has got egg in it. [unspecified amount]	This sauce has got an egg in it. [one]
She has blonde hair.	Waiter, there's a hair in my soup.
Is there life on the moon?	Fran leads a busy life.
Noise can damage your hearing.	I heard a loud noise just now.
I'm sorry I didn't have time to call.	Have a nice time!

Many words — particularly for abstractions, substances, and meals — are mass nouns in a general sense: cheese, dinner, time and count nouns when they mean an individual example or instance: <a dinner for fifty> <a nice time>, or a particular type: <fifty different cheeses>.

Also: brick, cake, chicken, death, food, hope, kindness, lamb, language, light, pain, pleasure, tea, town, trouble, worry.

B More distinct meanings

Mass	Count
Cloth is sold by the metre now.	Can we have a clean cloth on the table? [a tablecloth]
There's not much country near London now. [country vs town]	Is Scotland an independent country? [a nation]
Standards of dress have changed over the years. [fashions for men and women]	She always wears such pretty dresses.
It's difficult to get a job without experience. [without having worked]	Henry had some amazing experiences in the Amazon jungle. [memorable events]
Be careful. There's ice on the road.	The child was sucking an ice. [an ice cream]
Steel is made from iron.	Most people use electric irons today. [for ironing clothes, and they're not made of iron!]
There's so much sex in modern films!	It's normal to be interested in the opposite sex. [men or women]
This box is made of wood.	We walked through the woods. [group of trees]
Some people can't find work.	Have you read all the works of Shakespeare? [plays and poems]

With some related mass and count nouns, the count noun has a limited meaning that may not be deducible from the meaning of the mass noun.

Also: glass, paper, play and many others. Note man is sometimes used in an unmarked way with the meaning of mankind.

<The Ascent of Man> (book by J. Bronowski)

<Man does not live by bread alone.> (The Bible)

2.9 So-called idioms: (count nouns as mass nouns)

Mass (unmarked/or essential meaning)	*Count* usage
A **Institutions** Places [etc]	
He is going *to bed/church/college/court/gaol/hospital/market/prison/school/university.*	Don't sit *on the bed.* They sent their son *to a good school.*
I'm going *to bed* — I'm tired.	
He was sent *to prison* for theft.	She went *to the prison* to visit her brother.
It's late. Get *into bed.*	
Henry wasn't clever enough to get *into university.*	He couldn't get *into the school he wanted.*
He's *in bed/church/class/court/gaol/hospital/prison.*	My sister works *in a hospital.*
The poor child was *in hospital* for six months.	
He's *at church/college/school/university.*	
I met him *at college.* [when we were both students]	The bus stops right *at the college,* by the main entrance.
home	
He has gone/left/arrived/reached *home.*	I met him *at the home* of his aunt.
He is at/near/a long way from *home.*	The old man lives in *a home.* [one for old people].
town	
When are you/going to/leaving/coming to/in/*town?*	I live *in a small town.*
sea	I'd rather live *in a village* than a town.
We were *at sea* for three weeks.	There are many fish *in the sea.*
I like travelling *by sea.*	We live at/by/near *the sea.* The Caspian is *an inland sea.*
B **Means of travel**	
He came *by air/bicycle/boat/bus/car/plane/rail/road/sea/ship/train.*	He came by/on *the night train.* He came *on his bicycle/a boat/a bus/a plane/a ship/a train.*
He came *on foot.*	He came *in a boat, a car, a plane* [etc].
C **Times, seasons**	
at/before/after dawn/sunrise/sunset	*before/after* another dawn, a beautiful sunset
at/by night	*in/during* the day, the night
by day	
in (the) spring/summer/autumn/winter	*in* the morning/the afternoon/the evening.
D **Miscellaneous**	
The two countries were *at war.*	Thousands of people were killed *in/during* the two world wars.
All's fair *in love and war.*	
He's *at business/at work.*	He works *in a very small business.*
He's *in business/trade.*	Everyone needs *a trade.*

Some grammar books fall back on 'idioms' or 'exceptions' to explain the fact that many normally count nouns are frequently used without either *a/an* or final *-s* after certain prepositions. Though there certainly are many real idioms here (where the meaning is not clear even though the individual words are understood), many of these prepositional phrases — which are mainly of place or time — are perhaps better interpreted as examples of unmarked usage. The words are being used as mass nouns to denote their essential primary purpose, and number is irrelevant.

Compare, for example, mass and count usage in the following:
<He goes *to church* regularly.> [to pray]
<He loves looking at old *churches*.> [buildings]
<Everybody went *home*.> [to where they lived — possibly different people to different places.]
<They have *a home* in New York.> [house or flat]

Note also the mass usage in:
<What kind/make/sort of *fridge/car* do you want?>

Compare with count usage in:
<I need *a fridge/a car*.>

ADV **2.10 Other fixed expressions using unmarked nouns**

In addition to the examples in 2.9 there are many prepositional phrases and other fixed expressions where a noun that is usually countable is used in an unmarked way. In this usage the noun carries a general, more abstract sense, not a particular or concrete sense. (Consult a good dictionary for the meanings.)

A **Prepositional phrases**
at, hand, risk; *by* accident, arrangement, chance, contrast, hand, heart, mistake, order; *for* example, fear (of), instance; *in* addition, advance, case, effect, fact, favour, hand, mind, place, return, trouble, time; *on* account, call, demand, hand, oath, purpose, time; *out of* hand, sight; *to* measure, order; *under* contract.

B **Parallel structures**
arm in arm, day to day, door to door, eye to eye, heart to heart, time after time, from time to time, year after year, year by year

C **Double structures**
hand in glove, hand over fist, hand to mouth, head over heels, husband and wife, man and boy, man and wife

D **Verb + noun**
lose face, make conversation, take part, talk shop, give way — and many more

---

2.11 Count nouns as unmarked nouns in attributive use

A apple tree, armchair, bookshop, bus stop, department store, dress shop, football, house agent, matchbox, mousetrap, recipe book, sandwich bar, step ladder, toothbrush

B a three-hour exam, a two-part novel, a ten-pound note, a twenty-mile march, a twelve-foot pole, two dozen eggs

C a pyjama jacket, a spectacle case, a stair carpet, a trouser pocket

D an arms race, a customs officer, an economics exam, a goods train, a means test

---

A Many nouns that are usually count nouns are used in an unmarked form when used attributively (ie before a noun, like an adjective) or to form compound nouns. For example, *a bookshop* or *a book sale* are not offering only one book, but plurality is unimportant. All that matters is the kind of thing which is involved in the shop or sale.

It should be noted that attributive noun + head noun and a compound of two nouns fused together are not so much two separate phenomena as two ends of a continuum. Hence the real uncertainty that exists in some cases over whether to write a particular form as two words, one word or with a hyphen.

B The unmarked form is even used when the attributive noun is a countable unit of measurement preceded by a number: <a three-hour exam>.

C Some words which on their own have no singular form omit the -s when used attributively, as in <a pyjama jacket> from pyjamas.

D However some words need the -s in attributive position because the unmarked form might be interpreted as singular with a different meaning <*an arm race> or else as an adjective <*a mean test>.

Note: man/woman: When man or woman is the logical object in a compound noun, it is unmarked in both the singular and plural forms of the compound: <man-eaters> = animals that eat people; <a woman-hater> = a man who hates women.

But when the two parts of the compound are in apposition, then both parts are marked for plural: <men friends> <women doctors>.

This 'rule' does not apply to other compounds for people, which regularly have unmarked form for the first noun: <boy scouts> <child actors> <girl friends>.

2.12 Plurals only

A **Nouns without -s ending** — *Possible corresponding singular unit*

These *cattle* are valuable.	This cow is . . .
There are three *people* waving at us.	A person/man/woman is . . .
The *police* have arrived.	A policeman/policewoman has . . .
There are *vermin* here.	There is a rat/a flea/a louse, etc . . .

B **Nouns ending in -s — things with 2 equal parts**
Where *are* my glasses? *They* are on your nose.
I need a new pair/two pairs of glasses.
Also:
binoculars, glasses†, spectacles†, compasses†, scales†, scissors, shears, tweezers, tongs, jeans, pants, pyjamas, shorts, tights, trousers, etc

For † see below.

C **Other nouns ending in -s**
annals, arrears, belongings, clothes, congratulations, earnings, fumes, oats, odds, outskirts, remains, suds, surroundings, thanks, valuables, winnings
Most of these words can take plural-related determiners, but *not* numerals:
<many/few *clothes*>, but not <*ten clothes>.

D **folk/folks**
1 *folk* = people of a particular area, sharing the same (often primitive) life: <The remote hill *folk* . . .>
2 *folk(s)* [infml] = people as individuals <How are the old *folk(s)*?> and possibly one's family: <My *folk(s)* . . .>
3 *folks* [infml] = way of addressing friends: <Come on, *folks*, let's go.>

Some nouns are found as plurals only.

A Words in this group never take -s, except *people* with the different meaning of nation. With this sense, *people* is an ordinary count noun: <an ancient people> <the peoples of eastern Europe>.

B Nouns which end in -s and denote tools, clothes, etc consisting of two equal parts are plural. The words marked with † also have related singular nouns with other meanings, (2.13). To count, we use *a pair/pairs of* instead of <*three trousers>.

C Some other words ending in plural -s cannot be counted. That is, they cannot be used with numerals, although they can take some plural determiners.

D *Folk/folks* can cause problems. Both are plural words but they are used by many people with slightly different meanings.

2.13 Plurals only — but with related count nouns

Plural only	*Singular and plural*
Where do the rebels get their *arms* from? [weapons]	I have hurt my *arm*.
The *customs* officer seached all my cases.	It's not *the custom* to tip here. [social practice]
I'm short of *funds* until next pay day. [cash/money]	We're starting *a fund* to build a school swimming pool. [a collection of money for the purpose]
The castle has large *grounds*.	Where's the football *ground*?
You have no *grounds* for saying that. [reasons]	
She's lost her *looks* since she was so ill. [prettiness]	Take *a look* at this.
	Don't give me dirty *looks*. [glances]
He has disgusting table *manners*. [social behaviour]	He behaved in a strange *manner*. [way]
Some people have no *morals*. [morality]	The *moral* of the story is: Don't judge people hastily. [lesson, meaning]
You should invest your *savings* in these bonds.	I bought this in the sale and made quite *a saving*.
My eyesight is terrible — I need *spectacles*.	The royal procession was *a marvellous spectacle*. [a public show]
I'm feeling in *low/high spirits*. [depression/cheerfulness]	He felt the place was haunted by the *spirit(s)* of his ancestor(s). [ghosts]
I drink wine, but not *spirits*. [strong liquor]	

There are some nouns which in one sense are plural only; eg *arms* [weapons] but which have a corresponding regular count noun with singular and plural forms: *an arm/arms* [of the body].

Also: brain(s), draughts(s), glass(es), pain(s), premise(s), quarter(s), scale(s)

2.14 Plurals only — with related mass nouns

Plural only	*Mass noun*
After the cremation, his *ashes* were thrown into the sea.	Don't spill your cigarette *ash* on the carpet.
I have studied the *contents* page of this book and I don't want to read it.	I did not like the *content* [substance] of his speech.
The *contents* of this bottle could kill you.	
He won his lawsuit and was awarded £50,000 *damages*.	These storms have caused enormous *damage*.
A *goods* train	Nobody considered the common *good*.
For *spirits* see 2.13	That's the right *spirit* [attitude].
	You should obey the *spirit* as well as the letter of the law.

Here we have nouns which with one meaning are plural only, but which have a related mass noun with another meaning.

Collective nouns

2.15

This committee is/are		very proud of its/their achievements, isn't it?/aren't they?
The public	say/says	that nobody cares about it/them and its/their problems.
The staff	is/are	hardworking.
The staff	have	all gone for their lunch.

Collective nouns are a kind of count noun referring mainly to groups of people. In their singular form, collective nouns can take singular or partly plural concord. British English in particular uses collectives in a plural way when the group is thought of as consisting of separate individuals, (see also 4.29).

Some grammar books use the term *collective* to cover words like *people, cattle*, presumably for semantic reasons. But grammatically these are plurals only (2.12).

When a collective is used with plural inflection, plural verb concord is, of course, essential:

<The crews of several ships *were* in port.>

Collective nouns include such common count nouns as: *air force, army, cast, class, committee, company, couple, crew, crowd, family, firm, gang, government, group, herd, hospital, jury, majority, minority, navy, pair, the press* [journalists], *public* [rarely plural], *school, staff, team, tribe, university*.

Note: The word *youth* can be:
(a) mass noun <I was happy in my youth> [when I was young]
(b) count noun [young man/men] <Some youths were standing outside a pub.>
(c) collective noun [young people of both sexes] <Youth today has/have different problems from its/their predecessors.>

2.16 Proper nouns as collectives

The Department of Education	*say/says*	*they have/it has* no comment to make.
Arsenal	*is/are*	playing well this season.
Macmillan	*has/have*	made a good profit this year.
The Netherlands	*have/has*	a monarchy.

The names of many companies, sports teams and the like can also function as collective nouns.

Proper nouns

2.17

Just as the division between mass and count nouns is far from clear-cut (many nouns being used as both), so there is no absolute division between common and proper nouns (or names).

Features that characterise proper nouns (but see below) are:
(a) They are considered to have unique reference.
(b) They do not take determiners.

(c) In particular, they do not permit contrast between *a/an* and *the*.

(d) A proper noun is either singular or plural (but not both).

(e) They are written with initial capital letters.

([a] = definition by meaning; [b]-[e] = distinctions of form)

Proper nouns include the following. The first two categories are perhaps the most clearly proper nouns, while the later categories are on the borderline with common nouns.

- Personal names: *John, Mrs Smith, Dr Brown, Uncle Henry*
- Geographical names: *London, Scotland, Mount Snowdon*
- Religions: *Buddhism, Christianity, Islam*
- Days, months, festivals: *January, Sunday, Christmas*
- Names for streets, organisations etc are usually a combination of proper noun (or adj) and common noun: *The British Council, Scotland Yard, Piccadilly Circus.*
- Family relationships [when used as names]: *Mother, Grandma.* But <a young mother> = common noun
- Common nouns when personified and given unique reference: *Fate, Heaven, Liberty*
- Magazines: *Newsweek, Vogue*
- Languages: *English, Hindi*
- Nationalities: *an Englishman, the English* [but see 2.4 and 2.22]

2.18 Proper nouns with/without *the*

	Without *the*	With *the*
PEOPLE	*Personal names* Susan, Henry Mr and Mrs Brown President Reagan Pope John Paul Prince Charles	*Titles* [often really common nouns with unique reference] The President The Pope The Prince of Wales
GEOGRAPHICAL PLACES *continents,* *countries*	Argentina, Zaire Europe, northern Europe South-East Asia (sunny) Spain (Communist) China (modern) Mexico	*Exceptions* the Argentine, (the) Lebanon, the Soviet Union, the United States [common nouns], the Netherlands, the Philippines [plurals]
cities	(medieval) London Bangkok Rio	*Exception* — The Hague
lakes, *mountains*	Lake Geneva, Lake Michigan Mount Kilimanjaro (Mount) Etna (Mount) Everest	but: The Matterhorn The Peak [in England — common noun with unique reference]. *Plural mountain ranges:* the Andes, the Himalayas, the Rocky Mountains (or the Rockies). *Never* *an Ande *etc.*
islands	Borneo Jamaica Skye	but: The Isle of Skye The Isle of Wight *Plural island groups* the Cook Islands the Maldives

rivers		the (River) Congo the Irrawaddy the (River) Thames
canals, oceans		the Grand Union Canal, the Panama Canal, the Pacific (Ocean), the Caspian (Sea), the Mediterranean (Sea), the Black Sea, the Indian Ocean, the South-China Sea
street names, etc	Baker Street Hanover Square Hyde Park Kensington Gardens Cambridge Road	*Exceptions* the High Street [ordinary adj + n] the Haymarket, The Mall
public buildings	*Words with -s* Raffles (Hotel, Singapore) Claridges (Hotel, London) Simpsons-in-the-Strand [a London restaurant] St George's Hall St Paul's (Cathedral)	*but:* the Hilton (Hotel) the Sheraton the National (Theatre) the Albert Hall the Victoria & Albert (Museum)
newspapers, etc	*Many magazines:* Newsweek, Punch, Time, Vogue	The Times The Washington Post *Some magazines:* The Economist

Although proper nouns do not take the full range of determiners, some of them must always be preceded by *the* (ie *the* is part of the name.) Names taking *the* include rivers and groups of mountains and islands.

Personal names, and most names of continents, countries, cities, lakes and single mountains and islands are usually without *the,* even if premodified <sunny Spain>.

Many apparent exceptions to this latter rule are really common nouns with unique reference: <the United States>.

The names of canals and oceans usually include *the* for the same reason — the name is the + attributive name + common noun. The common nouns *sea* or *ocean* can be omitted if the attributive name is unique: <the Caspian (Sea)> but not if the name is an adjective commonly used for other things: <*The Black><*The Indian><*The South-China>.

Street names, etc are normally without *the*. But names based on common nouns use *the*: <*the* High Street>. Notice that <Oxford Street><Cambridge Road> etc are names, but <*the* Oxford road> is not — it means the road that leads to Oxford. In spoken English all 'town' place names of the type <Hanover Square><Cambridge Road> normally receive the main stress on the second word — except for combinations ending with *Street,* which are stressed on the first word.

For public buildings the common noun (eg *Hotel, Theatre*) is often dropped if the meaning remains clear. Where the name is probably a possessive form (even though no longer written with an apostrophe) there is no *the*: <Claridges>.

Most newspapers have *the* as part of the title. Magazine titles vary.

2.19 Proper nouns used as count nouns

A   Proper nouns as indefinite count nouns
There is *a Mr Smith* to see you. [a man who says his name is Smith. I don't know him]
This actress is hardly *a Garbo*. [an actress like Greta Garbo]
There are no *Garbos* around today. [actresses like G.G.]
There are several *Londons* in the world — for example there's *a London* in Canada.
Is that *a genuine Picasso*? *Picassos* fetch enormous prices these days. [pictures by Picasso]
I'd like *a Rolls*. [a Rolls-Royce car]
A Saturday would be more convenient than *a Sunday*.
There are not enough *Sundays*.
It was *a particularly cold November*.

B   Proper nouns with *the*
1   Do you mean THE Elvis Presley? [or some other man with the same name?]
2   Modified unique names:
   (a) the one and only / the unforgettable Elvis Presley
   (b) (the) young Shakespeare
       the England of Queen Victoria
       the London that Dr Johnson knew
   (c) the Henry Brown I went to school with   ⎫ [There is more than
       not the Henry Brown you know,   ⎬ one Henry Brown]
       not (the) Henry Brown next door.   ⎭
       the Saturday before last.
   (d) The Smiths are leaving. [Mr & Mrs Smith, or the Smith family]

C   Proper nouns with other determiners
   (a) every Saturday, many Henrys, several Susans
       Which River Avon do you mean?
   (b) My dear Henry, . . .

Even the most proper of proper nouns: <Elvis Presley><London> can be used as a common noun for various reasons. In every case the usage has changed because the reference is in some way no longer unique. Days and months are obviously only unique in a particular context, and frequently become common count nouns, but they are always written with an initial capital.

A   Proper nouns as indefinite count nouns
Names of people and places may be used as indefinite count nouns with a variety of meanings. But basically they are all either specific: <A Mr Smith to see you.> or classifying: <She is hardly a Garbo.> (3.6).

B   Proper nouns with *the*
1 If [*the* + name] is used without any other modification, then the meaning is that unique person/place as distinct from any other possible person/place of the same name. In speaking, the *the* is stressed.
2 When a name preceded by *the* is modified there are several possible meanings:
(a) A personal name may retain its unique reference and the modification is understook as non-defining, ie *the unforgettable Elvis Presley* does not suggest that there could be more than one.
(b) The reference remains unique, but the person/place is contrasted with himself/itself at some other time.
(c) The person/place is distinguished by the modification from others with the same name.

Notice that a following *of*-phrase often needs a preceding *the*. But other prepositions may be less bound to the noun phrase: <England under Queen Victoria>, <London as Dr Johnson knew it>.

See also 2.18 for modification of other geographical names.

(d) [*The* + a surname in the plural] means two or more members of that family.

C **Proper nouns with other determiners**

(a) Naturally, when proper names are used as common nouns, they can be used not only with *a/an* and *the*, but with other determiners and with adjectives.

(b) Even proper names, when clearly retaining their unique reference, can sometimes take other determiners.

2.20 Proper nouns as mass nouns

The category of proper nouns is not usually thought of as containing any mass nouns. However names of religions and names of languages are predominantly mass nouns:

<*Christianity* is a world religion.>

<She speaks *very little English*.>

Usage with *a* is possible, but much more unusual:

<They practise *a Christianity which would have surprised the Early Church.*>

<She is learning *an English that I feel is old-fashioned.*>

2.21 Proper nouns in attributive use

Proper nouns, like common nouns, can be used attributively: <The *Smith* family> <That *Jones* girl> <a *London* taxi-driver>.

2.22 Nationality words (including adjectives)

	Country	Adjective (+ Language)	People-Noun singular	plural
A	England	English	an Englishman	Englishmen the English
	Scotland	Scottish Scots (Scotch)	a Scotsman a Scot	Scotsmen the Scots
	Wales	Welsh	a Welshman	Welshmen the Welsh
	Ireland	Irish	an Irishman	Irishmen the Irish
	Britain	British	(a Briton)	(Britons) the British
	France	French	a Frenchman	Frenchmen the French
	Holland (The Netherlands)	Dutch	a Dutchman	Dutchmen the Dutch

	Adjective, Noun [sing and pl] = *the same*			
B	Burma	Burmese	a Burmese	(the) Burmese

Also China, Chinese; Japan, Japanese; Portugal, Portuguese; Vietnam, Vietnamese; Switzerland, Swiss.

<table>
<tr><td colspan="4">Adjective and Noun = the same, except add (-s) for plural</td></tr>
</table>

C **1** Africa   African   an African   (the) Africans

     Afghanistan   Afghan   an Afghan/   (the) Afghans/

               Afghani   Afghanis

Also: America, American; Australia, Australian; Belgium, Belgian; Bulgaria, Bulgarian; Brazil, Brazilian; Canada, Canadian; Egypt, Egyptian; Europe, European; Germany, German; Hungary, Hungarian; India, Indian; Indonesia, Indonesian; Iran, Iranian; Italy, Italian; Malaysia, Malay [ethnic]/Malaysian [national]; Mexico, Mexican; Nigeria, Nigerian; Norway, Norwegian; Russia, Russian; Saudi Arabia, Saudi (Arabian); Singapore, Singaporean.

2 Iraq, Iraqi; Israel, Israeli; Pakistan, Pakistani.

3 Nepal, Nepali/Nepalese [*Not* *Nepaleses].

4 Cyprus, Cypriot; Czechoslovakia, Czech (*or* Czechoslovakian); Greece, Greek; Jugoslavia, Jugoslav; Thailand, Thai; Philippines, Filipino.

<table>
<tr><td colspan="4">Adjective and Noun = different</td></tr>
</table>

D Denmark   Danish   a Dane   (the) Danes

Also: Finland, Finnish, Finn; Iceland, Icelandic, Icelander; Poland, Polish, Pole; Spain, Spanish, Spaniard (the Spanish); Sweden, Swedish, Swede; Turkey, Turkish, Turk.

<table>
<tr><td colspan="4">No Adjective (Country used attributively)</td></tr>
</table>

E New Zealand   New Zealand   a New Zealander   New Zealanders

Nationality words derived from the names of countries are grouped here for convenience of reference, but they include both nouns and adjectives. All are written with initial capital letters.

Languages are often denoted by the same form as the adjective, without articles. But there are many other cases where the language names are completely different. For example Indians speak *Hindi*, etc.

Language names resemble mass nouns in some ways: <Can you speak *English/Japanese/Thai?*> <I don't know much *Japanese*, but I speak *a little Thai*.>

People-nouns are felt to be names (hence the capital letters) but they share many characteristics of ordinary count nouns.

Although most names of countries have separate adjectival forms, the names of the countries are sometimes used attributively, with slightly different meanings:

<China tea>[= tea from China]   but <Chinese opera>

<India rubber>   but <an Indian summer>

<the Burma road>[the road to Burma]   but <Burmese temples>

A This group has two alternative people-words, with different usage. For example (a) *an/the Englishman* [noun only] and (b) *the English* [adjectival form].

(a) *nouns ending in* **man/men** [one word] If the reference is not exclusively to males, then some other noun is used. [Adj + *woman/women*] is also a one-word compound: <an/the Englishwoman>. Any other combination is written as two words <the/some/six English people>. This form, ie with *man/woman* etc, is the only form possible for singular in this group of words:

<An Englishman, an Irishman and a Welshman went into a pub. The Irishman said . . .> <*an English, an Irish . . . etc>

It is also used for indefinite plural (ie classifying reference): <Welshmen are fine singers.> and for specific indefinite or definite plural:

   <There were two Welshmen and some Scottish girls . . . The two Welshmen . . .>

(b) *the + adjective*

The adjective form as a noun can only be used preceded by *the,* so not <*a Welsh><*six Welshes>.

The meaning is either the nation as a whole or some representative group:

   The *Welsh* sang brilliantly at last month's festival.

   The *French* scored another rugby victory on Saturday.

(c) The Scots themselves prefer the adjectives *Scottish* <the Scottish Highlands> or *Scots* <Scots law>. The old adjective *Scotch* is mainly restricted to whisky, terriers and Scotch eggs. Never describe the people as Scotch <*the Scotch> <*He is Scotch.>.

   The word *Briton* used to be avoided when referring to individual inhabitants of present-day Britain, but it seems to be regaining acceptance. Collectively they can be called <the British>. (American English also uses *Britishers*).

B In this group the nouns for people are the same as the adjectives, and the same for singular and plural: <They're Chinese> <a Chinese> <ten Chinese>.

C Here the people form adds *-s* for plural: <an American> <some Americans>.

1 Adjectives and people-nouns mostly add -n to the name of the country.

2-4 form adjectives in miscellaneous ways.

D In another group the adjective is different from the word for people. We could include *Arab/Arabic/Arabian* here. All three words are used as adjectives. We speak of <Arabic numerals> and <the Arabic language> — or simply <Arabic> — and <The Arabian Nights> is a famous book, but the modern tendency is to use *Arab* as an adjective <the Arab world><Arab influence> etc.

   The noun for a native speaker of Arabic is (*an*) *Arab.* See also *Saudi* — Group C.

E A few countries have no real adjectival forms. For New Zealand we use the country attributively: <New Zealand butter> <New Zealand cricketers>.

   Hong Kong has no single word for its people — we can say <Hong Kong citizens> <a man from Hong Kong>.

Inflection in nouns

2.23 Regular

Final sound	Spoken	Written		
		sing gen	*pl*	*pl gen*
Voiceless except sibilant etc clock sunlight	/s/	clock's sunlight's	clocks —	clocks' —

Voiced except sibilant etc boy girl	/z/	boy's girl's	boys girls	boys' girls'
Sibilant or affricate bus judge Mrs Jones	/ɪz/	bus's judge's Mrs Jones's	buses judges the Joneses	buses' judges' the Joneses'

All regular common count nouns can be inflected for plural. Both count and mass can be inflected for genitive, and count plural can have a plural genitive.

In practice the use of genitive is somewhat limited (see below). There are no other noun cases. Contrast pronouns.

Pronunciation For any one regular noun, the inflections for all three cases (plural, and singular and plural genitive) are not distinguished. They all sound the same. But taking regular count nouns as a whole, this inflection has three pronunciation variants, depending on the final sound of the unmarked base form:

Add /ɪz/ after words ending with a sibilant (or affricate) sound whether voiced or not
/z/ after words ending in a voiced sound (except sibilants, etc)
/s/ after words ending in a voiceless sound (except sibilants, etc)

Written form By contrast, written forms distinguish the three meanings (cases) of the inflection, but not the pronunciations.

For plural add -s to the base
For genitive singular add 's } subject to normal spelling rules
For genitive plural add s'

Notice that in spoken English the grammar of a sentence usually makes it clear whether plural or genitive is meant; but the distinction between singular and plural genitive is often obscure: <the boy's/boys' mother>.

Compare the pronunciation and spelling rules with those for verb inflection of third person singular present tense (4.5). Any new words coming into the language are likely to follow the regular inflection system (except perhaps in the case of compounds formed with some of the exceptions listed below, eg *airman/airmen, spacecraft/spacecraft.*)

2.24 Irregular plurals

These can be divided into:
● words, with inflections retained from Old English (A, B) plus a few words derived from other languages (C), that are irregular in spelling, pronunciation or both. (2.25)
● zero plurals (2.26)
● foreign plurals (2.27)

2.25

A **Irregular spelling and pronunciation**
(a) Plurals derived from Old English:
man/men; woman/women; child/children; ox/oxen; brother/brothers [usual], brethren [rare]; foot/feet; tooth/teeth; mouse/mice; louse/lice; penny/pence [in amounts — fivepence], pennies [coins].

In compounds with *man/men*, the singular/plural distinction is often only in the spelling: *airman/airmen* [are both pronounced /eəmən/ but *snowman/snowmen* are /snəʊmæn/snəʊmen/.

Compounds with *woman/women* are distinguished in written and spoken forms.
(b) Nouns ending with sound /f/ and spelling (-f) or (-fe)
Regular: *belief/beliefs* /-f/fs/. Also *chief, cliff, proof,* etc
Irregular: *calf/calves,* ka:f/ka:vz/. Also *half, knife, leaf, life, loaf, self, sheaf, shelf, thief, wife, wolf*
Regular and irregular possible: *dwarf (dwarfs/dwarves)*
Also: hoof, scarf, wharf
Regular spelling, but pronunciation variants: *handkerchiefs, roofs* /-fs/ or /-vz/.

B **Irregular pronunciation** (but regular spelling)
(a) Base ending with sound /ə/.
Regular /əs/ *births, cloths†, deaths, earths, faiths, lengths, months.*
Irregular /ðz/. *baths, mouths, paths, youths*
†do not confuse with — *clothes*/kləʊðz/.
Both **regular and irregular** pronunciation used: *oaths, truths, wreaths*
(b) Note irregular pronunciation of *houses* /haʊzɪz/

C **Irregular spelling** (but regular pronunciation)
Base ending in sound /əʊ/ spelt (o)
Regular: *radios, solos, sopranos, studios.*
Shortened forms: *kilos, photos*
Names: *Filipinos, Eskimos*
Irregular : (add -es) *hero/heroes; potato/potatoes; tomato/tomatoes; Negro/Negroes*
Both possible: *cargos/cargoes; mosquitos/mosquitoes; volcanos/volcanoes*

2.26 Zero plurals

A Some names of **animals** etc: *deer, grouse, plaice, salmon, sheep, trout, wild fowl*:
<There were two sheep in the road.>
Other animal names have both mass and plural usage: *duck, fish* [*fishes* rare], *herring*:
<Two ducks waddled across the road.>
<Ian is out shooting duck.>

B **British measures** Some British measures also have ZERO and -s usage: *foot, hundredweight, pound, stone*:
<He weighs 12 *stone(s)* and is 6 *foot/feet* tall.>
<She is only 8 stone 5 pounds.>
<The baby weighed 7 pounds/7 *pound(s)* 2 ounces.>
<The tickets cost 5 pounds/5 *pound(s)* 10.> [£5.10p]
Dozen and *score* take ZERO plural when they are part of an exact number but are regular when vague and nominal:
<I'll take *two dozen*.>
<There were *dozens of* people about.>

C **Nationality words** ZERO when ending in a sibilant <*Swiss, Chinese*> ZERO or -s for *Bedouin, Eskimo*: <Six *Eskimo(s)*>.

D **Miscellaneous** *Craft* [boat, etc], *aircraft, spacecraft, offspring* [child/children]: <The harbour was full of small craft.> <one/two offspring>.

E **Singular and plural ending in** (*-s*). Although many words ending in *-s* have different plural forms (*bus, buses*), some remain unchanged such as *corps, innings, means, series*:

<It is a *means* to an end.>

<We've tried several different *means*.>

Some words ending in *-s* may use plural verb, even when the place referred to in the 'real world' is only felt to be one place: *barracks, crossroads, gallows, headquarters, works* [factory], *gas works, golf links, mews, shambles*:

<This crossroads is/These crossroads are . . . dangerous.>

2.27 Foreign plurals

Some words that are Greek, Latin or French in origin have foreign plurals. Often these are in variation with a regular English plural — the foreign plural being used in a more formal or technical context. The general tendency is for the normal English (*-s*) ending to be used as the word becomes more naturalised. But with many words there is no choice, so a good dictionary is advisable: *bonus/bonuses; stimulus/stimuli; terminus/terminuses/termini; diploma/diplomas; larva/larvae; erratum/errata; datum/data†; medium/mediums/media†; index/indexes* [in books] */indices* [scientific]; *appendix/appendixes* [of body] */appendices* [in books]; *analysis/analyses; crisis/crises; criterion/criterions/criteria†; phenomenon/phenomena*.

†*Data* is now being used as a mass noun:

<There *isn't much data*.>

Media is also used with a singular verb when it means the press etc:

<The mass media includes TV and the press.>

The use of *criteria* as a singular is generally regarded as substandard:

<*They applied a different criteria.>

2.28 Irregular genitive

Where the plural inflection is irregular, the 'rule' that plural and genitive (singular and plural) sound the same may, of course, not apply. In spelling, note that if the plural lacks *-s*, then the genitive plural is written *-'s*, not *-s'*.

Sing	sing gen	pl	pl gen
man	man's	men	men's
wife	wife's /fs/	wives /vz/	wives' /vz/
youth	youth's /əs/	youths /ðz/	youths' /ðz/
house	house's(sɪz)	houses/zɪz/	houses' /zɪz/
sheep	sheep's	sheep	sheep's

2.29 Inflection of proper names

Most current names ending in *-s* ə̃re inflected regularly: <Mrs Jones's son> <the Joneses' son> <St James's Park> although names that already have two sibilant sounds sometimes resist adding a third:

<This is Francis'/Francis's book.> /fra:nsɪz/ or fra:nsɪzɪz/

Classical names use the base without inflection, though case is indicated in writing. Other old names vary:

<Achilles' heel, Aristophanes' plays, Keats'/Keats's poetry, Dickens'/Dickens's realism>.

2.30 Inflection of compounds

Compounds may be inflected for plural and genitive, but in practice genitive usage is rare.

Two tendencies are at work in the inflection of compounds:
(a) Put the inflection at the end of the compound;
(b) Put the inflection after a noun.

A Regular

1 Where the second element is a noun (even if the first is too) no conflict usually arises. Add *-s* at the end of the compound:

noun + noun: *armchairs, lawsuits, crime reporters, hand signals, storm clouds*

verb + noun: *breakwaters, pickpockets*

2 For compounds with *man/woman* see 2.25

3 In the vast majority of other cases, (a) above also applies:

verb + adverb: *breakdowns, fly-overs, grown-ups, lay-bys*

adverb + verb: *also-rans*

Note also **noun** + *ful: handfuls, spoonfuls*

B Irregular

Difficulties arise in the plural mainly in 3 types of compound:

1 Noun + adverb, when derived from verb + adverb:

<a passer-by>   <some passers-by>

<a runner-up>   <two runners-up> but note:
                          [gen sing] <a runner-up's prize>
                          <these goings-on> [no sing]

2 Noun + adjective, mainly formal and old-fashioned:

<a court martial>   <courts martial>

<the poet-laureate>   <the poets laureate>

3 Noun + prepositional phrase

<my brother-in-law>   <my two brothers-in-law>
                           [gen sing] <my brother-in-law's mother>

<a Justice of the Peace>   <Justices of the Peace>

But so strong is 'rule (a)' above that in fact many people, except in the most formal contexts, would use final *-s* in many of the 2 and 3 examples:

<poet laureates>

C Group phrases

'Rule (a)' above (inflect at the end) also works for the genitive of longer noun phrases:

<Queens of England> [pl]   but <the Queen of England's clothes>

<the boys next door> [pl]   <the boy next door's bicycle> [infml]
                                      <somebody else's problem>

2.31 Uses and meanings of the genitive

A	**Possession**	my aunt's spectacles the Smiths' house the city's famous bridge
B	**Subjective genitive**	Henry's treachery [Henry was treacherous.] the plane's arrival [the plane arrived.] the President's death [the President died.] the lovers' quarrel [the lovers quarrelled.]

C	Objective genitive	Henry's admirers [people admire Henry] The President's murder [someone murdered the President]
D	Classifying	a girls' school [a school for girls] a day's pay [pay for a day] a stone's throw [the distance a stone can be thrown] a lovers' quarrel [that kind of argument]
E	Place — without following noun	St Paul's, Guy's the baker's, a grocer's I'm going to my cousin's

The genitive case occurs less frequently than the plural. It is widely used with people (both proper names and common count nouns), but has more limited use with nouns denoting things.

A **Possession** An important meaning of genitive is possession (hence one name for it — 'possessive'). But in fact it can express a great many other relationships.

B&C **Subjective and objective genitive** A potential source of ambiguity is the fact that the genitive word can represent either the 'logical' subject or the 'logical' object of the second word. Is *Henry's picture* (a) a picture that he owns (subjective genitive) or (b) a portrait showing him (objective)? In the absence of clues, the answer is probably (a). (See also 10.18).

D **Classifying** Commonly (as in **A-C**) the genitive word specifies either the owner or the subject or object of the second word. Any determiners or adjectives belong to the genitive and not the second word:

<(his new girl-friend's) second-hand car>
<(poor old Henry's) new house>.

But sometimes the genitive serves as a classifier of the following noun:

<the pretty new (dolls' house)>
<a mere (stone's throw)>.

In this case, determiners and adjectives belong to the whole item, and it is not possible to insert another word between the genitive and the second noun <*a dolls' wooden house>.

Fixed expressions, such as <*a stone's throw*>, also fall into this category. However, there are not always clear distinctions between

● fixed expressions where a genitive meaning is still felt: <*for goodness' sake*>

● near compounds: <a *bird's nest*> or perhaps <a *birds nest*> and

● words that are firmly one word: <a bridesmaid> <a statesman>.

From the point of view of position, notice that the genitive form of a noun, unlike other noun forms, is almost always followed by another noun. (For exceptions see below). In this, the genitive functions more like a determiner or an adjective than other nouns, and for this reason some grammarians include the genitive as a determiner. Once again we see how word-classes overlap.

E **Genitive without a following noun** The genitive is sometimes used alone without a following noun. Unless this is a case of ellipsis, the meaning is usually a place.

1 *Proper nouns* for certain well-known buildings:

<Have you been to *St Paul's*?> [St Paul's Cathedral]
<She's a nurse at *Guy's*.> [Guy's Hospital].

2 *Words for shops* denoted by the type of shopkeeper:
<at the baker's/butcher's/grocer's/greengrocer's/ hairdresser's>etc.
Similarly some other premises:
<She went to the doctor's/the dentist's.>
3 *Shop names* are frequently used with an *-s* inflection although the original personal name had no *-s*:
<in Boots/Marks and Spencers/ Selfridges>.
It is not always easy to say whether this *-s* is a plural or a genitive.
4 Names and nouns denoting people are sometimes used with genitive inflection to mean that person's home:
<I'm having dinner at my cousin's tonight.>
<See you at Henry's tomorrow.>
But this is only possible in this sort of position: <*My cousin's is in Scotland.> is unacceptable.

2.32 Genitive and *of* + noun

Textbooks sometimes describe [*of* + noun] as the *of-genitive*, but both constructions have many meanings and the two constructions are frequently not interchangeable.

A **The inflected genitive:**
1 is preferred (and sometimes essential) for people and animals, when there is some meaning of possession:
<Henry's age, the Smiths' house, the horse's hooves>.
2 can be used with some other names (mainly places): <New York's night life, London's West End, the third world's problems, India's neighbours>.
But <the excitement of Christmas> (see below).
3 can be used with common nouns (especially collectives, 2.15), also identified with people:
<the company's profits, the team's victory, the school's traditions, the ship's captain>.
4 is preferred for subjective genitive: [genitive as doer]
<the Prime Minister's speech>
<Henry's phoning me was a great surprise.> [essential here]
5 is essential (not replaceable by *of* + noun) for classifying genitives and various fixed expressions:
<a girls' school, a dentist's drill>
<a day's work, a moment's thought, today's weather, three weeks' pay, at arm's length, a stone's throw, for heaven's sake, donkeys' years>
6 is essential in many local expressions of the type <Guy's>
<the butcher's> (2.31E).

B **of + noun** is preferred for:
1 things [possession]:
<the end of the road, the top of the cupboard, the excitement of Christmas>.
2 objective genitive [people and things]
<the defeat of Napoleon, the sale of the house>.
3 subjective genitive when the noun phrase is [*the* + adj]
<the needs of the sick> and not <*the sicks' needs>.

2.33 Double genitive

For people, never for things, there is the so-called double genitive construction — double because it has both genitive inflection and *of*:
<a friend *of Henry's/hers/theirs*>
<some neighbours *of my grandparents'*>.

Notice that the first noun has indefinite reference (*a friend* . . .) and the second noun must be definite and human (*Henry's, hers, my grandparents'*).

This construction makes it possible to distinguish between <*neighbours of my grandparents*> [some indefinite neighbours] and <*my grandparents' neighbours*> [all the definite neighbours].

An exception to the 'rule' about indefinite reference are constructions with demonstratives or with relative clauses:

<*that* friend of Henry's/his>
<*those* neighbours of my grandparents'/theirs>
<*the* friend of Henry's *who came last week*>.

2.34 Gender

Gender is not an important feature of English nouns.

1 A few nouns have variant forms to denote the other sex: *actor/actress, bridegroom/bride, duke/duchess, heir/heiress, host/hostess, landlord/landlady, widower/widow.*

But these pairs do not always have strictly comparable meanings. For example, *an heir* (male or female) inherits a title, an estate etc; *an heiress* means a woman who will inherit a large fortune.

2 With some pairs there is no morphological connection between the words (ie they are not derived from each other): *brother/sister, father/mother, son/daughter, uncle/aunt, king/queen.*

3 With many animal pairs, one word is unmarked for sex. The sex-marked word is only used when the sex distinction is important:

unmarked:	*dog* [either sex or male]	marked:	*bitch* [female only]
	horse [either sex]		*mare* [female] *stallion* [male]
	duck [either or female]		*drake* [male]

4 Many words for people can be used for male or female: *cousin, doctor* etc.

Gender can be shown by the addition of markers: *male nurse, a boy-friend, men friends, a woman doctor, women students* etc.

Some words which have distinctly one-sex connotation, such as *barmaid, chairman*, are avoided by feminists, who favour such neologisms as *bar person, chairperson* and so on. See 3.29 for common use of *they* as unmarked third person singular pronoun.

Noun phrases

ADV **2.35** A noun phrase (NP) is a word or words functioning in a sentence like a noun. It usually consists of a noun (or verbal noun), alone or expanded. The noun is said to be 'head' of the phrase. For example, in <*All these rules*> (2.36), *rules* is head. Less often, a pronoun or an adjective functions as head of a noun phrase. Modification of pronouns is limited, (though see 2.37.3) but modification of the noun can be elaborate. It can involve (a) *premodification* (before the noun), usually by single words and (b) *postmodification* (after the noun), which often takes the form of a reduced clause. (*Note:* some grammarians use the term 'modification' differently. In *Current English Grammar* it means ways of modifying the head noun.)

Proper nouns, like pronouns, usually occur alone as noun phrases because they do not need further identification, but there are exceptions: <*my sister Mary*> <*something different*>.

2.36 Premodification consists of one or more of the following:

1 *Determiners* — essential except where noun can have ZERO article.	*All these* rules!
2 *Adjectives* (for adjective order in noun phrases — see 8.27) Adjectives may themselves be modified, eg by adverbs.	All these *difficult grammatical* rules. These *rather more difficult* rules.
3 *Participles* (8.29)	*frozen* foods / a *sickening* thud
4 *Other nouns* [nouns in attributive use including genitive]	*grammar* rules the *British Broadcasting Corporation World* Service the *BBC's* programmes
5 *Adverbs* Only some are possible (see 9.21 for some focusing adverbs and 9.33 for *quite/rather*)	*Only* Harry can afford it. *rather* a problem
6 *Miscellaneous* Various word compounds, and even finite clauses, are possible.	a *best-selling* author a *stainless steel* knife that *never-to-be-forgotten* day He had an 'I *told you so*' look on his face.

2.37 Postmodification consists of one or more of the following:

1 *Prepositional phrases* (see chap 10) Usually the head of the NP is also the 'thing' we are talking about (eg a visitor). (a) But in one large class of nouns + PP it is the second noun, the one in the *of-*phrase (eg cheese) that is semantically more important. (b) Sometimes a premodifying adjective can be attached to either noun and refer to the 'thing as a whole'. But an adjective belonging only to the first noun may be unacceptable. So <*a cracked cup of coffee> is impossible. Contrast: <a tall visitor from Mars> (where the true 'head noun' can have its own adjective)	(a) a girl *with red hair* a visitor *from Mars* pleasure *at your success* a world record *out of the blue* (b) a piece *of cheese* a loaf *of bread* a box *of chocolates* a stale piece of cheese a piece of stale cheese a hot cup of coffee a cup of hot coffee
2 *Adjectives* — see postposition (8.31)	the Festival *proper* something *different*
3 *Relative clauses* [finite] (11.27)	the girl *who/that lives next door* a place *where I should hate to live* <the hearts and minds of the many *who had voted for the alliance with secret misgivings*>

4 *Non-finite clauses* See 8.31 for reduced clauses with participles. Nouns can also be postmodified by *to*-infinitives. The structure can imply different relationships. The noun may be: ● the 'logical' object of the *to*-infinitive ● the object of a preposition ● verb-related so that *noun + to-infinitive* is more like a catenative group	bricks *flying in all directions* a lorry *loaded with amusement machines* a book *to read* salt *to put on the potatoes* the last person *(for you) to tell* a corkscrew *to open the bottle with* his decision *not to go* [compare: He decided not to go.]
5 *Adverbs* Only some adverbs can postmodify — mainly common adverbs of place and time (see also 9.21 for *exactly/alone*).	the way *up*/ the river *below* the morning *after* what *exactly* . . . Harry *alone* . . .
6 *'Split' patterns* See 8.16 for complementation of adjectives	a *hopeless* child *at games* a *hard* story *to swallow* the *first* thing *to say*
7 *Apposition* — see next section	

ADV **2.38 Apposition**

Apposition can be regarded as a kind of postmodification, or as a separate function of noun phrases. Instead of a head noun followed by some description, we have two noun phrases in an equal relationship:
<the chairman, Mr Jeremy Brown>
<Mr Jeremy Brown, the chairman>.
Noun clauses can be in apposition to abstract words like *fact, belief, report*. Notice the difference between a noun clause in apposition and a relative (adjectival) clause:
<The report *that the prisoners had escaped* alarmed the villagers.> [apposition]
<The report *(that/which) the papers published* was inaccurate.> [relative]
Like adjectives and relative clauses, nouns and clauses in apposition can be defining or non-defining:
<the name Wessex> [defining]
<a rumour that the prisoners had escaped> [defining]
<Jane Reid, *my cousin*> [non-defining]
<This alarming report — *that the prisoners had escaped* — was denied.> [non-defining].
See also (11.37).

3. DETERMINERS AND PRONOUNS

Determiners		Pronouns
		(one, ones)
+	Articles	
+	Demonstratives	+
	Quantifiers:	
+	some, any	+
+	no	—
—	none	+
—	somebody, nobody etc	+
+	many, much	+
+	enough, a lot (of), several	+
+	few, little	+
+	a few, a little	+
+	more, most	+
+	fewer, fewest	+
+	less, least	+
+	either, neither	+
+	each	+
+	every	—
+	all, half, both	+
+	Numbers	+
+	another	+
+	other	(another, the other)
—	others	+
—	Personal forms:	I/me, he/him etc
my/his etc	Possessive	mine, his, one's etc
—	Reflexive	myself, himself, oneself etc
	Wh- series:	
what(ever), which(ever), whose	Interrogative and relative	what (ever), which (ever), who (ever), whom, whose; + (relative only) that, ZERO

What are determiners?

3.1   'Determiners' is not a category that occurs in older grammars. Instead, the words dealt with here (including sometimes even the articles) were often treated as adjectives.

This is now felt to be unsatisfactory. Words like *my*, *every*, *this* do not behave like ordinary adjectives. In addition, they often have corresponding or identical pronouns, eg *mine*, *everyone*, *this*, which ordinary adjectives do not. Yet to label them as pronouns, as older grammars often do, fails to show how differently they function from that word-class too.

Modern grammar therefore uses the label 'determiner' for words with the following characteristics:

Form They are mostly closed category words (1.17) having corresponding pronouns.

Position They must come before ordinary open-class adjectives (if present) in a noun phrase.

Function They determine or limit the noun that follows.

Exclusive use A fourth characteristic that distinguishes determiners from adjectives is that, whereas there is theoretically no limit to the number of adjectives in a noun phrase, most determiners are mutually exclusive.

It must be admitted, however, that there are still problems of overlap with other classes: for example, *few* has comparative (*fewer*) and superlative (*fewest*) like adjectives; *this/that* have plurals like nouns.

What are pronouns?

3.2   **Form** Pronouns are closed category words (1.17) and formally related to determiners. In many cases the same word, eg *that*, can function as both parts of speech:

    <Look at that!> [pronoun]
    <Look at that dog!> [determiner]

Position Pronouns occupy the same positions in sentences as noun phrases (2.35) or single nouns.

Function Despite the name 'pronoun', pronouns do not always stand for a noun phrase within the text. They may have direct reference to the outside situation, particularly *I*, *you*, or refer to a whole clause, eg *that* (3.11).

Restricted use with count and mass nouns

3.3

	Determiners		Nouns		Pronoun reference
1	with count singular only — A a/an/one each/every either/neither	**A**	**Count singular** dollar story apple suggestion tourist	**1**	one each either/neither he/she/him/her [people]
2	with count singular — A or mass — B (ie non-plural) this that	**B**	**Mass** money information tourism advice fruit	**2**	this that it
3	with mass only — B (a) little/less/least (but see 3.19) much a bit of a great amount of a good/great deal of			**3**	(a) little/less/least much a bit a great amount a good/great deal
4	with mass — B or count plural — C (ie non-singular) all (but see 3.20) enough more/most a lot of/lots of plenty of ZERO some/any (but see 3.13)	**C**	**Count plural** dollars stories tourists suggestions apples	**4**	all enough a lot/lots plenty some/any
5	with count plural only — C (a) few/fewer/fewest both many several these/those a good/great many a great/large number of Numbers			**5**	(a) few/fewer/fewest both many several these/those a good many etc ones they/them Numbers

Although the definite article *the* can be used with count and mass nouns (singular and plural) and with mass nouns, many determiners are restricted to use with certain types of nouns only. Their corresponding pronouns are similarly restricted. The most important restrictions are shown in the table. ZERO means the absence of any articles or other determiner.

Articles

3.4 *the* (definite), *a, an,* ZERO (indefinite)

	Singular	Plural	Mass
a/an	a furniture shop a factory a carpet factory		
ZERO		furniture shops carpet factories carpets	furniture factory furniture
the	the furniture shop the factory the carpet factory	the furniture shops the carpet factories the carpets	the furniture the factory furniture

Usage

A/an is only used when the head of the noun phrase is a singular count noun. It is not used with plural count or with mass nouns, which do not necessarily require determiners at all — that is, they can take ZERO article. *A/an* therefore alternates with ZERO in the indefinite system. Another way of looking at this is to think of mass as unmarked. Indefinite plural is then marked by inflection, and indefinite singular by *a/an*. *The* is possible with all common nouns.

Pronunciation

Although *the* has only one written form, both definite and indefinite articles have two commonly spoken forms, depending on the sound that follows.

● Before a consonant sound: *the* = /ðə/; *a* = /ə/
● Before a vowel sound: *the* = /ðɪ/; *an* = /ən/.

These are the so-called weak forms of the articles. Strong forms — /ðiː/eɪ/æn/— are rarely used except for unusual emphasis.

Examples: (weak forms) /ðə/ or /ə/ +

European, ewe, head, unicorn, Fellow of the Royal Society, hydrogen bomb, long-playing record, Member of Parliament, non-commissioned officer, State Registered Nurse, xylophone, youth

/ðɪ/ or /ən/ +

emperor, hour, FRS, H-bomb, lp, MP, nco, SRN, x-film.

Meaning

The traditional names 'definite' (*the*) and 'indefinite' (*a/an* plus ZERO in modern grammar) indicate some of the semantic implications of article usage. Cutting across this division is another distinction, between *specific meaning*, pointing to identifiable units and no other and *generic meaning* referring to the class in general.

3.5 Meaning of *the* (definite)

	Count	Mass
specific	the dolphin [sing] the dolphins [pl]	the music
generic	the dolphin [sing]	

[*The* + count noun] (sing and pl) and [*the* + mass noun] can all have specific reference (A below). Specific definiteness may be established in the text (A1, A2), or in the context of the external situation (A3). Only [*the* + count singular noun] can be generic (B).

A   Definite meaning — specific

1 *text-reference back* — 'anaphoric' reference: <There's a dolphin over there, apparently listening to music. *The* dolphin looks happy, but *the* music sounds terrible to me.>

2 *text-reference forward* — 'cataphoric' reference: <*The* dolphins *here* are fascinating, but *the* music *here* is not very good.>
<They are *the* *most intelligent* animals I *know*.> [reference forward + uniqueness]

3 *Context of external situation*
unique, eg *the* sun, *the* moon
unique in the situation [even though others exist elsewhere]:
<Oh look at *the* *dolphins*.> [here in this zoo]
<Do you think *the* *water* is warm?>
Also: The Prime Minister made a speech.
        It happened in *the fifties*. [the 1950s]
        Please pass *the* salt.
        Put *the* kettle on.
        I'm going to *the post-office/the doctor's/the bank*.
        What's in *the* paper today?
        We live in *the* south.

B   Definite meaning — generic
The dolphin is in no danger of extinction.
Do you think man exploits *the* *dolphin*?
The violin is a subtle instrument.
Do you like *the* theatre?

A   Definite meaning — specific
1 It is not true, as is sometimes stated, that the indefinite article is always used for 'first mention' and that the definite article is used subsequently for reference back (as happens in 1 above). *The* can in fact be used for first mention (see 2 and 3 above), or indefiniteness may persist in second and subsequent mentions, as in:
        <I wish I had *a* dolphin — *a* dolphin of my own.>
2 *The* plus postmodification (ie *the* with reference forward) establishes specific definiteness. But notice that indefiniteness can persist despite postmodification:
        <*A* dolphin I *saw here last week* was incredible.>
        <Music *on tape* isn't the same as live music.>
3 Since uniqueness is a form of definiteness, *the* is used when referring to unique and specific things in the 'real world'. But the uniqueness is not absolute; it is in the speaker's mind. *The moon* is unique in our world; *the kettle* is the only one where the speaker is.

B   Definite meaning — generic
As used here, these singular nouns denote a whole class (dolphins in general, violins contrasted with other instruments, the theatre as an art form, not a specific building etc). [*The* + plural noun] and [*the* + mass noun] are specific only: <*What is the meaning of *the* life?>

Other uses of *the* [definite]:
For *the* + adjective, eg *the rich/the helpless* — see 8.28.
For *the* + nationality adjectives, eg *the English* — see 2.22.
For *the* + names (specific usage) — see 2.18-19.
For *the* instead of possessive pronouns — see 3.32.
For *the sooner, the better* — see 11.24.

3.6 Meaning of *a/an/*zero (indefinite)

	Count	Mass
specific	a dolphin (some) dolphins	(some) music (some) food
classifying	a dolphin dolphins	music food

The indefinite article also has two distinct meanings. But the label 'generic' is less appropriate here. The indefinite plural <*Dolphins have been exploited by man.> does not strictly have the generic meaning sometimes claimed for it, and it is not comparable with definite singular <The dolphin has been exploited.>

The dolphin can mean the whole genus or class; indefinite *dolphins* means members or examples of that class. And there is nothing generic about indefinite singular, which can only be specific: <*A dolphin has been exploited by man.>

A better label for the indefinite and non-specific usage of *a/an/*zero therefore is 'classifying', an indication of class membership.

The difference between specific and classifying usage of the indefinite article is brought out by
- what happens in the plural for count nouns (the possibility of *some* for specific, but not for classifying);
- whether 'second mention' is definite or indefinite. (The second mention of specific is definite; the second mention of classifying remains indefinite.)

A   Indefinite meaning — specific
   a particular, actual example of the class — *and no other* — even though indefinite:
   A dolphin has just leapt out of the water.
   The zoo has/have just bought *a new dolphin*.
   There's *a dolphin* asleep over there.
   Perhaps that dolphin is trying to catch *food*.
1   *plural* of indefinite-specific can be *some* or zero:
   Some dolphins have just leapt out of the water.
   The zoo have just bought *(some) new dolphins*.
2   *second mention* — first mention was earlier — is **definite**:
   The (new) dolphin is very young.
   The dolphin (asleep over there) looks comic.
   The food looks unsuitable.

B **Indefinite meaning — classifying** (unit(s) of a class)
> *A dolphin* is *a highly intelligent animal.*
> I wish I had *a dolphin* of my very own.
> That is not *a dolphin* — it's *a whale.*
> Don't throw *food.*

1 *plural* of indefinite classifying must be ZERO:
> *Dolphins* are *highly intelligent animals.* not <*Some dolphins . . .>
> Those aren't *dolphins* — they're *whales.* not <*Those aren't some dolphins . . .>

2 *second mention* of classifying remains still indefinite (*a/an*/ZERO — never *the*)
> If I had a *dolphin* of my own I would communicate with it.
> *Food* must not be thrown.

3.7 Other uses of a/an

1 *distributive* twice *a* week, 20p. *a* pint, [twice every week , etc]
2 *with some numerical expressions* a dozen, *a* score, *a* hundred, etc.
This is perfectly regular if we think of these words as representing single units, and the words themselves as count nouns.
3 *a/an + mass noun* can denote a separate unit of the material, etc, eg, a coffee = [a cup of coffee] a good cheese = [a good variety].
4 *a/an + verb base* [some verbs only] can be used as a singular noun [but not plural]:
> <I must have *a think.*>   <This book is *a good read.*>

For *a/an* with names — see 2.19.
For quite/rather *a bargain* — see 9.33.
For such/what *a clever girl* — see 3.36.

3.8 Zero article with singular count nouns

Apparent exceptions to the rule that singular count nouns need an article include:
1 *Ellipsis* — ie omission — before the second count noun in linked pairs seen as a single unit:
> <a knife and __ fork> <a blouse and __ skirt>
> <the cup and __ saucer>.

2 *Noun phrases in apposition to a name* Here it is probably *the* rather than *a* that is omitted:
> <John le Carré, __ author of some gripping spy stories, . . .>

3 *Job/profession words* after linking verbs normally require *a/an*: <My cousin is/became *a* dentist/*an* airline pilot> etc [classifying]
But when the noun means a unique role or job, definite *the* is sometimes omitted. This is a sort of proper name usage:
> <They made a Polish cardinal __ Pope.>
> <Harry's just been appointed (the) deputy editor.>

4 Articles are often omitted in special forms of English such as *headlines, notices,* etc (12.9):
> < __ Plane Crashes on __ House>.

For common nouns with ZERO article (*by hand, in hospital*) see 2.9-2.10.

Demonstratives

3.9 Usage and meaning

this that	money [Mass] cheque bank manager } [Count sing]	these those	dollars cheques [Count pl] managers

In general *this* is the basic unmarked form in this set — unmarked for number or for distance in time and space.

- *This/these*, unmarked for distance, mean near the speaker or writer (here, now, today).
- *That/those* mean farther away (there, then, yesterday, tomorrow).
- *These/those* are marked for plural. Notice that demonstratives distinguish between non-plural and plural, whereas most determiners make other distinctions (3.3).

As determiners (ie followed by nouns), all four demonstratives can be used with people and things (see tables above), but as pronouns, their reference is sometimes restricted to things.

3.10 Demonstrative pronouns in classifying sentences

A

What	is	this? that?
Who		[people & things]

C

What are	these? those? [Count pl, mainly things]

D

What	are	those people? these children? [Count pl; determiners are more usual than pronouns for people]
Who		

B

This [including introducing plural people]	is	my money [Mass]
		my wallet [Count sing, Mr Smith people & things] the bank manager
That [people & things]		Mr & Mrs Smith my mother and father [Count pl, people]

E

These	are	travellers cheques French francs [things]
Those [people & things]		bank managers my cousins [people]

The main usage of demonstrative pronouns to refer to people is in classifying sentences of the kind shown. (For the difference between *what* and *who* see 3.34.) But notice that in questions (A, C and D) *these/those* are not very usual if people are meant.

In statements (B and E), *these/those* are acceptable in subject position. Notice that in introducing people we say *This is* + *plural* if the people are seen as a unit.

3.11 Demonstrative pronouns and determiners — other uses

Pronouns

A	*This/that* puzzles me. *These/those* look interesting. Come and look at *this/these*.
B	Those children look all right. But *these* are tired.
C	It's rather hard on *those of us who pay our taxes.* Will all *those in favour* please raise their hands?
D	Heavens, what was *that?* What's happening? What is all *this?*
E	Listen to *this.* There's been a heatwave at the South Pole. I lost my wallet and my house was burgled. Oh dear, when did *this/that* happen? <*When did these/those happen?>

A Except in classifying sentences (3.10), demonstrative pronouns are normally only used with things, and all the sentences here would be so understood.

B *These/those* (but not *this/that*) can sometimes refer to people. But identity must have been clearly established, so perhaps this is really a case of determiner + ellipsis.

C [*Those* + postmodification] can mean people.

D *This/that* can refer not only to things (ie something for which a mass noun or a singular count noun exists) but also to events, happenings.

E *This/that* can also stand for a clause or sentence. Notice that *this* can point backwards — 'anaphoric' reference — or forward — 'cataphoric', but *that* can only have backward reference.

Determiners

A	'What's *that child* doing?' 'I don't know, but *this one* is half asleep.'
B	Who's *that noisy silly one?* Where are *those expensive ones?*
C	I was on my way home when I saw *this stunning blonde.* [infml]

A Although *this/that* [pronouns] are not normally used for a person, we can refer to a person as *this one/ that one* 12.2.

B When adjectives follow demonstratives, whether for people or things, *one/ones* (or nouns) are needed: <*Who's that noisy silly?> <*Where are those expensive?> are not acceptable.

C Informally [*this/these* + noun] are used to suggest that the things or people referred to are familiar to us, or the speaker is about to make them familiar.

Quantifiers

	Count	Mass	
m	all		**m**
o	every [+ count sing]	all	**o**
r			**r**
e	most		**e**
	many	much	
f l	some		**l**
e e	(a) few	(a) little	**e**
w s			**s**
e s	fewest	least	**s**
r	any		
	no/none		

3.12 A large group of determiners and pronouns indicate quantity on a scale from *all* to *no/none* and the general term *quantifier* can be given to them. The table gives a general indication of where most of these words come on the scale and shows which are restricted to count or mass nouns.

Quantifiers also include *enough* and *several*, but these cannot reasonably be shown on the scale. In terms of meaning we could also include numbers among quantifiers, but most grammarians treat these separately (3.37).

3.13 *some/any/no/none*

Some/any [determiners and pronouns] have two main meanings:

1 Indefinite quantity or amount — with count plural and mass nouns only.

2 Identity — with count (singular and plural) and mass.

No (determiner) *none* (pronoun), both with the sense of negative amount, have comparable usage to **1**, but *no* can also be used with reference to count-singular. All four words can apply to people and things.

1 Indefinite quantity or amount

	Count sing	Count pl	Mass
Affirmative statements		There are { some eggs. some plates. some.	There is { some meat. some.
Non-assertive		There aren't { any eggs. any plates. any.	There isn't { any meat. any.
Negative	There is no plate.	There are { no eggs. no plates. none.	There is { no meat. none.

Questions	open assertive	Have you had *any* (food) today? Would you like *some* (sandwiches)? [to encourage the answer Yes]
Statements of uncertainty		I *don't* think he's had *any* food today. Telephone me *if* you hear *any* news. *Don't* write *unless* there's *any/some* news.

The determiners in this quantifier usage are usually weak (*some* = /səm/). The pronouns are strong /sʌm/, though not necessarily stressed.

Some suggests a positive quantity. It is used in positive (affirmative) statements and questions that in some way expect a positive answer. It is not used in ordinary negative statements. Do not confuse this use of the term 'positive' with the degree usage for adjectives and adverbs (8.6).

Any is non-assertive (1.7). It is used in negatives, open questions and in complex statements containing some doubt or uncertainty.

2 Identity

Positive meaning	Count singular	*Some* careless driver has hit my car. *Any* fool can learn to drive. *Any* stick to beat a dog!
	Count plural	*Some* people will do anything for money. *Any* people who drive when they're drunk are mad.
	Mass	*Some* cheese is made from goat's milk. *Any* food would be better than none.
Negative	Count singular Count plural Mass	I'm *no* saint; I'm just an ordinary human being. I'm not afraid of *some* insects. [but I am of others] I can't eat *some* food — fish heads, for example. I won't just eat *any* food — only nicely cooked food. I can't eat *any old* food.

In this usage, *some* is always strong /sʌm/, and *any* receives some stress.

Some here roughly means 'particular one/ones'. It can be used in negatives.

Any — meaning 'one or some person or thing': of unspecified identity, but existing — can be used in positive statements.

3.14 Verb concord — *some/any/none* as pronouns

Some		these plates are this china is	yours
	of		
Do you think any None		these plates are these plates is this china is	broken valuable

Some/any/none take singular or plural verb according to meaning and the type of nouns they relate to. Prescriptive grammar says *none* always takes a singular verb. Actually *none* (and *any*) take singular verb in relation to count-nouns if they imply 'not (even) one', and plural if they imply 'all . . . not':

<A British diplomat said, 'Mark is OK, and *none* of them seem __ to be suffering any ill-effects from what must have been quite an ordeal.'>

3.15 *someone* series: pronouns only

Person		Thing
someone	somebody	something
anyone	anybody	anything
no one	nobody	nothing
everyone	everybody	everything

1 The meaning and usage of *some-* and *any-* compounds, with regard to positive and negative, and assertive and non-assertive are the same as for *some* and *any*. (There are also corresponding adverbs: *somewhere*, *anywhere*, *nowhere*, and *everywhere*).

<I can hear *someone/somebody* coming — listen!>
<Does *anyone/anybody* here speak Chinese?>
<I $\left\{ \begin{array}{l} \text{don't know } anything \\ \text{know } nothing \end{array} \right\}$ about it.>

2 There is virtually no difference in meaning between the *-one* and the *-body* series. But notice the difference between *everyone* etc as one word [all people] and *every one* [each person/thing] as two words:

<We hope *everyone/everybody* will enjoy the film.>
<We hope *every one* of you will enjoy it.>
<*Every one* of the films we've shown this year has been a success.>

3.16 *someone* series: concord

Verb concord for this series is regular (ie singular), but pronoun concord is usually *they/their/them*:

<Everybody had his own way of doing things.> [fml]
<Everybody has their own way . . .> [usual]
<Everybody knows that, don't they?> [usual; <*Everybody knows that, doesn't he?> is impossible.]

For *one*, *oneself* — see 3.29.

3.17 *many, much, a lot (of), enough, several*

A	How questions	How	many travellers cheques [pl] much money [mass]	have you got? did you get?
B	Other questions & negatives	Are there There aren't	many days [pl] enough boxes [pl]	left(?)
		Is there There isn't	much time [mass] enough time [mass]	
		Did you get	many enough $\}$ cheques? [pl]	
		I haven't	much enough $\}$ money. [mass]	

C Statements			
	She has won	enough/a lot of/several	prizes. [pl]
		so / too } many	
		many valuable	
		many [fml]	
		enough/a lot of	money. [mass]
		so / too } much	
		much [fml and rare]	
	Many/A lot of/ Several	intelligent people believe in luck.	
	Much [fml] A lot of	nonsense is talked about luck. time is wasted deciding what to buy.	

Both *many* and *much* are neutral as to quantity in *how*-questions, but
otherwise are near the top of the quantity scale. *Many/much* —
particularly *much* — tend to be non-assertive, except with *so* and *too*.
Much alone in positive statements is usually very formal as in the
formula: <*I have much pleasure in* declaring this fête open.> *Much* is
particularly rare in object position. *Many* is used with count nouns-
plural, and *much* with mass.

A *lot of* (or *lots of* — very informal) is preferred to *many/much* in
informal positive statements. Both can be used with count plural and
mass. Although determiners are mainly closed class, it is possible to
add items here like *a great deal of* [mass] and *a large number of* [count
plural].

Enough is used mainly with count-plural and mass.
It can follow nouns but this tends to be formal: <There will be time
enough for that later.>
Several relates to count-plural only.

3.18 *few/little, a few/ a little*

Positive meaning:	Let's take a picnic — I've got *a few* rolls and *a little* cheese.
Negative meaning:	The people were starving. There were (*so/too*) *few* vegetables and (*so/too*) *little* meat in the shops.

A *few/a little* have 'positive' meaning [some, even if not many].
Few/little have negative meaning [almost none]. *So* and *too* can be used
with *few/little* in this sense, but not with positive *a few/a little*.

3.19 *more/most, few/fewer/fewest, little/less/least*

A	More Fewer (Less)	people went abroad for their holidays last year. [count]		
	More Less	wine is drunk nowadays than years ago. [mass]		
	Who's got (the)	most fewest	coins? apples?	[count]
		most least	money? food?	[mass]

Much, many, few, little are unusual determiners/pronouns in that they have comparative and superlative forms like adjectives. *More/most* are the comparative and superlative for both *many* and *much*. Note that *few* has regular inflection.

B Theoretically, *little, less, least* are used with mass nouns and *few, fewer, fewest* with count plural. Careful speakers/writers make this distinction and it must be made with *(a) little* and *(a) few*: <A few people> <little money>. (Do not confuse determiner *little* with the adjective *little*, which can of course be used with count nouns — *a little boy*). There is however a growing tendency to use *less* (not *fewer*) for all nouns:

> <There's *less* money around.>
> <*Less/Fewer* people took holidays abroad last year.>

For *much, more, enough* etc as adverbs — see 9.22.
For *more, most, fewer*, etc in comparative and superlative — see 8.18 and 8.21.

3.20 *both/either/neither, each/every, all/half*

A ***Both, either, neither*** [all det and pro] refer to count nouns in a set of two only.
- *Both* views the two together: <both grandfathers> and takes a plural verb.
- *Either* usually views the two as exclusive alternatives: <either man> [not both] and takes a singular verb. But if the meaning is 'neither' [both . . . not], then a plural verb is possible in pronoun use.
  > <I don't suppose either of them know/knows.> <I suppose neither of them know/knows.> (see below).
- *Neither* <neither man, neither of them> is not strictly comparable to *either*. The meaning is nearer to 'both . . . not', and a plural verb is usually possible. But *neither/either* as determiners take singular nouns and singular verbs:
  > <Neither of them know/knows.> <Neither man knows.>

B ***Each*** [det and pro] ***every*** [det only] refer to a count noun in a set of two or more.
- *Each* sees the units separately, often with distributive meaning [one at a time].
- *Every* also sees the units separately, but at the same time there is a group meaning rather like *all*.
- *Each/every* normally take a singular verb.

C ***All/half*** [det and pro] refer to count nouns [sing and pl] and mass nouns.
- *All* with count plural usually means the group together; *all* with count sing or mass usually means the whole.

Meaning

Meaning and concord is shown in the box above.

Position

1 All of the pronouns in this group (ie excluding determiner *every*) can appear in the pattern:

<Both (etc) of ^{the men> [noun]}
them> [pronoun]

But not <*both they> <*both them> (etc); ie as determiners these words never precede a personal pronoun (3.21, 3.23-24).

2 *All/both/half* occur before other determiners (articles, demonstratives, possessives) and are sometimes called predeterminers. Only *half* occurs before the indefinite article *a*, and it cannot occur without determiners unless used as a pronoun (3.24 and 3.25).

3 *All the* (or *all* + *his*, *this* etc — not plain *all*) is usually needed with singular count nouns:

<I walked *all the way*.> <I've read *all his* new book.>

But notice: *all day*, *all night*. (3.24 and 3.25).

4 *All/both/each* (but not *half*) can occur after nouns and pronouns in subject or indirect object position; *all/both* can occur after nouns as direct objects (3.26).

5 *All* as a pronoun + a following clause can mean 'everything' or 'the only thing':

<*All you say is true.*> [Everything . . .]

<*All I want* is peace and quiet.> [The only thing . . .]

6 *Each* can occur finally with distributive meaning (3.23).

For *both*, *either*, *neither* as conjunctions — see 11.11.

3.21 *Both/either/neither*

Both (of) my grandfathers Both of them Both (those) men Both	have gone. [plural verb] are deaf.
Neither of my grandfathers Neither of them Neither	wear/wears glasses. [sing or pl] know/knows.
Neither man I wonder if either (man)	wears glasses. [sing]

I don't think I *doubt* if [negative meaning]	either of them either of the men either	is/are here. [sing or pl]

3.22 *Both/either/each*

[determiner + noun]		
You can park on	either each	side [sing]	of the road.
	both	sides [pl]	

3.23 Each/every

Each child Every child Each (of them) Each one Each of the children	has [sing verb]	£1 (each). [distributive]

3.24 All/both/half

		Determiner	Noun	
All Half	(of)	the this my	bread [mass] loaf [count sing]	is . . .
	of	—	it [pronoun]	
Half	—	a an	loaf hour [count sing only]	is . . .
All Half Both	(of)	the these my	loaves [count pl]	are . . .
	of	—	them [pronoun]	

3.25 All/both without other determiners

All	bread [mass] is . . .
All Both	loaves [count plural] are . . .

3.26 All/both/each with noun/pronoun subjects and objects

[Plural subjects]	[after subject NP] all both each	[Verb] have £1 (each).		
They				
The children	[auxiliary] have	[after operator] all both each	[Verb] got been sent	£1.
My sisters				
We	[BE] are	[after BE] all both		well. wondering what to do.
		each		doing their/our bit.

He	gave	[Indirect obj] them us the children	[after IO] all both each	£1. sweets.
They		[Direct obj] them us the children	[after DO] all both [not each]	
	took			to London.

Personal pronouns and determiners

3.27 Form of personal pronouns

		Subject	Object	Reflexive
1st person	sing pl	I we	me us	myself ourselves
2nd person	sing pl	you		yourself yourselves
3rd person	sing	he [male] she [female] it [neuter]	him her it	himself herself itself
	pl	they	them	themselves

	one	one	oneself

3.28 Usage of personal pronouns

A Subject	*He and I* are just good friends. What is *she* going to do? You're luckier than *I* am. [subject of 2nd clause]
B Object	The Smiths have asked my husband and *me* to dinner. Don't tell *them* anything. Please explain this to *us*. We want *them* to come. [grammatically object of *want*] It's *me/him/them*. [*It's I*, etc = old-fashioned, fml] You're luckier than *me*. [Compare A above]. She looked around *her*, surprised. } [in prepositional I haven't got my cheque-book on *me*. } phrases of place]

C **Reflexive**	Help *yourself*. [subject understood] Tom's found *himself* a new job. He hurt *himself*, and asked me to help *him*. [not *himself*] You have nobody but *yourself* to blame. Don't talk to *yourself*, Susan. You and Henry should talk to *each other/one another* more. In this situation one must look after *oneself*. Everyone enjoyed *themselves/himself*. Nobody likes to talk about *themselves/himself*. I *myself* saw it. I saw it *myself*. [emphatic] I went *by myself*. [alone] I went *myself*. [I didn't send someone else.]
D **choice after some prepositions**	This is worrying for people like *us/ourselves*. Who is involved besides *me/myself*? Nobody except *you/yourself*. Between *you and me/between ourselves*, I think she's left her husband. *Between us*, we could surely repair the car. Tom and Dick did the job *between them*.

A & B **Subject & object pronouns** Broadly speaking, subject pronouns are used as subjects of a finite verb, and object pronouns anywhere else: so <*They have asked my husband and I> is substandard. Object pronouns (not reflexives) are used in phrases of place like *around her/on me*, even though there is reference back.

C **Reflexive pronouns** are used as objects etc where these refer back to an element in *the same* clause. Notice the difference between

<They were talking to *themselves*.> [separately] and
<They were talking to *each other/one another*.> [reciprocal]

One is unlike the indefinite pronouns of the *someone* series (see 3.15) in having a reflexive form. *Someone* etc usually uses *themselves* [pl] or *himself* etc [sing].

Reflexive pronouns for emphasis can follow the noun or take final position in the clause.

D **After prepositions** Object pronouns are normally used (and see B) except in reflexive positions: <You have nobody but *yourself* to blame.> But a few prepositions alternate between object and reflexive pronouns — mainly when 1st or 2nd person.

Notice the different usage and meaning with *between* in

<between you and me/between ourselves> [in confidence]
<between us/them/you> [sharing something].

Subject pronouns after prepositions are substandard: <*between you and I>.

3.29 Meaning of personal pronouns

Despite the name, pronouns do not always stand for nouns. It should be noticed too that the traditional terms, '1st person' (*I/we*), '2nd' (*you*) and '3rd' (*he, she, it, they*) are more accurate formally than functionally.

1 *I/we/you* usually have reference outside the text. *I* means the speaker or writer. *We* may include the listener/reader(s), or it may exclude them and include some other people.

2 *She/her; he/him* are mainly used for people. Both can be used for animals which are felt to have some personality:

<Where's that dog of mine? I want to take *him* for a walk.>

3 *She/her* can be used for countries, ships and sometimes cars:
> <India needs to increase *her* exports.>
>
> <'How's your new car?' 'Great! *She* can do 100 miles an hour.'>

4 *They/them* can refer to people or things. Because there is no third person singular pronoun in English which is neutral between male and female, informal English often uses *they/them/their* etc in sentences such as
> <Will *everyone* please bring *their* passports with *them*.> and
>
> <If *anybody* calls, tells *them* I'm out.>

5 *They/you* can be used as vague informal personal pronouns. *They* often means 'the authorities'; *you* means people generally:
> <*They* fine *you* in Singapore if *you* drop litter in the streets.>

6 *One* is a formal personal pronoun in the sort of context where *you* means 'people'. It often means people including the speaker, and sometimes seems to be a modest substitute for I:
> <*One* can't do anything these days without breaking some law.>
>
> <'Did you enjoy your boarding-school?' 'Oh, *one* got used to it.'>

British and American usage following *one* are different: <If *one* is going to fish or hunt, *he* will want to bring along clothes suitable for such activities.> [**Am. Eng** guide book].

British Eng here would have to continue with *one will want* . . . and similarly with *one's, oneself* etc (see also 3.31).

3.30   *It/itself*

It/itself would more accurately be described as 'non-personal' pronouns as far as meaning is concerned, but normally these are included among personal pronouns. The meaning is not, however, always inanimate.

1 *It* can be used of animals and even human babies if the sex is unknown or unimportant:
> <What's the matter with that child? *It* looks ill.>

2 *It* can also have more general textual reference:
> <Her mother's just died. *It's* been a terrible shock for her.>

3 *It* is the pronoun for *all/everything* etc in question-tags:
> <*Nothing's* the same now, is *it*?>

Note: *it's* = it has/it is. *its* = possessive (3.32)

4 *'Empty' it* (also called 'dummy' it). It is used as an empty subject with no meaning when talking about the weather, time, etc. and in some other structures:
> <*It's* raining.> <*It's* cold today.> <*It's* November already.>
>
> <*It* says here that income tax is going up.> [Notice that transformation here is impossible: <*That income tax is going up says here.>]
>
> <Who is *it*?' '*It's* Tom.'>
>
> <That's torn *it*.> [vague object].

5 *Introductory it:* (also called 'anticipatory' or 'preparatory' it). Again *it* is used to fill the initial subject slot in the sentence, but in this structure the actual subject comes later:
> <*It* is difficult *to speak Chinese well*.>
>
> <*It's* bad luck *being an invalid*.>
>
> <*It* is sad *that he refuses to come*.> [Transformation here is possible: <That he refuses to come is sad.> etc]

Notice also:
> <We thought *it* wrong *to conceal the facts*.> [introductory object].

3.31 *one* (pronoun and determiner)

1 For *one* as a formal pronoun referring to people (never <*ones> in this use) — see 3.29.

2 *One/ones* can be pronoun substitutes for count nouns — people and things:

<The teapot's broken, and we do need *one*.>

<And what about cups? There were some pretty *ones* here yesterday.>

For the difference between substitution and reference — see 12.2.

3 *One* can contrast with *the other/another*:

<*One* is broken, and *another* is lost.>

<The twins are so alike, I can't tell *one* from *the other*.>

4 *One* as a numeral contrasts with *two*, *three*, etc:

<I've only got *one* brother; not two.>

<That's the *one* thing I'm afraid of.> [= the only thing]

But if there is no emphasis on number, we use *a* rather than *one*:

<I haven't got a sister, only a brother.>

5 As a number pronoun, *one* may be followed by *of* and preceded by *any/each/every*:

<You may have *any/each/every one* of these books.>

6 *One* may be an indefinite determiner:

<*One* day you'll understand.>

<*One* evening I was watching TV when . . .>

3.32 Possessive pronouns and determiners

Determiners	Pronouns
This is *my* (own) money.	It's *mine*.
He should use *his* (own) car.	He should use *his*.
She even lost *her* (own) car.	She lost *hers*.
That's *our* (own) copy.	That's *ours*.
These are *their* (own) keys.	Yes, these are *theirs*.
Where are *your* (own) books?	Where are *yours*?
The dog is asleep in *its* (own) chair.	It has really made that chair *its own*.
	([det + *own*) as pronoun — not <*its>]

Forms

Forms for possessive determiners and possessive pronouns are slightly different (except *his* which is both). *Its*, unlike the other forms, is not normally used as a pronoun by itself.

Possessive determiners + *own*

Own may be added to any determiner form for emphasis or contrast. This can be used with or without a following noun but does not normally take *one/ones*. So:

<my money/my *own* money/my *own*/mine>.

But not <*my own one/ones>.

Own can also be used in the patterns <my *very own*> <a car *of my own*>.

Usage

Possessives are normally used rather than articles with reference to parts of the body:

<*My* head hurts.>

<Tom's broken *his* leg.>

But *the* is possible in some prepositional phrases when talking of pains or injuries:

<The dog bit me in *the* leg.> But — <It bit *my* leg.>
<I was hit on *the* head.> <Something hit *my* head.>
<He received a terrible blow in *the* stomach.>

wh- series and *such*

3.33
- *Who, whom, whose, what, which* are used as interrogative determiners and pronouns, (3.34)
- The *wh*-series, with the addition of *that* and ZERO, are used as relative pronouns, (3.35)
- *such* has predeterminer, determiner and pronoun usage. *What* too can be a predeterminer, (3.36)

3.34 Interrogative determiners and pronouns

who [pro] 1. Personal subject	Who(ever)	is the Foreign Minister? wants to know? are those people? gave you that?	
2. Personal object [infml]		does he mean? are you looking for?	
whom [pro] Personal object [fml]	Whom	do they mean? are you looking for? [very formal = For whom are you looking?]	
whose [pro & det] Personal genitive	Whose	(coat) (teacher) is (money)	this? that?
		(coats) (teachers) are	these? those?
what Unlimited reference. 1. [pro] non-personal, subject & object	What(ever)	happened? is the matter? are those? did you say? was she worrying about?	
2. [det] Personal and non-personal, subject & object	What(ever)	idiot(s) book(s) child(ren)	gave you that idea? do you mean? did you learn that from?
which [pro & det] Reference to a limited set of people/things. Personal and non-personal subject & object	Which(ever)	book/books child/children of the books/children of those (books/children)	do you want? is/are yours? is/are his? is/are hers? is/are Tom's?

69

1 *People or things?*

Who/whom/whoever are pronouns only, and refer to people only. *What* as a pronoun is non-personal only, but as a determiner *what* can be personal and non-personal. *Which* both as a pronoun and a determiner can be both personal and non-personal. Contrast *what/which* as relative pronouns.

2 *Limited or unlimited?*

What has unlimited reference; *which* suggests the choice is limited:

    <*What* kind of books/people do you like?>
    <*Which* do you prefer — fiction or non-fiction?>

3 *Form of following verb*

When *who/whose/what/which* are subject in a question, the question takes statement order <*Who* told you?> but if the interrogative word is object then we have interrogative order, and if necessary operator DO (1.3):

    <*Who* did you tell?>

4 **-ever** *Ever* can be added for emphasis to produce *whoever/whatever/whichever*. *Whichever* is not used with mass nouns. For these forms as adverbial and nominal subordinating conjunctions — see chapter 11.

5 *Verb concord*

Verbs agree (singular or plural) with the following noun or pronoun, or according to the number of the implied subject:

    <*Who is* that child?> <*Who are* those children?>
    <*Whose (book) is* this?> <*Whose (books) are* these?>
    <*Which of you wants* this ticket?> [only one person can have it.]
    <*Which of you want* to come?> [hopefully more than one].

6 *What* has many meanings:

    <*What is* your father?> [He's a bank manager.]
    <*What is* he *like*?> [He's kind; a bit old-fashioned.]
    <*What* does he *look like*?> [He's tall and rather good-looking.]
    <*What* did you do that *for*?> [Because I wanted to.]
    <*What's* the time?> <*What* time is it?>
    <*What's* the matter?>
    <Guess *what*! Henry and Mary have got married.> [infml]

3.35 Relative pronouns

		Defining	*defining and Non-defining*
Subject	PEOPLE	that	who
	THINGS		which
Object	PEOPLE	that/ZERO	who(m)
	THINGS		which
Possessive	PEOPLE	whose	
	THINGS	whose of which	
Nominal relative S & O	THINGS	what	

Relative pronouns introduce (subordinate) relative clauses — see 11.27 for examples.

That can be used for people and things in all defining clauses, except when a possessive pronoun is needed (*whose*).

Who/whom are mainly for people only. They can be used for animals thought of as individuals (eg family pets), but on the whole animals are treated as non-personal (*that* or *which*):

<They had a big dog, which bit me.>

Which is for things (and animals) only.

Whose is possessive for people, and to a limited extent for things.

What is always non-personal. It is unlike other relative pronouns because

- it has sort of determiner meaning [*that* which / *the* thing which]
- it forms an essential grammatical part of both the preceding and following clause:

  <I'll tell you *what* happened.> [I'll tell you *what*/What happened.]

  <*What* she bought was a secret.> [She bought *what*/What was a secret.]

The whole phrase (eg *what happened*) functions as a noun phrase. *What* is not used in ordinary relative clauses but only in this special type, called nominal relative clauses (11.35).

3.36 *such/what*

<table>
<tr><td>A Predeterminers
What</td><td colspan="3">a stupid man (he is)! [sing]
lovely flowers (you sent)! [pl]
wonderful news (they brought)! [mass]</td></tr>
<tr><td>He is
You sent   such
They brought</td><td>a stupid man.
lovely flowers.
wonderful news.</td><td>Such   a stupid man
lovely flowers
wonderful news</td><td>can't be ignored.</td></tr>
<tr><td>B Such
There is   ←→ no
There must be ←→ some
I don't know ←→ any   such
Are there   ←→ many
I'm fascinated by ←→ all</td><td colspan="3">←→ address.
←→ person.
←→ person.
←→ people?
←→ men.</td></tr>
<tr><td>C Such/what

Stamps</td><td>such as</td><td>these
first-day issues
I collect</td><td>are worth having.</td></tr>
<tr><td>I'll show you</td><td>such

what</td><td>stamps   as

information</td><td>exist(s).

I have.</td></tr>
<tr><td colspan="4">D Such [pro]
He's a keen stamp collector, and as such he's always pestering me for stamps.
His request was such that I couldn't refuse.</td></tr>
</table>

Such and *what* cause grammarians a lot of headaches. One modern grammar calls them adverbs on one page, and predeterminers in an identical context on another. It may be easier to think of them as both (pre-)determiners and pronouns.

A **Predeterminers** *What* takes first place in sentences of exclamation. It precedes singular [*a* + singular noun]. The noun phrase is a complete exclamation in itself, though subject and verb can follow. *Such* also is a predeterminer in noun phrases and is similarly used to express

71

admiration, criticism etc. But noun phrases containing *such* usually function in a sentence containing a verb.

<He is such a stupid man.>

<Such a stupid man oughtn't to get the job.>

B **Such** can be a determiner and follow some other determiners as shown. The *such* here is anaphoric, referring back to something (unless there is postmodification — see C). For example, the examples given in B could be replies to an enquiry like 'I'm looking for a Mr. P. Piper of Hamelin.'

C ***such/what* and postmodification**

Such as can postmodify a noun phrase: <stamps *such as* these> and *such* and *what* can also enter into split structures. In both patterns *such* requires *as*. Notice also that there is no subject pronoun following *as* if the preceding noun is understood as subject (11.10, 11.23).

D **Such as a pronoun** refers back in the phrase *as such* (eg as a keen stamp collector), but forward to result in the phrases *such that*, *such as to*.

For *such . . . that/as to* (compared with *so*) in result clauses — see 11.19, 11.25

For *such* in comparison — see 8.22.

For *what* compared with *how* in exclamations — see 1.3.

For other uses of *what* — see 3.33-35.

Numbers

3.37 **Cardinal and ordinal (determiners and pronouns)**

1. one	first (1st)	**11.** eleven	(th)
2. two	second (2nd)	**12.** twelve	twelfth
3. three	third (3rd)	**13.** thirteen	(th)
4. four	fourth (4th)	**14.** fourteen	(th)
5. five	fifth (5th)	**15.** fifteen	(th)
6. six	sixth (6th)	**16.** sixteen	(th)
7. seven	seventh (7th)	**17.** seventeen	(th)
8. eight	eighth (8th)	**18.** eighteen	(th)
9. nine	ninth (9th)	**19.** nineteen	(th)
10. ten	tenth (10th)	**20.** twenty	twentieth

21. twenty-one	twenty-first
22. twenty-two	twenty-second
30. thirty	thirtieth
40. forty	fortieth
50. fifty	fiftieth
60. sixty	sixtieth
70. seventy	seventieth
80. eighty	eightieth
90. ninety	ninetieth
100. (a/one) hundred	hundredth
1000. (a/one) thousand	thousandth
1,000,000. (a/one) million	millionth

1 Apart from *first, second, third* (and higher figures incorporating them) most ordinal numbers are formed by adding the sound /ə/, spelt (*th*) to the cardinal numbers, but note some irregular spellings. With 20, 30 etc, the spelling changes from -y to -*ieth* and /əə/ is added in speech.

2 When both are used together, ordinal numbers normally precede cardinal: <the first three prizes> [eg the gold, silver and bronze medals]. Contrast: <three first prizes> [There were three equal winners].

3 Both cardinal and ordinal numbers usually follow rather than precede other determiners, though cardinal numbers can precede some quantifiers: <those six months> <a third child> <the first few days>.

4 The words *hundred, thousand, million* are used without *-s* in definite numbers: <three hundred (days)> <two thousand five hundred (pounds)>. Contrast: <hundreds of times> <He's worth millions.>

In speaking these figures or writing them as words, a single hundred etc needs a determiner — usually *a*: for example <£100> becomes <*a* hundred pounds>, though *one* can be used for emphasis <You should only pay *one* hundred, not two>.

5 *And* is used in spoken British English (not in American English) with numbers above 100, between the last two spoken 'units' if these include figures other than 00 in the last two places:

101		a hundred and one
2003	} are spoken as {	two thousand and three
3120		three thousand, one hundred and twenty

but 8,100 becomes <eight thousand, one hundred>.

Numbers from 1,100 to 1,900 can be spoken as eleven hundred or as one thousand one hundred etc. 0 is often *nought* (British English) or *zero* (American English).

Telephone numbers are usually pronounced figure by figure, with 0 as '*oh*' or '*zero*'. When the same digit is repeated this can be given as 'double -'. For example, <240 . 2044> is <two-four-0, two-0-double four>.

6 *Dates* Four-digit years are usually said in two halves. So <1945> becomes <nineteen forty-five>. But <1905> can be <nineteen hundred and five> or <nineteen-0-five>.

3.38 *double/twice/three times*

These can occur with count nouns [singular and plural] and mass. They can precede some other determiners.

<twice this quantity> <double these amounts> <six times the normal rate>

Another, other, others

3.39

A	That was a delicious *apple*. Can I have *another* (one)?		
	This apple is bad. Can I have *another* (one)?		

B	*another*	three	(people)
	the next	six dozen	(apples)
	the last	few	(weeks)

C	the		bread
	my (etc)		loaf/loaves
	this (etc)	*other*	friend
	some/any		one/ones
	no		
	many/several [+pl]	*others*	—

73

A As a pronoun *another* means one more of the same category — though possibly not identical. (Notice the two meanings above: 'another (apple)' does not mean 'another bad apple!') *Another* usually stands for a count-singular thing, not a person <*Let's ask another.> Compare <Let's invite *another* person/someone else/an extra person.>

B As a determiner (usually meaning 'in addition'), *another* can be used — like *the next* and *the last* — before numbers and before *few*, with plural nouns.

C *Other* as a determiner (meaning different) can be used with count nouns [singular and plural] and mass. It can follow other determiners as shown. In the singular, *the other one* is perhaps more usual than *the other*, particularly for people, but plural *others/the others* often mean people:

<I'm glad you're here, but where are *the others*?>
<Some people are always punctual; *others* aren't.>

For each *other/one another* (people) — see 3.28.

Order of determiners

3.40 Some determiners can be used with others, but only normally in the order indicated. This table does not mean that any word in column **1** can be followed by any word in column **2**, etc — some are semantically mutually exclusive. But where determiners can combine, the order is important. *More* can itself follow *many/much/a few/a little/ several*, and cardinal numbers.

1	2	3	4
pre-determiners	main determiners	post determiners	other quantifiers
all	ARTICLES	ORDINALS	many/much
both	a/an/the	first	more/most
half	DEMONSTRATIVES	second (etc)	(a) few/(a) little
	this/that	last	less/least
double	these/those	next	several
twice	QUANTIFIERS		CARDINALS
three times	each/every		one/two (etc)
(etc)	either/neither		
	some/any/no	other	
	POSSESSIVES		
	my (etc)		
	Tom's		

Examples:
<*all these last few* cold days>
<*both my next* novels>
<*half Tom's* juicy orange>
<*twice that* amount>
<*the first two* days>
<*every few* hours>
<*some more* fresh bread>
<*a little more* time>
<*another three more* weeks>
<*the least* money>

4. INTRODUCTION TO VERBS

What are verbs?

4.1 Verbs are defined partly by position/function and partly by inflection. To oversimplify greatly, we can say that any word that fulfils the following two conditions is a verb:

1 *Position* Any single word that can fit into one or more of the following patterns and make a complete sentence (with no further words):

The boy
[subject] · · ·
(a) *clever.* [adj]
(b) *carefully.* [adv]
(c) *the dog.* [noun phrase]

eg (a) *is, seems looks;* (b) *works, wrote, spoke;* (c) *has loved, hits, fed.*

2 *Inflection* Any word that has a set of inflections similar to the following:

walk   walked   walked   walks   walking
begin   began   begun   begins   beginning

4.2 Classification

This two-fold definition partly fits BE/DO/HAVE. But it totally excludes a number of other words (eg *can, must*) because

(a) they cannot be used alone except when a verb is ellipted (12.3) and
(b) they do not have a set of inflections as in 2 above. Yet these words always form groups with verbs, and they share some of the formal characteristics of BE/DO/HAVE (eg negative and question formation). So it is reasonable to classify them as a sub-division of verbs.

On formal grounds, therefore, we divide verbs into:

A **Lexical verbs** (so-called because they carry full dictionary meanings). This group includes BE/DO/HAVE when used with full meanings — eg BE = exist, have quality of; DO = perform; HAVE = take, experience.
B **Auxiliaries** These may be subdivided into:
(a) BE/DO/HAVE when used as auxiliaries to other verbs.
(b) Modals (*can, must*, etc), which are always used as auxiliaries to other verbs. So-called because they indicate mood.

The tense system and the meaning of tense forms

4.3 English verbs have only two simple tenses (present and past), plus six complex tenses using auxiliaries. In addition, transitive verbs form eight passive tenses, also with auxiliaries. Using the modals, a further eight 'modal tenses' can be formed (including the traditional 'future tense'). Four of these 'modal tenses' are active, and four are passive.

The meanings of the individual tenses and of the modals are discussed in chapters 5 and 6. But a few generalisations need to be made.

A **Time and tense** Time and tense are not the same thing. 'Time' (consisting of past, present and future) is a concept; 'tense' is a grammatical device. A great deal of confusion is created by text-books that seem to feel that any tense system is abnormal unless the present tense relates only to the moment of speaking, and that anything before or after needs past or future tenses. But people (including textbook writers!) do not always view time like that. (What do we mean, for example, by 'the present time' or 'these days'? Where does 'now' begin and end?) In English, the present simple is the unmarked tense. This means it is used for very general time where specific marking for non-present time is unimportant and so unnecessary. To put this another way, any period that includes the moment of speaking (whether extending into the past or the future) can be regarded as present time and use a present tense. The past simple, marked usually by inflection, is a marked tense, and is not so much past as non-present. English has no future simple tense, though plenty of ways of talking about future time (5.16).

B **Aspect — perfective or progressive** Both present simple and past simple are unmarked for aspect. But if we wish, we can emphasise:
(a) that the action or state referred to by the verb is in some way completed or achieved, though still relevant. This is called *perfective* aspect, and is indicated by the use of [HAVE + past participle of the lexical verb]:
    <I have written> [so *now* . . .]
    <I had written> [so *then*] (4.17)
(b) that the action or state is/was in progress or temporary or uncompleted. This is called *progressive* aspect, and is indicated by using [BE + the present participle].
    <I am writing/was writing.> (4.17)

C **Voice: active or passive** The distinction between active and passive — often called a distinction of 'voice' — can be made with most transitive verbs. It offers different ways of focusing attention on different parts of the information. Choice of the passive, therefore, like choosing to mark for time or aspect, is the selection of a grammatical device that contributes to meaning (4.18-4.22).

D **Dynamic vs stative** In their intrinsic lexical meanings, most verbs refer to actions or happenings (eg *arrive*, *hit*, *speak*) which
(a) occur as a single action,
(b) are repeated several times, or
(c) are seen as in progress.
These verbs are called dynamic (or action or event) verbs. For (a) single events and (b) a repeated series of actions (habit), they usually use simple tenses, but for (c) actions temporarily in progress they use progressive tenses.

A smaller group of verbs refer to states of affairs (eg *be*, *belong*, *know*, *see*) which exist more or less permanently. These verbs are called 'statives' (from the word 'state') and do not normally occur in progressive tenses. One reason for preferring the name 'progressive' to 'continuous' for the -ing tenses is that these tenses are stressing the temporary nature of the action in progress, whereas stative verbs (in the simple tenses) may refer to states of affairs that in fact continue for a long time.

E **Mood: subjunctive** A distinction between indicative (for facts) and subjunctive (for hypotheses, suppositions etc), which is usually called a distinction of mood, hardly exists in the tense system of modern English. Where there are separate subjunctive tense forms, they are usually replaceable by other tenses and by modals (4.2). But subjunctive forms are obligatory in a few usages. (4.28).

Inflected forms of the verb (and the two simple tenses)

4.4   English verbs have very few inflections. Only BE has more than five forms — it has eight. DO has five; HAVE and regular lexical verbs have only four because past simple and past participle are the same; irregular lexical verbs have three, four or five.

Modals have only one. (On a different analysis (4.7) some have two.)

4.5   Lexical verbs, plus DO and HAVE

	1 Base	2 Past simple -ed	3 Past participle -en	4 Present simple 3rd pers sing	5 Present participle -ing
Regular	walk hope	walked hoped	walked hoped	walks hopes	walking hoping
Irregular	shut make run write	shut made ran wrote	shut made run written	shuts makes runs writes	shutting making running writing
DO	do	did	done	does	doing
HAVE	have	had	had	has	having

Lexical verbs, DO and HAVE have a maximum of five forms. Two forms are *finite* (they can function as the only verb in a sentence, and they contain a time reference). Two are *non-finite* (they cannot function as the only verb in a complete sentence). And one can be used as both finite and non-finite. The five forms are:

1	**Base,** the unmarked form, used alone as (a) **Imperative** [finite]	*Walk* there. *Write* your name. *Do* this.
	(b) **Present simple** — except for 3rd pers sing (see 4) [finite]	They *walk* everywhere. We *write* novels. You *have* lovely eyes.
	(c) **Infinitive** [ie non-finite]	I want to *walk*. There's no paper to *write* on. It's difficult to *do* this crossword puzzle.
2	**Past simple** — same for all persons [finite]	They *walked* twenty miles. He *wrote* to me last month. She *did* a funny thing yesterday.

3	**Past participle** [non-finite by itself, though used to form finite complex tenses]	They have *walked* twenty miles. There's a note for you, *written* in pencil. It is *done*.
4	**Present simple** 3rd pers sing [finite]	He *walks*. She *writes*. It *has* a guarantee.
5	**Present participle** [non-finite by itself, though used to form finite complex tenses]	*Walking* is good for you. What are you *doing*? *Having* finished, he left.

A **Past simple and past participle (2 & 3)**

In *regular* verbs and HAVE, these two forms are the same — ie these verbs have only four different forms. Regular verbs add spelling *-ed* to the base, subject to normal spelling rules.

(a) *Pronunciation of -ed:*

● After final /t/ or /d/ sound, *-ed* is pronounced /ɪd/, eg *patted* /pætɪd/; *added* /ædɪd/.

● After other *voiceless* sounds, -ed is pronounced as /t/ (itself voiceless) eg *hoped* /həupt/; *placed* /pleɪst/ *wished* wɪʃt/; *watched* /wɒtʃt/.

● After other *voiced* sounds, -ed is pronounced as voiced /d/, eg *timed* /taɪmd/; *judged* /dʒʌdʒd/; *pleased* /pli:zd/; *viewed* /vju:d/.

(b) Irregular verbs have various patterns for forms **1**, **2** and **3**. Sometimes all three are different (*write*, *wrote*, *written*). Sometimes all three forms are the same (*shut*). Sometimes base, **2** or **3** are different and the other two forms are the same (see Appendix IV).

The majority of irregular verbs, and HAVE and DO, have the characteristic /t/ or /d/ ending for **2**. Where **2** and **3** are different, the typical past participle is *-en*. Notice also DO — *done*; BE — *been*. Hence the common practice of referring to the past simple as *-ed*, and the past participle as *-en*, irrespective of the actual forms.

B **3rd person present singular (4)**

All lexical verbs (and BE/DO/HAVE) add the ending *-s*. The spelling for all lexical verbs, both regular and irregular (but excluding BE/DO/HAVE) is completely regular: add *-s* to the base, subject to normal spelling rules. Two common verbs have irregular pronunciation: *says* /sez/ and *does* /dʌz/.

Pronunciation of *-s*:

The pronunciation of the 3rd person singular ending is the same as for the plural of nouns (see 2.23): that is, spelling *-s* is pronounced /ɪz/, /s/ or /z/ depending on whether the preceding sound is:

● sibilant or affricate /ɪz/: places, wishes, watches, judges, pleases.

● other voiceless sounds /s/: pats, hopes.

● other voiced sounds /z/: adds, times, views.

C **The present participle (5)** is also regular in *all* verbs — subject to normal spelling rules.

Thus the three parts of irregular verbs given in dictionaries (**1**, **2** and **3**, eg *write*, *wrote*, *written*) enable one to form all possible complex tenses.

4.6 BE

1 Base	2 Past simple	3 Past participle	4 Present simple	5 Present participle
be [imperative, infinitive]	I he she it } was (2) we you they } were (6)	been	he she it } is (4) I am (7) we you they } are (8)	being

BE is unique among English verbs. It has eight forms (instead of a maximum of five), and only two of its forms are derived from the base: past participle 3 (*been*) and present participle 5 (*being*). The past simple 2 (*was*) and the third person singular 4 (*is*) are unrelated to the base form, and both need extra forms for various persons as shown (6 *were*, 7 *am*, 8 *are*).

4.7 Modals

Group A	1 can 2 could	3 shall 4 should	5 will 6 would	7 may 8 might	9 must 10 ought to
Group B	11 need	12 dare	13 used to		

The first eight words in Group A are often treated as pairs, and analysed as present and past of the same verb (eg *can, could*). But in fact the second words in these pairs (2, 4, 6, 8) have very limited past meaning and are mainly non-past in usage. So they are all better treated separately, as verbs having one form each.

Modal forms are not base forms. They cannot be used as imperative or infinitive. They are finite, but need a lexical verb with them. There is no inflection for third person singular.

Group B verbs behave partly like modals and partly like lexical verbs (4.24-26).

Questions and negatives (simple tenses)

4.8 BE, auxiliaries DO, HAVE, and modals

Formation with inversion and *not*

Positive and negative	Short form positive [cannot stand alone]	Short negative	Short questions positive & negative
BE — present I am (not) we you } are (not) they he she } is (not) it	I'm (here) we're you're } (ready) they're he's she's } (walking) it's	I'm not (never *n't) we *etc* aren't (or we're *etc* not) he *etc* isn't (or he's *etc* not)	am I? aren't I? [Br Eng] are(n't) { we? you? they? is(n't) { he? she? it?
BE — past we you } were (not) they I he she } was (not) it		we you } weren't they I he she } wasn't it	were(n't) { we? you? they? was(n't) { I? he? she? it?
DO — present I we you } do (not) they he she } does (not) it		I *etc* don't he *etc* doesn't	do(n't) I *etc*? does(n't) he *etc*?
DO — past [one form for all persons] I *etc* did		I *etc* didn't	did(n't) I?
HAVE — present [+ Past participle] I we you } have (not) they he she } has (not) it	I've *etc* (walked) he's *etc* (walked)	I *etc* haven't (or I've *etc* not) he *etc* hasn't (or he's *etc* not)	have(n't) I *etc*? has(n't) he *etc*?

HAVE — past I *etc* had (not)	I'd *etc* (walked)	I hadn't (I'd not)	had(n't) I?
Modals [+ infinitive] can (cannot) walk could (not) walk will (not) walk would (not) walk shall (not) walk should (not) walk may (not) walk might (not) walk must (not) walk ought (not) to walk	 — — I'll etc I'd (walk) I'll I'd — — — —	 can't couldn't won't wouldn't shan't [rare in Am Eng] shouldn't (mayn't) [rare] mightn't mustn't oughtn't to	 can (can't) could(n't) will (won't) would(n't) shall (shan't) I *etc*? should(n't) may might(n't) must(n't) ought(n't) I etc to?

BE and the modals, and DO and HAVE as auxiliaries, all form questions and negatives in the same way:

A   **Questions** The subject and verb are inverted:

    <Are we? Do I? Has he? Can you?>

B   **Negatives** Add *n't*, or more rarely *not*, to the verb: <We *aren't*. / We are *not*.> <I *don't*/I do *not*.> <He *hasn't*/He has *not*.>

An alternative is to add *not* to short (ie contracted) forms of the verbs if they exist: <We're *not*.> <I've *not*.>

Notice: only *not* (never *n't*) is added to *I am*: <I am *not*./I'm *not*.>

Mayn't is very rare, and *shan't* is rare in American English.

C   **Negative questions** Add *n't* to the verb:

    <Aren't they ready?> <Don't you like it?>

Not can be added after the subject, but this is formal: <Are we *not* ready?> <Do you *not* like it?>

The negative question form for *Am I?* in British English — American avoids it — is *Aren't I?* The spelling looks odd, but the vowel change in standard pronunciation is comparable to *can/can't* /kæn, kɑ:nt/ or *shall/shan't* /ʃæl, ʃɑ:nt/.

D   **Short negatives** can stand alone, eg in answer to a question:

    <'Are you ready?' 'Sorry, I'm not/we aren't/we're not.'>

E   **Short forms — positive** are only used when followed by another word. Otherwise the full form must be used:

    <Yes, we're here/ready/waiting.> BUT: <Yes, we are.>

Notice: *I'd* = *I had* or *I would*. *He's* = *he is* or *he has*.

4.9 Lexical verbs — including lexical DO and HAVE

Formation of questions and negatives with DO

Statements	Questions	Negatives

Present simple
 	
I
we   } walk there
       } do the homework
you
       } have lessons
they
	I
	     } walk . . ?
	Do we
	     } do . . ?
	   you
	(Don't) } have ..?
	they
		} walk . . .
		   don't
		I *etc* } do . . .
		   do not
		        } have . . .

he } walks . . .
she } does . . .
it   } has . . .
	he } walk . . ?
	Does she } do . . ?
	(Doesn't)
	it } have . . ?
		} walk . . .
		  doesn't
		he *etc* } do . . .
		  does not
		      } have . . .

Past simple
 	
      } walked . . .
I *etc* } did . . .
      } had . . .
	} walk . . ?
	Did
	  I *etc* } do . . ?
	(Didn't)
	     } have . . ?
		} walk ...
		  didn't
		I *etc* } do ...
		  did not
		      } have ...

Lexical verbs, and DO and HAVE as lexical verbs, form questions and negatives of their two simple tenses by using DO as an operator with infinitive of the lexical verb for both tenses and all persons. Thus the past simple inflected forms are only used in positive statements.
Negative questions are commonly formed by adding *n't* after DO:
    <(Why) didn't you walk there?>
    <Doesn't she do any homework?>
There is also a formal alternative of adding *not* immediately after the subject:
    <(Why) did you not walk there?> [fml]
Auxiliary DO is also used with lexical verbs and with BE/DO/HAVE for:
(a) *Emphatic imperative*
    <*Do* hurry, please.>   <*Do* be sensible.>   <Oh *do do* it.>
    <*Do have* a second helping.>
(b) *Emphasis in positive statements* (but not with BE) — especially to point a contrast with a previous statement:
    <I always *do* hurry.>   <I usually *did* do my homework.>
    <'I don't think he has guitar lessons any more.' 'Oh yes he *does have* them — he told me yesterday.'>
(c) *Negative imperative*
    <*Don't* spend all your money.>   <*Don't* be stupid.>   <*Don't do* that!>   <*Don't have* any more ice cream — you'll be ill.>
For DO in tags, short answers, etc — see chapter 12.

BE/DO/HAVE as lexical verbs

4.10 *BE* as lexical verb

---

1 He *is* an engineer/my brother. (classifying, identifying)
He *is* clever/tall/warm/twenty-five. (states, permanent conditions, etc)
He *is* here/in Edinburgh. (location)
He wants *to be* an engineer. (become)
Are there mountains on the moon? (exist)

2 He *is/was being* silly/difficult.

3 Why *don't you be* a nurse?
Why *don't you be* a good boy and help Mummy?

---

1 As a lexical verb, BE has a wide variety of meanings and can be followed by various parts of speech.

2 Lexical BE does not usually take progressive tense, but can do so to imply temporary behaviour.

3 BE does not normally form tenses with DO (except for emphatic or negative imperative — see 4.9), but the phrase *Why don't you be . . .?* functions as a suggestion.

4.11 *BE to*

---

1 You *are to do* as your mother says — don't argue. [obligation]
Nobody *is to leave* this room.
Tim and Marian *are to be* married in June. [future arrangement, somewhat formal]
Henry *is to be* their best man.
If we *are to catch* the train, we must hurry.
It was to be 27 years before she published another successful novel. [future destiny in the past]

---

2 I can't stop — *I'm just about to* go out.

---

1 [BE to + infinitive] occurs in the present and past simple and not in complex tenses. The underlying meaning, as with many [verb + infinitive] combinations (7.31) is future.

Common meanings are obligation (commands); and arrangements for the future. In the past this structure becomes a future-in-the-past, possibly with a sense of destiny.

2 To be *about to* DO something refers to the immediate future. 'I can't stop — I'm on the point of going out.'

4.12 *DO* as lexical verb

> I *didn't do* very well in my exam.   <*I didn't very well . . .>
> *Did* you *do* the shopping yesterday?   <*Did you the shopping . . .>
> What *does* he *do* all day?   <*What does he all day?>
> *Don't do* that.   <*Don't that.>
> What *have* you *been doing*?

As a lexical verb (meaning 'perform', etc), DO behaves like any other lexical verb, using auxiliary DO as operator in questions and negatives of simple tenses, and also appearing freely in complex tenses.

4.13 *HAVE/HAVE GOT/*do *HAVE*

> **A** HAVE/HAVE GOT — **basic meanings** [stative]
> *Has* she *(got)* blue eyes/a brother? [Am Eng *Does* she *have* . . .?]
> Henry *has (got)* flu/measles/a cold.
> *Have* you *(got)* any avocadoes today? [Am Eng *Do* you *have* . . .?]
> I *haven't (got)* any sugar in this coffee. [Am Eng I *don't have* . . .]
> *Had* you *(got)*/*Did* you *have* any idea that this could happen?
> I *hadn't (got)*/I *didn't have* a hope/a chance of getting to university.
> I *haven't* a clue.
>
> **B** HAVE/do HAVE [dynamic]
> *Does* he often *have* flu/colds?
> She's *having* a baby in June.
> I've *been having* an argument with my bank manager.
> We *are having* a party/a holiday next month.
> *Do* you ever *have* avocadoes?
> I *didn't have* any difficulty/trouble finding the way here.
> *Don't have* an accident.
> *Have* fun!

As a lexical (not auxiliary) verb HAVE can mean:
(a) possession, permanent relationship (ie stative meanings)
(b) take, experience, etc (ie dynamic meanings).

A **Basic meanings** In the basic meaning of possess, HAVE uses question-inversion and *not*-negation (like the auxiliaries):
<Has he any?>   <They hadn't any.>
A common alternative is HAVE GOT. In form, this is a regular perfect tense of *get*, but its meaning is more like present HAVE. HAVE GOT must take question-inversion and *not*-negation:
<Has he got any?>   <They *hadn't got* any last week.>
'Basic possession' can include illnesses, even when temporary, and also various mental processes (a *clue*, a *hope*, an *idea*; also a *chance*).

B **do** HAVE
HAVE can also be treated in a third way — as a regular lexical verb using DO as an operator:
<Does he *have* any?> <They *didn't have* any.>
This form of HAVE must be used when HAVE has dynamic meaning, eg 'take' (a bath), 'experience' (difficulty), etc. This dynamic HAVE can be used with progressive tenses, imperative and even occasionally passive. It is referred to as *do* HAVE in this book.

For basic possession British English tends to prefer HAVE GOT (to plain HAVE), but American English frequently uses *do* HAVE for this too.

British English uses *do* HAVE when there is a sense of habit or repetition:

<Does your grocer ever have avocadoes?>

and often even for basic possession in the past:

<My sister had blonde hair as a child, but I *didn't*.>

Note: HAVE GOT, meaning permanent possession, does not use infinitives or participles, but the dynamic verb GET (to obtain) can use perfect infinitives and participles:

<It's clever of you to *have got/get* six A levels.>

<*Having got* them, you should use them.>

In American English, the past participle of dynamic GET (but not of course in HAVE GOT as permanent possession) is *gotten*:

<*I've only just gotten to hear of this.*> [Am Eng]

<Dwight's *gotten* tickets for the big match.> [Am Eng]

For GET vs BE in passive — see 4.20.

4.14 *HAVE GOT to/do HAVE to*

We *have (got) to* go now/soon, or we'll miss the train. [future]

I've got to work on Friday evenings next term. [future series] But Betty *hasn't got to*. [absence of obligation for future]

'*Does Henry have to* work on Saturdays?' [present habit]

'No, *he doesn't have to* now.' [absence of repeated/external obligation]

'I *had to* telephone William yesterday.'

'Why *did you have to* do that?'

'I knew I *had (got) to* telephone him in the evening.'

'*Did Bill have to* work last Saturday?'

'No, *he didn't have to*. He's never *had to* work on Saturdays.'

You have to be joking! [Am Eng]

HAVE GOT *to* and *do* HAVE *to* when followed by the infinitive of another verb both have the meaning of obligation or necessity. As with HAVE GOT and *do* HAVE, American English favours the forms with *do* for all usages. British English uses *do* HAVE to where the obligation is for habitual/repeated actions already taking place, but often uses HAVE GOT *to* where there is an obligation now for a future action or series of actions. The essential difference between the two forms is therefore one of time reference, and not between one action and a series as is sometimes stated, since a future series can happily use HAVE GOT *to*. This time reference is often clear in the past. <I had to telephone William yesterday.> suggests 'and I did', but <I had got to telephone William yesterday.> is a sort of future-in-the-past, with some sort of implication like 'I'd got to telephone him so I was worried until I did'. The *do* HAVE *to* forms (rather than HAVE GOT *to*) are therefore common in the past, since they are concerned not only with a past obligation to act, but with whether that action was performed.

The negatives *haven't got to* and *don't have to* both express absence of obligation (compare *needn't*, 6.14). Again regular *don't have to* suggests the absence of repeated or external obligation.

HAVE vs MUST

ADV HAVE *to* — particularly *do* HAVE *to* — is a more external obligation than MUST (6.13). Compare:

<Robert *must* find another job.> [my recommendation]

<Robert *has (got) to* find another job.> [his firm has closed down.]

In American English, *have to* shares with *must* a meaning of deduction: <You *have to* be joking.>

85

Confusingly, usage of *have to/must,* etc is not standard throughout Britain. For example, well-educated northern speakers may use plain *haven't to* with the sense of prohibition (like *mustn't*) imposed by someone else. It sounds like concealed reported speech:
<It's a secret — I *haven't to* tell anyone.>

4.15 *HAVE* + **object** + *DONE/DOING*

1	• cause something to be done by someone else [passive] • cause something to happen [active] • not allow something to happen [negative]	We're *having/getting* the car *serviced.* I must *get* my suit *cleaned.* He *had* us all *guessing.* I'll soon *have/get* the TV *working* again. I *won't have* you *laughing* at me. I *won't have* Rachel *laughed* at.
2	experience something (usually undesirable)	He *had* his car *stolen* while he was away. You'll *have/get* everyone *asking* you for money if they find out you've won the pools.

Have (and *get*) are used in the pattern [*have* + object + participle] with the dynamic meaning of 'get/cause/experience'. If the resulting event is desirable, *have* is often interpreted as deliberate cause (in positive statements); if undesirable, as unintended experience. *Won't have* in this pattern (not *get*) means 'don't allow'.

ADV More rarely we find a similar usage with [*have* + object + infinitive]:
<I'll *have* you know that . . .>
<I won't *have* you behave like that.>
<I *had* an odd thing happen the other day.>
With *get* [= cause] the pattern here is
<He *got* the TV *to* work . . .> (7.36)

4.16 *Had better* — and *would rather/would sooner*

1	I had or I'd *etc* better (or best)	go tomorrow, hadn't I *etc*? not go, } had I *etc*? not, }

2	He would rather	(not) go,	
		you went/didn't go on Saturday, I had(n't) told Tom,	wouldn't he?
	He would sooner	die *than* go through that again,	

1 *Had better* (rarely *had best*) — meaning 'it would be advisable' — is followed by the infinitive. *Had* is invariable. Time reference is present/future unless in a subordinate clause with past meaning.
2 *Would rather/would sooner* (roughly 'prefer') take infinitive or a clause with past tense for unreality. (Compare conditionals.) The *-er* of *rather* and *sooner* still actively carries a comparative meaning, so both phrases can be followed by a *than*-clause. (This does not happen with *had better*.) The tag is usually *wouldn't*, both for '*would* rather' (go) and '*would* rather not' (go).

Complex tenses — active

4.17 Formation of present and past with *BE/HAVE*

Active tenses	HAVE for *perfect*	BE for *progressive*	Lexical verb (+ ending)
1 Pres } simple 2 Past }			walk/walks write/writes (-s) walked wrote -ed
3 Pres } perfect 4 Past } simple	*have/has* (not) *had*		walked written been -en done had
5 Pres } prog 6 Past }		*am/is/are* (not) *was/were*	walking writing being doing -ing
7 Pres } perfect 8 Past } prog	*have/has* (not) *been* *had*		having

Examples:

1 Present simple	I . . .		write to Ian regularly.
2 Past simple	I . . .		wrote to him yesterday.
3 Pres perf simple	I have . . .		written to Ian.
	He has . . .		had a busy week.
4 Past perf simple	I had already . . .		posted my letter when . . .
5 Present prog	He . . .	is . . .	writing regularly now.
	You . . .	are . . .	being foolish.
6 Past prog	They . . .	were . . .	doing nothing.
	I . . .	was . . .	hoping to hear.
7 Pres perf prog	We have . . .	been . . .	writing to each other.
8 Past perf prog	He had . . .	been . . .	meaning to write for ages.

Lexical verbs (including BE/DO/HAVE) have eight active tenses — the two simple tenses (repeated here for completeness), plus six complex ones. These are formed with BE and HAVE, and show perfect and progressive aspect and combinations of both.

Perfect tenses (3,4,7 and 8) use [HAVE +-en (past participle)]. A past participle of a lexical verb gives a present or past perfect simple tense (3 and 4). If the past participle is *been*, this may be a perfect tense of BE (3 or 4). Or the *been* can be followed by an -ing form (7 and 8) to give perfect progressive tenses.

Progressive tenses (5, 6, 7 and 8) must use [BE + -ing]. HAVE (auxiliary) precedes BE (auxiliary) in perfect progressive (7 and 8).

The first word of a finite tense (simple or complex) establishes present or past. The lexical word comes last. In the two simple tenses, the single word carries both bits of information. Questions in complex tenses invert subject and operator, and negatives add *not/n't* to the operator. Negative questions have a formal alternative (compare 4.9):

    <Haven't you written?>

    <Have you not written?> [fml]

Complex tenses — passive

4.18 Formation of present and past with BE/HAVE

Passive tenses	Active tense of BE		Lexical verb adds -en
1 Pres **2** Past simple	*am/is/are* *was/were*		written
3 Pres **4** Past perfect	*have/has* *had*	been	done
5 Pres **6** Past prog	*am/is/are* *was/were*	being	had
7 Pres **8** Past perf prog	*have/has* *had*	been being [rare]	

Examples:
2 *Were* you *fined* for that parking offence?
6 The car *was being towed* away when I got there.

A   To form the passive voice, all tenses (including present and past simple) use the corresponding active tense of BE and add the -en form of the lexical verb. All passive tenses therefore include a form of BE plus an -en form. As in active tenses, the first word establishes present or past and the last word is the lexical verb. Questions are formed by inversion, and negatives by adding *not/n't*. Passive perfect progressive tenses with *been being* are disliked by some speakers, but certainly occur:

    <He's been being interviewed for the past hour.>

Get sometimes replaces BE where there could otherwise be ambiguity. For example: *The chair was broken* could mean 'it had been broken for ages' — ie stative BE + adj — or 'it was broken in the fight' — ie dynamic passive. The second meaning is more clearly expressed as <It got broken.>

B **Formal relationship of passive to active sentences** The grammatical subject of a passive sentence corresponds to the object of an active one, and the 'agent', (or doer — see Chapter 1) usually signalled by *by*, replaces the subject of the active sentence. Thus, the active

<A man bit a dog.> becomes <A dog was bitten by a man.>
[S + v + O]   [S + pasv v + agent]

From this formula it would appear that (a) all transitive verbs have interchangeable active and passive forms and (b) intransitive verbs cannot have passive forms because they have no objects. This is nearly true but not quite (4.20-21).

By is not used if the active subject is not felt to be the agent: <1981 saw a world recession.> becomes <A world recession was seen in 1981.>

With is used for instrument:

<He appears to have been attacked with an axe.>

4.19 The meaning of the passive

A	Grammatical subject is *new* topic. Note indefinite or ZERO articles [no agent]	A silver collection will be taken. An inquiry is to be held. Carbon monoxide is produced as a result.
B	Grammatical subject is 'given' topic. Main focus in predicate [no agent]	Trespassers will be prosecuted. I like being met at airports. Timothy has been killed in an aircrash. [active not possible — no doer.] It is believed that Charles is a millionaire. Charles is supposed to [said to] be a millionaire. He was asked to leave. You are supposed to [meant to] buy a dog licence. Diana was given some wonderful presents when she retired. [S = IO of active]
C	Focus on agent	The exhibition is to be opened by the Queen. Surely tiddly winks is only played by children. [*length also a factor* — meaningless without agent] Another plane has been hijacked by a gang of international terrorists.

A & B **Omission of agent** It is sometimes said that the passive emphasises the grammatical subject — because it is fronted — at the expense of the doer. This is only so in a few cases, as in A, where the grammatical subject is clearly a new topic. In many other cases (B) the passive certainly omits the agent altogether because the doer is unimportant, unknown or too obvious to mention. (Scientific English is always cited as an example of this.) But if the grammatical subject is 'given' or known information, this too receives little emphasis, and the big focus is on the new information in the predicate (B).

The new information in the predicate also receives strong focus in
● two structures involving verbs of *mental states and processes*:

<It is believed that . . .> <He is believed to . . .>

Also: *consider, declare, expect, feel, know, report, say, suppose, think, understand.*

- some verbs of *ordering* which in the active take the pattern
  S + V + O + *to* infin (7.36):
  <He was asked to . . .>
  Also: *advise, ask, command, order, tell.*

  The usual 'given theme' nature of the subject may also account for the fact that in the passive version of an active sentence containing both direct and indirect object: <They gave Diana some wonderful presents.> it is usually the known human recipient who becomes the passive subject, while the direct object (probably the new information) comes later:
  <Diana was given some wonderful presents.>
  (This type of active-passive transformation must be distinguished from a sentence with 'object complement': <They made Diana secretary.> which can only become <Diana was made secretary.>)

C **Focus on agent** Although the agent is often omitted, when it is present its position in the predicate usually gives it special emphasis. So corresponding active and passive sentences are rarely two ways of 'saying the same thing'. Notice, for example, the inappropriateness of the passive transformation of a common notice in buses: <Smokers must occupy rear seats.> This tells smokers what they must do. The passive <Rear seats must be occupied by smokers> would imply that the rear seats are to receive special treatment.

4.20 Incomplete active and passive verbs

1	'Where/When *were you born?*' 'I *was born* in Edinburgh in 1960.' Jenny and Al *were married/got married* in June. They *were married* by Jenny's uncle, the Vicar of St. Mary's. But: Janet *has married* an American. Richard never *married.*

2	This box *costs* £10, *weighs* 4lb and *measures* 2 feet by 3. [stative] But: All these boxes *have been weighed* and *measured*. [dynamic] My clothes *don't fit* me now I'm so thin. [stative] But: Nothing more can *be fitted* into this case. [dynamic] This bottle *holds* a litre. [stative] But: This box *is held* together with rusty nails. [dynamic] Henry *resembles* his grandfather. [stative] He *lacks* commonsense. [stative] She *has* blue eyes. [stative] But: There was no food to *be had*. [dynamic = obtained] You've *been had*. [infml dynamic = *cheated*]

1 Three factors described in 4.19 (the agent may not merit mention; the subject is already known; and the predicate, including the verb, will contain new information) explain why two common verbs are used mainly in the passive. *To be born* is the passive of *to bear*, but the verb is rarely used actively in this meaning.

To be married has alternative *to get married*. This second form avoids the potential ambiguity of <They were married.>, which can mean 'They were married in June', which is dynamic, or it can have stative meaning, 'They were married when I first met them (but they have since got divorced)'. The active verb *to marry* exists, but the usage is different: <They both married American girls.>

2 Another principle explains why some transitive verbs when used statively have no passive forms. The subject of a passive verb needs to be 'affected' by the action of the verb, but with some active transitive verbs the grammatical object is in no way seen as the recipient of the action: <*Ten pounds is cost by this box.>

Some of these verbs, however, when used with different meanings, can have passive forms as shown.

4.21 Prepositional verbs in the passive

Some prepositional verbs (that is, verbs that take prepositions before an object) are felt to 'affect' their objects just like straight transitive verbs or transitive phrasal verbs, and they can therefore be used in the passive:

<These cats *are well looked after*.> [Someone looks after these cats . . .]

<You'll *get yourself talked about*. [People will talk about you.]

The structure can be used with other verb + prep + n, where there is a similar feel of 'affected' subject:

<That house hasn't been lived in for years.>

But not <*London is lived in by seven million people.>

4.22 Reflexive and 'possessive' objects

Sentences such as <Tom hurt himself> or <Tom stretched his legs> cannot meaningfully take a passive, since clearly *himself* or *his legs* are not mere passive recipients of external action.

Modals: complex tenses

4.23

		Modal	Infinitive	+ -en	+ -ing	+ -en
1	Active simple	will	write			
2	Active progressive	would / shall			writing	
3	Passive simple	should / can	be			written
4	prog (rare)	could			being	written
5	Active perfect simple	may	have [for perfect]	written		
6	perfect prog	might		been	writing	
7	Passive perfect simple	must		been		written
8	perfect prog (rare)	ought to		been	being	written

Examples	S + modal	infin	+ -en	+ -ing	+ -en
1 act	I may	complain.			
2 act	They will	be		considering the matter.	
3 pasv	Oughtn't the lock to	be			changed?
4 pasv	It could	be		being	fitted now.
5 act	They would	have	told me.		
6 act	Who can	have	been	trying to get in?	
7 pasv	It might	have	been		injured.
8 pasv	It should	have	been	being	followed up.

Four active 'modal tenses' and four passive tenses can be formed beginning with any of the modals. Four may be considered 'present' (1-4) and four 'perfect' (5-8), but none are past as such. Passive progressive forms with *be being* and *been being* (4 and 8) are rare. So are combinations with contracted *mayn't*.

The modals do not stand alone but must always be associated with the infinitive of another verb, just like operator DO.
Compare: Can/Did you write to him?
For apparent exceptions — see chapter 12.

The modals have no infinitives (so they cannot follow other verbs) and no imperatives.

Traditional grammars give *will/shall write* etc as the 'future tense'. This verb phrase can refer to future time, but it has other meanings and there are other ways of referring to the future. Formally *will/shall* pattern like other modals, and they are treated with them here.

In the formation of these complex 'modal tenses', some of the 'rules' governing other complex tenses apply, namely: BE is followed by -ing or -en, HAVE is immediately followed by -en. Only the first word (ie the modal) is finite, and the lexical verb completes the group. Question-inversion and *not*-negation follow the usual rules.

For the meaning of the modals — see chapter 6.

Semi-modals
DARE/NEED/USED *to* (4.24-26)

These three verbs are partly like modals and partly like ordinary lexical verbs, because they sometimes use question-inversion and *not*-negation and they sometimes use DO. Tag questions are usually with DO.

As modals, DARE and NEED are mainly used in questions and negatives only; they have no -s inflection for third person singular, and they are followed by bare infinitive. As regular verbs they take -s inflection, and regular NEED always takes *to*-infinitive. But see below.

4.24 Dare

<table>
<tr><td>A</td><td>Set phrases
I daresay everything will be all right. [one word]
How dare you (speak to me like that)!
You dare/Don't you dare (do that again)!</td></tr>
<tr><td>B</td><td>Negative
She daren't tell him. [past or present]
She doesn't/didn't dare (to) tell him.
I wouldn't dare (to) tell him either, would you?
They didn't dare (to)/dared not complain.</td></tr>
<tr><td>C</td><td>Non-assertive
I wonder if I dare go.
I don't know how he dares to/dare show his face here.</td></tr>
</table>

Modal *dare* mainly occurs in:

A **A few set phrases** *I daresay* (one word, first pers. sing. only) roughly means 'I expect' or 'probably'. *How dare you/he*, etc expresses annoyance at something already done. *You dare* or *Don't you dare* expresses annoyance at a proposed action and is a kind of prohibition. All these last three expressions can be complete in themselves.

B **Negative** *Daren't* is used for past and present, but there are alternative regular forms (as shown.)

C **Non-assertive** Modal *dare* is also common in subordinate clauses after expressions of doubt, uncertainty, though again there are regular alternatives. Notice that even when used like a regular lexical verb (eg with another modal — *don't/wouldn't dare*, etc) *dare* can take bare infinitive.

    Dare in the pattern *dare* [challenge] *someone to* DO *something* is always regular:

        <I dare you to jump off the top diving board.>

4.25 Need

Need is the only one of these three verbs that fits into the modal meaning scale of possibility-necessity (6.14). As explained there,

(a) modal NEED is non-assertive and has one form only.

(b) regular *need to*, with DO, can make a complete range of complex tenses:

        <You'll need to book seats in advance — it's a popular play.>

(c) both must be distinguished from regular *need* + DO:

        <I needed some aspirins.>   <The whole place needs cleaning.>

4.26 Used to

<table>
<tr><td>1</td><td>I used to live in Brighton.
She used to be slim, didn't she?
You used to know her well, didn't you?
They often used to swim before breakfast, didn't they?
I used not to/I didn't use to enjoy pop music, but now I do.
Did/Didn't you use to play tennis at school?
Usedn't you to play tennis? [fml]
What games used you to play?
Where did you use to play?</td></tr>
</table>

1 *Used to* has past simple only, and means past habits and states, usually no longer existing. It takes the infinitive. Questions and negatives with *did* seem to be increasingly gaining favour. *I used not to* DO is still fairly common for straight negatives, but *did* questions are usual, and *did* is virtually essential in tags. *Usedn't you to . . .* now appears formal.

Compare *would* for past habit (6.9). Notice that only *used to* (not *would*) is possible with reference to a past state: <She used to be slim.> *Used to* is pronounced /ju:st tʊ or tə/.

2			NP	optional tag
	You are		London	aren't you?
	They got	used to	pop music	didn't they?
	They'll get/be		walking to work	won't they?
	He's never got		living in London	has he?
3	Don't break that knife — *use* a tin-opener. She disliked tin-openers and never *used* one.			

Used to DO must be distinguished from two similar forms:
2 To BE/GET used to something/DOING something, meaning 'to be/get accustomed'. This can form complex tenses and refer to any time.
3 Ordinary verb use /ju:z/ju:zd/ + DO.

Stative verbs

4.27

A	**Being and having** **Relationships**	
	appear, seem, sound;	He *appears* to be worried.
	mean, equal;	What does 'stative' *mean*?
	own, possess, belong to;	The house once *belonged* to Henry's aunt.
	consist of, comprise, contain, include, involve, hold;	The bottle *holds* 1 litre. [can take]
	concern, depend on, apply to, deserve;	This new law *concerns* us all.
	cost, owe, measure, weigh;	These regulations *don't apply* to me.
	resemble	
	Contrast non-stative:	Tom's *appearing* in a play next month.
		I've *been meaning* to write for ages.
		Henry and Jane *were holding* hands.
		I'm *applying* for a new job.
B	**Involuntary sensations**	
	hear, notice, see;	Oh I (can) *see* Henry over there.
	feel, smell, taste	This pudding *smells/tastes* of lemon. [inherent state]
		I *smell* gas. [involuntary sensation]
		It *didn't feel* like an ordinary parcel. [inherent]
	Contrast: non-stative:	I'm *seeing* Tom tomorrow. [meeting]
		He *was carefully feeling* it when it exploded. [touching]

C	**Mental states & processes**	
	agree, believe, doubt, know, understand, feel [=think], think [opinion], see [= understand], forget, remember Contrast: non-stative:	I *feel* Henry needs a holiday, but I *don't think* he'll take one. I *forget* where he went last time. He's *thinking about* one. Heavens, I'm *forgetting* the time.

D	**Emotions**	
	adore, care, mind matter, prefer (and sometimes: detest, dislike, hate, love, want, wish, etc) Contrast: non-stative	I *don't care* what the neighbours say, but I *mind* [rare] what Henry thinks. Surely it *doesn't matter*? She *was caring* for her sick father all the time, and someone else *was minding* the baby. 'How *does* Duncan *like*/ how *is* Duncan *liking* his new job?' 'He *hates/is hating* it.'

Strictly speaking, we should speak of stative meaning or use, rather than stative verbs, since some of these verbs can be used with dynamic meaning in progressive tenses. (Compare the way some nouns can be both count and mass.)

Here they are divided into four groups roughly according to meaning:

A **Being and having relationships** *Look* is marginal, because even when it means 'involuntarily appear', progressive tense is possible: <You look/are looking ill.> Contrast <You appear ill.> <*You are appearing ill.>

B **Involuntary sensations** When used to denote involuntary sensations, these B group verbs are true statives. You do not deliberately *hear* or *see* (though you probably deliberately *listen* and *look*, and the latter verbs are dynamic.) *Hear* and *see* are often preceded by *can* (6.3).

Feel, smell and taste. When these verbs mean (a) inherent state or (b) involuntary sense, they are usually stative. (But like *look*, *feel* is often used progressively: <I *feel*/ I *am feeling* ill.>. As deliberate activity with object, they are dynamic.

C & D **Mental states & emotions** These verbs are sometimes called the 'private verbs', as they report private opinions and emotions. Group C verbs when referring to states of mind are almost always stative, but many verbs of emotions (Group D) are used both in simple and progressive tenses (though progressive tends to imply the emotion is temporary). *Mind* in an emotional sense is mainly non-assertive.

Subjunctive mood

4.28

ADV	**A**	**Base of the verb**	
	1	God *save* the Queen!	Long *live* the President!
		Bless you!	Heaven *help* us!
	2	They { ordered / have ordered / gave the order }	(that) the prisoner (not) *be released*.
		It is/was essential	(that) he *remain* in custody.

<table>
<tr><td>3</td><td>If that be (not) the case
Whether she be willing or not }</td><td>I shall leave.</td></tr>
</table>

<table>
<tr><td>B</td><td>Were — subjunctive
If I were (not) rich, I would . . .
If/Suppose he were to win the lottery.
If only I were young again.
As if that were all he wanted. [He talks as if . . . but . . .]
They have an understanding, as it were.</td></tr>
</table>

There are few subjunctive forms in modern English, which usually finds other ways of indicating that the events being talked about are uncertain or hypothetical. There are two types of subjunctive.

Forms

A **Base of the verb** For all verbs and all persons, with both present and past reference, eg: *be, go*. No other forms of the verb (eg *goes, went*) are used.

B **Were-subjunctive** The verb BE can use *were* for all persons in certain constructions (ie I/he/she/it/we/you/they *were*).

Usage

A **Base of the verb**

1 In simple sentences, all with present or future reference, the subjunctive expresses wishes etc. It is largely confined to a few set expressions.

2 The same base form is used, with both present and past reference, in two types of subordinate clauses, where *should* structures are an alternative. These are after *suggest*-verbs (and similar nouns) and after *advisable/anxious* adjectives (6.11). Notice the position of *not*.

3 *Be* has only present reference after *if/whether*. The patterns in both 2 and 3 are commoner in American English. In British English they are very formal.

Notice also the set expressions:

If need be, I'll come myself. ['If there is a need/a necessity . . .']
Be that as it may, I'm leaving. ['That may or may not be true, but . . .']

B **Were-subjunctive** For unreality this is used in hypothetical clauses of condition, after *wish* and in expressions that are really concealed conditions (6.24 & 6.27).

Verb concord

4.29

<table>
<tr><td>1</td><td>This box of chocolates is for you.
What was the cost of the tickets?
A number of pupils have chosen this new course.</td></tr>
<tr><td>2</td><td>£5/Five pounds is cheap.
Twelve days is too long.</td></tr>
<tr><td>3</td><td>Decline and Fall is a great book.
The bread and butter was too thin.</td></tr>
<tr><td>4</td><td>Australian and New Zealand butter come in refrigerated ships.</td></tr>
</table>

Verb concord means the correspondence or 'agreement' between singular or plural subjects and their verbs. As there are few verb inflections in English, this only applies with BE, DO and HAVE and tenses using them, and the present simple tense of lexical verbs.

Actually 'singular' is the wrong word. The distinction is between non-plural and plural, since mass nouns take 'singular' verbs. Clauses (whether finite or non-finite) also count as non-plural:

<Buying *all those tickets was* extravagant.>

Problems arise where there is a conflict between grammatical and 'notional' number:

1 When the subject is a noun phrase (not a simple noun), the verb should agree with the head. But if the head is felt to be unimportant: <*a number of . . .*> the verb may agree with another noun, particularly if this noun is closer.

2 Noun phrases involving times and prices are usually felt notionally to represent single units (Compare: *a mere 30 seconds*). They take singular verbs.

3 Co-ordinate subjects felt to constitute single units also take singular verbs.

4 But a singular noun phrase with a mass noun that in fact has double reference <*Australian (butter) and New Zealand butter*> can take plural verb.

For verb and pronoun concord of collective nouns — see 2.15.

For verb and pronoun concord of *everybody* etc, *either, neither, none,* etc, — see relevant sections of chapter 3.

5. THE TENSES: USE AND MEANING

Present and past

5.1   The forms of the English tense system are set out in Chapter 4. Here we see in more detail the meaning of the interacting choices between present and past, progressive or simple, perfect or non-perfect, and how these tenses are used.

It has been noted that English has no future tenses. This perhaps reflects a realistic attitude to the world — the past and present can be spoken of with certainty, the future may never happen! We have, however, plenty of ways of talking about the future. Some appear under present tenses, and there is a summary in 5.16. As for present and past, the essential difference is not the real time of the action in relation to the moment-of-speaking, but whether the period containing the action is regarded as present or past.

The four past tenses correspond to the four present tenses in form, but they are not always parallel in usage. Present tenses are unmarked for time, and so include certain 'timeless' uses. The past tenses are marked for past time, but also for other non-present or 'remote-from-the-present' concepts, including:

(a) unreality or hypothesis (mainly in subordinate clauses — 5.20)
(b) social distancing. This is often a way of being formal and polite, but if it is too formal it is a sign of coldness.
    <Did you want to see me?> could be rude or polite, depending on context and intonation.

Sections 5.2-5.16 are mainly concerned with the primary uses of tenses in simple sentences and main clauses. The use of tenses in subordinate clauses is discussed in 5.17-20.

5.2 Present simple

A	**Timeless** (States, repeated actions)	Air *contains* oxygen and nitrogen. Water *boils* at 100°C. The earth *goes* round the sun.
B	**Long-term present period** (States, habits, repeated actions)	The house *belongs* to me. We *know* the Smiths well. Paul *lives* in Brighton. Jane *wears* glasses. We *visit* Aunt Dorothy every summer. *Do you borrow* many books from the library? 'What *does* Susan *do*?' 'She *writes* children's books.' Henry always *buys* me flowers for my birthday. The 8.20 train *is often cancelled*.

	C	**Actual present moment** (States, single actions)	This meat *smells* bad. 'What *do you advise*?' 'I *think* you should go.' I *understand* now. I *declare* the meeting closed. I *apologise* for the trouble I've caused. Now McEnroe *serves* and . . . [TV commentary] Now I *add* the chocolate powder. [demonstration]
ADV	D	**Future already fixed now** (Mainly single actions, time marking needed)	Next Tuesday *is* my birthday. Christmas Day *falls* on a Saturday next year. Uncle Ben's plane *leaves* at 18.00 hours. We *have* a meeting every day next week.
ADV	E	**Past related as present** (Usually recent single actions)	Chancellor *Announces* Tough Budget [newspaper headline] Henry *tells* me you're ill. I'm sitting there minding my own business, when in *walks* this stunning blonde.

The present simple is the unmarked tense — unmarked for time, progressive or perfective. The *period* covered may be timeless, long-term present or more immediate present, often the actual present moment. The *actions/events* can be:

1 *States* This includes stative verbs, but also dynamic verbs used statively for what may roughly be described as habits: <Jane wears glasses.>

2 *Repeated actions* in a timeless or long-term period.

3 *Single actions* at the actual present moment or in the near past or future (C, D and E).

A **Timeless** For general truths, such as the so-called natural laws, the concepts of past, present and future are irrelevant.

B **Long-term-present** Present time can be seen as having indefinite length, so there is no clear distinction between a timeless period and the long-term present (which might stretch to cover your lifetime or even 'the modern world'.) A sort of general truth and timelessness is the basic meaning of this tense. Notice that most of the examples require no time adverbials.

C **Actual present moment**

1 Stative verbs commonly use this tense. Sometimes the meaning is a long-term state: <We know the Smiths.> but the meaning may also be present moment: <Now I understand.>

2 Not many actions are so short that they can be completed at the moment of speaking, but the tense can be used for example in radio and TV commentaries on fast sports like tennis or football, and in demonstrations: <Now I add . . .>

3 It is also used in a special group of verbs, where the speaking is itself the action, at any rate in the first person. For example in saying *I congratulate you, I promise . . ., I guess, I forbid . . .*, I am performing the action simply by saying the words.

ADV **D** **Future** The use of the present simple with future reference is largely confined to events already fixed, such as events on the calendar or definite travel arrangements. In a way, the future is so certain that it is felt to be part of the present. But the tense is not used for prediction: <*It is cold next winter.> <*I die before I'm 100.> Time adverbials are needed, unless future is clear from the general context. The usage is formal.

ADV **E Past related as present** This is sometimes called the historic present, and is used for greater immediacy. Time adverbials are not required, and the implication is of very recent events. This usage is popular with writers of newspaper headlines. A similar usage is found in captions to pictures, though here one might interpret as 'actual present moment', ie the action now in the picture. The usage is also a quite common device in certain types of story-telling.

An alternative to <Henry tells me you're ill> <Tom says he'll help.> etc is <Henry has just told me you're ill.> etc.

A and B, and in a limited way C, are the main uses of the present simple.

5.3 Present progressive

A Actual present moment (Single activities in progress)	Oh look — it's *raining* hard and the children *are still playing* in the garden. The kettle's *boiling*; the telephone's *ringing*, and someone's *knocking* at the door. Why *aren't you wearing* your glasses, Jane? 'What *are you doing*?' 'I'm *watching* TV.'
B Short-term present period (Temporary habits, and repeated actions)	The Smiths *are living* in a hotel at present. Henry *is writing* a book. Tom *is staying* with friends in Ireland. Susan Smith *is learning* to drive. She's *eating* only one meal a day, to get slim for her holiday. Whenever I call, they're *watching* TV.
C Existing arrangements for future (Often single actions — time marking needed)	What *are you doing* tomorrow? We're *having* dinner with the Smiths tomorrow. Jane *is going* to New York this summer. Uncle Ben *is returning* to Canada tomorrow.
ADV **D Past related as present**	I'm *sitting* there minding my own business when in walks this stunning blonde.
ADV **E Long-term present period** (With some frequency adverbs)	I'm *always missing* the train. He's *constantly buying* me flowers. Elizabeth *is always coming* to see me.

The present progressive is marked for action in progress. This often implies
(a) that the action is not complete, and
(b) that it may be temporary, rather than habitual.

The period of this tense, as of the present simple, may be the actual moment or some more extended period, but the marking for 'in progress now' suggests a fairly short-term period. Activity in progress now (A) or repeated over a short-term period (B) is the basic meaning of this tense — the meaning implied without time adverbials or other markers. It does not suggest states.

A Actual present moment Action happening at the moment of speaking often contrasts with the present simple:

<Why *aren't you wearing* your glasses, Jane?> [now]
<Jane *wears* glasses.> [habit]

B **Short-term present** Activity (including repeated actions) in the short-term similarly contrasts with present simple (habit). Compare:

<Paul *lives* in Brighton.> [and may do so all his life] with
<The Smiths *are living* in a hotel.> [a temporary measure]

Compare also: <What *are you doing*?> [a question about the actual moment or temporary activity] with <What *do you do*?>, which out of context almost certainly means 'What is your job?' — a question about the long-term present.

Notice also the present progressive as a repeated background to a repeated series of actions:

<Whenever I call, they're *watching* TV.>

C **Existing arrangements for future** Usage of this tense for the future is much commoner than the limited use of the present simple for the same purpose. Like the present simple, it is not for unarranged certainty: <*I am dying before the year 2100.>

The difference between the two tenses with future reference is that the present simple sees the action as a short complete, rather impersonal fixed event due to take place at the time specified, while the present progressive emphasises personal arrangement and activity, and lacks the formality of the present-simple. Compare: <Christmas Day *falls* on a Saturday next year . . .> [a fixed event] with <We're *having* dinner with the Smiths tomorrow.> [arranged activity]

ADV **D** **Past related as present** Not a very common usage (compare present simple 5.2). Again, use of this tense makes the action seem as if it were happening now.

ADV **E** **Long-term present period** For continuous or repeated activity over a period, a simple tense is normal. But, unusually, the idea of very frequent activity, or accidentally repeated activity, occurs with progressive tenses and some frequency adverbs (*always, continually, constantly, forever, repeatedly*):

<He *always buys* me flowers for my birthday.> [regular habit]
<He's *always/constantly buying* me flowers.> [? a bit surprising]
<He *always catches* the train.> [means literally *always*]
<I'm *always missing* the train.> [means *frequently*, but quite definitely NOT always.]

Notice that this usage does not — despite an often repeated 'rule' — necessarily imply annoyance.

Another odd possibility exists with *always*: <She *is always coming* to see me.> could mean this is an existing arrangement for the future (C) — ie she keeps saying she is coming, but the implication is that in fact she never does!

5.4 Present perfect simple

Period containing the action extends to *now*.

A **Long-term present period** (States, single and repeated actions)	The house *hasn't always belonged* to me.
	Tom *has visited* Ireland more than twenty times.
	Has Susan (*ever*) *been* to Egypt?
	He *has* (*often*) *appeared* on TV.
	There *have always been* wars.
	I *have never flown* in a helicopter before.
	This is the first time I *have ever flown* in one.

B	**Short-term present period** (Often recent single actions)		*Has* the kettle *boiled?* I *have invited* 50 people to a party. *Have you locked* the door yet? Tom's *just locked* it. Susan *has (already) gone* to Paris. The car's *been serviced* — thank goodness. Henry's father *has (just) died.*
C	**Present period** (Long or short-term) is mentioned as	**1**	I've *known* them all my life. Henry *has been* to New York twice this year. *Have you seen* the Smiths this week?
1	a still present period		There *have been* two world wars in my lifetime. Man *has exploited* man throughout history.
2	a length of time starting earlier (with *for*)	**2**	The house *has belonged* to my family for 80 years. We've *known* the Smiths for years. I *have waited* for two hours already. We've *visited* Stratford every summer for the past ten years.
3	a period starting at a definite point (with *since*)	**3**	It's *belonged* to us since 1900. I've *lived* in London since I was three. We've *visited* Stratford every summer since 1971. Susan's *learned* Arabic since 1980. Paul's *bought* a car since you last saw him.

The present perfect simple is often described as used for 'past events
with present reference'. This is true in a sense, but the old name is a
good one. The tense has present reference and relevance because the
period containing the action extends from some time in the past until
now, and is therefore still present. The tense is perfect, because the
action is partly 'perfected' or achieved. Whether the action is actually
over or continuing depends on various factors such as whether the
verb refers to a single action, repeated actions, a state and so on. But
the choice of this tense is a rejection of 'past and finished'. The time
period may end at the moment of speaking or continue beyond, but it
is not separated from the speaker's *now* by any gap. (The smallest gap
would require the past.) This is the basic meaning of this tense.

A **Long-term present** The present implied may be long-term, especially if
states or repeated actions are involved.

Frequency adverbs often imply an extensive period — though notice
that very recent *action* is implied [in the more extensive period of my
life to date] by <I have never . . . before> or <This is the first time I
have ever . . .>

Note the difference between *been* and *gone* as verbs of movement.
Been = gone and returned; *gone* = left here. Compare
<Has she *been* to Egypt?> [Has she *visited* Egypt at any time?] with
<Has she *gone* to Paris?> [Has she *left* for Paris? Is she there or
on her way?]

B **Short-term present** Without other information, this tense usually
implies recent action, with perhaps some present result:
<Have you locked the door?> [I want to know if it is secure now.]
Just, lately, already, yet can emphasise recentness and are often
associated with perfect tenses. But American English can use *just* with
the past simple tense: <Tom just locked it.>

C **Present period actually mentioned**

1 Time expressions with this tense refer to a still present period, eg *this week, throughout history* (but see 5.8). If these adverbials are modified to make a gap between them and *now*, they become past and need the past simple: <I saw the Smiths *earlier this week*.> <Henry went to New York *at the beginning of this year*.>

2 and 3 The extent of the period extending until now can be mentioned as a length of time (with *for*), or as a period starting at a definite point (with *since*): <*for* an hour / six months / thirty years.> <*since* ten o'clock / last week / 1970.> *For* may sometimes be omitted: <She's been here a week.>, but not *since*: <*She's been here last week.>

Notice that *the past* week/month etc are periods extending right up to now. But *last* week/month etc are past and completed periods. Compare:

<I have been ill *for the past week*.> [a seven-day period extending to now]

<I have been ill *since last week*.> [the period began sometime in the week ending last Saturday and has continued until now]

<I was ill *last week*.> [during the period that ended last Saturday].

ADV *Since* is sometimes followed, not by a noun or noun phrase, but by a clause. The reference is similarly to a past point of time and so the *since*-clause usually contains a past-tense verb. The main clause (like the sentences of C3 above) takes the present perfect, and not present or past tenses: <*I live / lived / am living here since I left home / since 1980.>

But if *since* partly indicates cause, and not solely time, then this 'rule' about the present perfect no longer holds good and present tenses are possible:

<I am feeling better
<I feel better
<I've been feeling better
<I've felt much better

} since the doctor gave me these pills.>

5.5 Present perfect progressive

Period containing the action extends to *now*.

A	**Short-term present period** (Recent activities — single or repeated)		Susan *has been cooking*. Tom *has been visiting* Ireland. He *has been staying* with friends. Henry *has been appearing* on TV. You've *been drinking*. [Your breath smells!] *Have you been waiting* long?
B 1	**Present period** (Long or short term) is mentioned as a still present period	1	Henry's *been travelling* on business this month. Susan's *been cooking* this afternoon. Hello! At last! I've *been telephoning* you all (the) evening. I've *been hoping* to visit Africa all my life.

103

2	a length of time starting earlier (with *for*)	**2**	I *have been waiting* for ages. They'*ve been living* in Edinburgh for the past ten years. We'*ve been visiting* Stratford every summer for the past ten years. You'*ve been coming* to see me for ages.
3	a period starting at a definite point (with *since*)	**3**	Susan's *been learning* Arabic since 1980. People *have been behaving* like that since the world began. I'*ve only been wearing* glasses since last year.

The present perfect progressive tense takes the same viewpoint to real time as the present perfect simple. But the progressive emphasises activity. This has two implications:

(a) If there is no time adverbial (**A**), the present perfect progressive usually implies recent activity. This is the basic meaning of this tense. (Contrast the present perfect simple, where the tense without time adverbials can imply an extensive period.) The sense of recentness can however be overruled by the addition of adverbials referring to some longer period (**B**).

(b) The achievement may be incomplete. This does not mean, as is sometimes said, that the action of the verb is unfinished and therefore continuing up to the moment of speaking. What it means is that we are more concerned with activity than with result, so that the final result may be left vague.

5.6 Difference between the two present perfect tenses

<Susan has been cooking.> <Susan has been cooking dinner.> <Susan has been cooking this afternoon.> These statements with the progressive are all neutral as to whether Susan has finished or not. But they might be offered as reasons why she has not had time to do something else, because they all emphasise activity.

Contrast the present perfect simple:

<Susan has cooked the dinner.> This stresses achievement — the dinner which is now ready.

<Susan has cooked.> This is an unlikely sentence, since it suggests achievement without stating what has been achieved.

In some contexts, both present perfect tenses are possible: <I *have lived* / I *have been living* here ten years.> but, as with the present simple and the present progressive, the implications are often very different and only one tense, and not the other, is possible.

Simple (Achievement)	Progressive (Activity)
I have visited *Ireland*. [prior, long-term achievement]	I have been visiting Ireland. [recent: this tense is *not* possible with *twice,* etc.]
I have visited Ireland *twice/many times.*	
He has drunk *the wine.* [There is none left.] *But not:* *He has drunk.	Tom has been drinking.
	Tom has been drinking the wine. [In both cases there may or may not be some wine left.]
I have run */all the way here/ six miles.* *But not* *I have run.	I've been running. [That's why I'm hot and tired.]
Susan has learnt *Arabic since 1980.* [A complete achievement in the period since 1980. She did not know Arabic before, and now she does.]	Susan has been learning Arabic since 1980. [Maybe she is still learning.]
Susan has won. [ie a race, match etc is understood. Here, unusually, the verb alone stands for the complete achievement.]	Susan has been winning a lot of prizes. [recent repeated activity. But <Susan has been winning> would be odd because *to win,* by itself, is a verb of achievement rather than activity.]
What *have you done* about that job you wanted? [Have you applied? etc]	What *have you been doing* since I last saw you?
	What *have you been doing?* [Why are your hands dirty?]
Have you *eaten?* [infml — Have you had lunch/dinner?]	*Have you been eating?* [I think you eat too much/too little.]

5.7 Past simple

Period containing the action is over.

A	**Past period**	**1**	We *lived* in Brighton years ago.
1	States, habits, repeated actions		The house *belonged* to my grandfather.
			Jane *wore* glasses as a child.
			We *visited* Aunt Dorothy in Scotland every summer for twenty years.
			I *went* to school by bus.
2	Single actions	**2**	Henry *wrote* a book that year.
			Susan *learned* to drive in 1975.
			Tom *stayed* with friends in Ireland that summer.
			I *telephoned* Aunt Dorothy last night.
			One day Jane *left* her glasses on a bus.
3	Very recent past [mental states]	**3**	I *didn't know* (you were here).
			I *expected* you to be home earlier.
B	**Future in the past** (Already fixed) time marking needed		[I was getting excited.] The following Tuesday *was* my birthday.
			Uncle Ben asked the taxi-driver to hurry because his plane *left* at 6.
ADV **C**	**Social distancing** [Present context]		*Did you want* to see me?
			I *wondered* if you could lend me £5?

The past simple like the present simple can refer to states, habits and repeated actions (Compare A1 with 5.2.B). But in other respects usage of the two tenses is not entirely parallel. The present simple tense (5.2) is also used for:

(a) Timeless general truths: <Water boils at 100°C.> but only rarely for
(b) Single actions at the moment of speaking: <Now I add the chocolate powder.>

A **Past period**

However, in marking for past period, we specifically reject the timelessness of present simple. On the other hand, we also lose the sense that only a few actions are brief enough to be completed at the moment of speaking. Consequently while losing timelessness, past simple has a greatly increased usage for single actions. In fact this is *the* tense for past actions and events which perhaps were of more than momentary duration at the time, but which are *now* seen as single complete events:

<Susan learned to drive in 1975.>

Use of past tenses to refer to very recent past (A3) is common with a number of mental-state verbs. It is easy to see that use of a past tense, with a time-gap from *now*, however small, implies that the opposite is now true: <I didn't know . . .> [but I know now.] Of course such verbs can be used with the present perfect if the state still holds: <*I knew/I have known all along* that you would come in the end.>

B **Future in the past** Usage parallels the usage of present simple as a fixed arrangement for the future.

ADV C **Social distancing** The use of past tenses with present reference as a means of social distancing is common in spoken English. It is often a marker of politeness.

The main usage of past tenses without past reference is for unreality in various subordinate clauses. See especially 6.24.

5.8 Difference between the past simple and the present perfect

A **Adverbials** The use of past adverbials (*yesterday, last year, 1980*) normally makes past tense obligatory. Notice *ago*: <an hour ago> <two years ago.> It measures the time-gap between *now* and a past point and requires past tenses. Contrast *for/since*:

<We left Brighton two years ago.>
<We have lived in London for the past two years.>

'Perfect' adverbials (*already, since, yet*) usually require perfect tenses. Present adverbials (*this week, today*), however, go with past or perfect tenses according to viewpoint or fact:

(a) <I haven't seen Jane today/this week.>
(b) <I didn't see her today/this week.>

In (a) *today/this week* is not over.
In (b) *today* etc stands for some understood past point: perhaps I usually see her at breakfast/on Mondays, but today/this week I didn't.

B **No adverbials**

If there are no obviously time-linked adverbials, then use of past tenses implies a period now finished, and conversely a finished period must use past tenses. The present perfect goes with still present time.

<Queen Victoria *reigned* for over sixty years.> [Her reign is past.]
<*Did you have* a happy childhood? [said to an adult]
<I *saw* Henry in New York.> [I am now somewhere else.]
<My father *lived* here all his life.> [He is dead now.]
But <He *has lived* here all his life.> [He is still alive.]

5.9 Past progressive

Period containing the action is over.

A	**Actual past moment** (Single activities in progress)	It *was raining* hard, but the children *were playing* in the garden. The kettle *was boiling*, the telephone *was ringing* and someone *was knocking* at the door.
B	**Short-term past period** (Temporary habits, repeated actions)	The Smiths *were living* in a hotel at that time. Henry *was writing* a book that year. This time last year, Tom *was staying* with friends in Ireland. Susan *was having* driving lessons twice a week. She *was only eating* one meal a day at that time.
C	**Past arrangements for future-in-the-past**	We *were having* dinner with the Smiths the following day. Jane *was going* to New York that summer. I *was meeting* Tom tomorrow.
ADV **D**	**Long-term past period** (Continually repeated actions)	I *was always missing* the train. He *was constantly buying* me flowers. Elizabeth *was always coming* to see me.
ADV **E**	**Social distancing** (Present context)	Were *you looking* for somebody? I *was wondering* if ⎫ I *was hoping* that ⎭ you could lend me £5?

A & B Past progressive shares the pastness of the past simple, plus the temporary aspect of present progressive. Either the activity was happening at the *actual past moment* we are talking about, or we are referring to some *short-term past period*.

C **Past arrangements for future-in-the-past** Just as the present progressive can mean an arrangement now for the future, so the past progressive can mean an arrangement *then* for what was then the future. However, if the *was* or *were* is stressed for contrast, this can imply that this was the arrangement only, and the opposite of what actually happened. It is therefore possible to say <I *was meeting* Tom tomorrow.> that is, tomorrow in relation to my speaking now; the meaning is that that was the arrangement, but now I am not going to meet him.

ADV **D** **Long-term past** With certain frequency adverbs, the past progressive parallels present progressive usage. Again, <Elizabeth was always coming to see me.> could mean either (a) she did, or (b) if an unfulfilled 'future-in-the-past', that she did not come.

ADV **E** **Social distancing** Compare the similar usage with the past simple. <I *was wondering*> is even more tentative (and polite) than <I *wondered* if . . .>.

5.10 Difference between the past simple and the past progressive

A common contrast between the present simple and the present progressive is between habits or repeated actions (simple) and an action of limited duration at the moment of speaking (progressive):

<I *smoke* 30 cigarettes a day, but — as you can see — I'm *not smoking* now, because I know you don't like it.>

This contrast is possible with the corresponding *past* tenses, but a much commoner contrast between the two tenses is what appears to be a reverse situation, due to the common use of the past simple for single actions. A shortish, single past simple action takes place against a background activity of limited, but longer duration: <I *was smoking* a cigarette [actual past moment] when Tom *walked* in.> [single action] We can of course add to this: <I *smoked* 30 cigarettes a day in those days.> [past habit]

Other contrasts:	
Simple	*Progressive*
She *learnt* to drive. [achievement seen as single action/event]	She *was learning* to drive. [unfinished activity — we don't know if she succeeded]
We *had* dinner with the Smiths. [single event]	We *were having* dinner with the Smiths. [out of context — fact or future-in-the-past]
We *lived* in Brighton. [long-term state of affairs/habit]	They *were living* in a hotel. [temporary activity]
Elizabeth *always came* to see me. [repeated actions]	Elizabeth *was always coming* to see me. [may be fact, may be future-in-the-past]
His plane *left* at 6. [fact or future-in-the-past]	His plane *was leaving*. [fact or future-in-the-past]

5.11 Past perfect simple

Period containing the actions, etc extended to *then*. The past point of time (to which the actions etc are related) is mentioned or implied.

A	**Pre-past period** (Long- or short-term)		*By 1980*, Paul *had had* enough. He *had been* ill the winter before. He *had visited* America twenty times in the previous thirty years. He *had never, at that time, been* to India. [He went to India in 1981.] He *had never visited* Asia before. [ie before 1981] It *was* the first time he *had visited* India. He *had visited* New York the year before.
B	**Past period** (Long- or short-term) is mentioned as		
	still continuing at past point	1	Henry *had been* to New York twice *that year*. Paul *had worked* hard *all his life*.
	a length of time (with *for*)	2	He'd *got up* at 7 am every day *for forty years*.
	a period starting at a definite point (with *since*)	3	Paul *had bought* a car. [since I'd last seen him] He *had worked* at the bank *since 1940*.

108

C	**Social distancing** [Present context]	I *had hoped* you would lend me £5. I *had intended* to go to London tomorrow.

The past perfect simple is marked for past and perfective. The combination implies some measure of achievement before some past point or period of time. It refers to pre-*then*, not to pre-*now* as the present perfect does.

However, the need to distinguish between some pre-past and the past is not always so keenly felt as the distinction between pre-present (present perfect tenses) and present. Both pre-past and past are both, after all, past — so often past simple is sufficient, and in fact 'correct'. The past perfect is only obligatory in contexts where perfectiveness, not mere prior happening, must be stressed. This is usually in subordinate clauses (eg in some conditionals, some reported speech, and some time clauses (5.12), and with some adverbials).

Adverbials

(a) A number of adverbials establish a past point or *then* (corresponding to the present's moment-of-speaking or *now*) to which prior achievement is related. They include *at that time, by then, up till then*. Used in this way, they need the past perfect with dynamic verbs, although not with stative: <By then he *had visited* America twenty times.> But <He *knew* America well *by then*.>

Alternatively the time period of the prior action can be expressed in relation to the past *then*. For example, <the year before> corresponds to present *now*'s <last year>. Adverbials relating the past to *now* (eg *yesterday*) are not normally used with the past perfect (11.45).

(b) *just, yet, already, since, for* are other adverbials that often need a past perfect tense, not a plain past. (Again, compare present perfect.)

5.12 The past perfect in time clauses

A sequence of two or more past events is often recounted with the past simple, using the chronological order:

<I *came*, I *saw*, I *conquered*.>

<Paul *worked* at the bank for forty years, and *retired* in 1980.>

However, if the events are mentioned in a different order, then the chronological sequence has to be indicated. This can be done with adverbials (eg *later*) or conjunctions, (eg *before*). But since the reason for putting the chronological events out of sequence is probably to focus on a particular point in time, the past perfect is often used to emphasise the completion of the prior event:

<Paul visited India in 1981. He *(had) retired* the year before.>

<Paul visited India after he *(had) retired*.>

<Before Paul retired he *was/had been* ill.>

The past perfect must be used if there is no other indication that the events are out of sequence:

<Paul visited India in 1981. He *had retired*.>

When-clauses A *when*-clause in a sequence of two simple tenses introduces the prior event, even if the *when*-clause comes second:

<When Paul retired he went to India.>

<Paul went to India when he retired.>

It is only if the *when*-clause contains the later event that we need a past perfect in the main clause:

<Paul *had (already) retired* when he went to India.>

Some grammar books remark with surprise on the 'special' use of past perfect with *before* and *until* for a later, (not an earlier) event, and indeed for an event that probably did not happen, as in:

<She disappeared *before he'd had* a chance to apologise.>
<He died *before he had completed* his autobiography.>
<They refused to come *until we had explained.*>

There is nothing odd about this if we stop thinking of the past perfect as a 'before-past' and remember that:
(a) perfect tenses are marked primarily for perfectiveness; and
(b) English divides time into two main periods — present and past.

Just as present tenses can be used for future happenings (one could call this 'future in the present', though nobody ever does!), so past tenses can be used for 'future-in-the-past' events. With subordinate clauses, this means that the 'perfectiveness' of perfect tenses is contained within the present or past period of the main clause, but not necessarily achieved before the main clause action. Compare

(a) <He is going to go to India   when
    <He can't go   before   he has retired.>
    <He is waiting   until
(b) <He was going to go to India   when
    <He couldn't go   before   he had retired.>
    <He was waiting   until

In all of these six sentences, the reality of the perfected action is in doubt. But the parallel between present and past is not complete. There are two important differences:

1 In the subordinate clauses in (a) if the prior achievement were not important we could use the present simple: <when/before/until he retires> and this would still not make *he retires* a certain future fact. But in talking now about the past, we may be presumed to know what happened. So *when/before/until he retired* in (b) could imply an actual happening (ie, he retired).

2 In the main clause, we can use the past simple tense in (b) as a single complete achievement: <He waited until . . .> but we cannot use the present simple in (a): <*He waits until . . .>

A combination of two past simples suggests that both events were past facts: <He waited until he retired.> But past perfect in the time clause may, depending on context, either leave the possibility open, as in (b), or clearly imply that the event did not happen — exactly as it does in an *if*-clause: <If he had completed his autobiography . . .>

5.14 Past perfect progressive

Period containing the actions etc extended to *then*. The past point of time (to which the actions etc are related) is mentioned or implied.

A	**Short-term pre-past period**		He *had been feeling* depressed. He'*d been drinking*.
B	**Past period** (Long- or short-term) is mentioned as		
	1	period still continuing in past	He *had been travelling* on business *that year*. Paul *had been hoping* to visit India *all his life*.
	2	length (with *for*)	He'*d been getting up* at 7 am every day *for forty years*. He'*d been working* at the bank *for ages*.
	3	period [starting with *since*]	He'*d been living* in Brighton *since 1940*.
ADV	**C**	**Social distancing** [Present context]	I *had been hoping* you would lend me £5. I *had been intending* to go to London tomorrow.

Most of what has been said about the past perfect simple applies to the progressive, except that:

(a) without indications to the contrary, the progressive on its own implies recent activity (compare other progressive tenses);

(b) the emphasis is on activity rather than on completed achievement.

ADV **Social distancing** The use of past perfect tenses, whether simple or progressive, arguably has past, not present, reference. But the point is that by saying <I had hoped>, <I had been hoping> — or <I was hoping> — the speaker implies that perhaps he does not hope now. In using past perfect tenses, he is expressing himself even more diffidently than if he were using past tenses.

5.15 Difference between the two past perfect tenses

The main difference between the two past perfect tenses parallels that between the two present perfect tenses (compare 5.6).

Simple [**Achievement**]	*Progressive* [**Activity**]
Paul had visited America *twenty times*.	He'*d been visiting* America for years.
He had saved up *£2,000*.	He *had been saving* hard.
He had bought *a very good guide book*.	He'*d been planning* the trip for years.
He'*d read* *thirty books on India*.	He *had been reading* travel books throughout the previous year.

Talking about the future

5.16

A	**Present simple** Future timetable already fixed now	Uncle Ben *leaves* tonight. His train *leaves* at 10 pm. We *have* a meeting every day next week. According to the brochure, we *stay* in Rome for five days and then *fly* to Athens.
B	**Present progressive** Future already arranged now	Uncle Ben *is leaving* tonight. What *are* you *doing* tomorrow? We're *having* lunch with the Smiths. *Are* you *going* to the Post Office? Monica and Adrian *are getting married* in August. 'How *are* you *paying*?' 'I'm *paying* by credit card.' (you said I could)
C	**will/shall + infin** 'pure future' (prediction) or volition now (decision now)	I'll *be* 21 next month. ['pure future'] You'll *be* cold in Scotland in January. [prediction] Oh well, perhaps I'll *wait* till the summer. [decision now] *Will* I *see* Susan tomorrow? [Predict!] *Shall* I *see* her? [Advise me!] I've spilt my coffee — I'll *get* a cloth. [decision now] 'What *will you do* if you can't use a credit card?' 'I'll *pay* cash.' *Will* you *go* to the Post Office for me? [request] *Will* you *have* a cup of tea? [invitation]
D	**will/shall + be + ing** Prediction	This time next week I'll *be sunbathing* in Florida. *Will* you *be going* to the Post Office? [because, if so, I'd like some stamps]
E **1**	**going to + infin** prior decision or	Monica and Adrian *are going to get* married in August. [their prior decision] I've put the kettle on because I'm *going to have* a cup of tea. [my prior decision]
2	speaker's certainty because causes exist now	I'm *going to be* sick: I feel terrible. James *is going to be* a tall man.

Here we bring together the main ways of talking about the future.

A **Present simple** The future is already fixed now. This usage often feels formal and impersonal. It is not very common, except with travel arrangements and fixed timetables.

B **Present progressive** A very common usage: an arrangement already exists now for the future. It is sometimes interchangeable with (E) because arrangement and decision overlap, but <I'm staying at the Ritz.> suggests I have booked a room, whereas <I'm going to stay at the Ritz.> emphasises my decision and intention.

C **will/shall** With future reference, this tense is concerned either with 'pure future' and prediction or with volition, which means a decision now at this moment. <What will you do . . .?> [if or when something happens] has a sort of 'Predict!' or 'Decide now!' meaning, which is quite different from the present progressive (B) — <What are you doing?> [Tell me about the arrangements], or from *going to* (E) — <What are you going to do?> [roughly = What have you already decided to do?]

Will you DO..? is therefore the normal form for straight invitations and requests.

Only *will* (not *going to*) can be used for a decision at the moment of speaking. Not therefore, in the context here, <I'm going to get a cloth.> And not <I'm getting a cloth.>, which would mean 'I'm already on my way to fetch one.'

D **will/shall be + ing** The progressive tense puts emphasis on the activity rather than on volition, so this form implies a predictable future, perhaps as a background to some other action. <Will you be going to the Post Office?> is therefore an enquiry about a future action, not a request, but with the possible implication that something else might be done if the answer is 'yes'.

E **going to** *Going to* expressing prior decision **1** contrasts with *will* [decision now]. *Going to* expressing the speaker's certainty **2** is sometimes interchangeable with *will* expressing prediction <I am going to be 21 next month>. But since *going to* is a present tense in form it implies that there is already evidence for the future event. <James is going to be a tall man *because he is a tall boy*>. *Will*, on the other hand, is 'purer' prediction.

See also chapter 6 for variants on (C) and (D).

Tenses in subordinate clauses

ADV **5.17**   The popular way of looking at tenses in subordinate clauses is rather misleading. Starting from misconceptions about the relationships that should hold between time and tense, we get dubious rules like 'the future perfect becomes the present perfect in future time clauses' or 'past tenses in main clauses must have past tenses in subordinate clauses'. These are the so-called 'sequence of tense' rules, which have very limited use.

It is safer to remember a few basic principles:

1 The speaker/writer is speaking *now*, and events (in both main and subordinate clauses) are seen from now, the moment-of-speaking.

2 The time references in the main and subordinate clauses may be different. Conditionals are an obvious example. Notice also subordinate clauses after expressions like *I hope, It doesn't matter . . .* where any time is possible:

   <I hope you didn't/don't/won't upset her.>

3 The fundamental division of the English tenses is into present and past. This means that future time and 'future-in-the-past', which seem to cause most problems, fall within these divisions.

5.18 Future time in subordinate clauses

Adverbial clauses	I'll give you that book *when I see you.* [time] I'd like it back *when you've finished it.* [time] She'll tell you *when you're having lunch.* [time] I'm going to buy one, *however much it costs.* (concession) I'll get there *as quickly as you do/as you will.* [comparison] I'll do the shopping *because you'll be busy.* [predicted reason] I'll do it *because you're busy.* [reason now]
Relative clauses	We're going to tell anyone *who calls* to go away.
Nominal clauses	Let us know *how you get on.* I hope (that) *they have/they will have a rosy future.* It doesn't matter *where we go next week.* I don't care *what happens.*

1 The fact that we are talking about the future is usually indicated in the main clause (by a modal, an imperative, an adverbial, etc). Therefore an unmarked present simple is normally sufficient and 'correct' in the subordinate clause(s). This applies not only in conditional 'type 1' clauses (6.23) but in many other adverbial clauses (including purpose and result, 11.19), relative clauses and nominal clauses.

2 Naturally there may be reasons why we wish to indicate modality or use present tenses other than present simple in the subordinate clause. We can distinguish, for example, between reasons existing now and predicted reasons.

We must of course indicate future in the subordinate clause if it is not clearly indicated by the main clause (for example, if the main clause is past — see 5.19).

5.19 Tenses after past main clauses

Showing past, present or future reference

Straight narrative	I did the shopping *because she was busy.* [past] I did the shopping *because she was going to be busy.* [future in the past] It didn't matter *where we went the following week.* [future in the past]
Reported speech (and see chapter 11)	I told you $\left\{\begin{array}{l}\text{I would}\\\text{I would}\\\text{I will}\dagger\end{array}\right.$ give him the book when $\left\{\begin{array}{l}\text{I saw him.}\\\text{I see}\dagger\text{ him.}\\\text{I see}\dagger\text{ him.}\end{array}\right.$ (†These forms denote the speaker's future) I told you *I'm never going to eat snails again.*
Result Comparison	He was so successful that $\left\{\begin{array}{l}\text{he never worked again.}\\\text{he doesn't work now.}\\\text{he'll never work again.}\end{array}\right.$ The prize money was more than $\left\{\begin{array}{l}\text{he (had) expected.}\\\text{most people win.}\\\text{I'll ever win.}\end{array}\right.$

When the main clause is past, the question to consider is whether the subordinate clause also relates to the past from our point of view now. If it does, then the 'sequence of tenses' and 'future-in-the-past' rules apply, as in most straight narrative, and in some reported speech with past reporting verbs (see chapter 11). But frequently main and subordinate clauses have different time reference (eg in adverbial clauses of result or comparison and in much reported speech), and then the only rule is: Use the tense that is relevant *now*.

5.20 Hypotheses

In *hypothetical conditions*, where both main and subordinate clauses are hypothetical, both clauses use 'past' tenses marked for unreality (6.24-25).

Hypotheses in only the subordinate clauses may be indicated by:
past tenses — after *wish/It's time* (6.27-28);
subjunctive (4.28); and
should (6.10).

6. MODAL VERBS AND CONDITIONALS

Modal verbs

6.1   The modals are often described as defective verbs, because they lack a full set of forms, and many course books fill in the 'gaps' in the system with other verbs: *must* with *have to*, *can* with *be able to*, etc. From a practical teaching point of view this may be reasonable, but it is worth asking why the modals are defective. Formally, they may be. In terms of meaning, they are less so.

    Take *must*. This imposes the speaker's obligation for now or the future. One can, of course, report that one imposed an obligation in the past: <I told them they must.> but one cannot retrospectively lay an obligation: <*I insist now they must/musted do it last week.> There is no such form because there is no such meaning. Stating now that an obligation existed in the past is a different concept, and requires a different verb (*They had to . . .*).

    Could/might/would/should are classified as separate modals (and not as past forms of *can/may/shall/will*) because
(a) it is only in reported speech that they are regularly used as pasts;
(b) all four forms have present and future reference. However, they are like the past tenses of lexical verbs in being used for unreality (hypotheses) and tentativeness (for politeness or some other 'social distancing'.)

6.2 Meaning: possibility — necessity

		Degrees of freedom to act	Theoretical possibility
Scale		Complete freedom (*top*) to necessity to act/not to act (*bottom*)	Possibly true (*top*) to necessarily true/not true (*bottom*)
can (*+ needn't*)	6.3 6.14	general possibility (opportunity)	general theoretical possibility
could	6.7	sometimes past or tentative/hypothetical *can*	
may/may not	6.4	permission	likelihood
might/might not *mightn't*	6.8	occasionally past or tentative/hypothetical *may*	
ought/ought not to *oughtn't to* *should/should not* *shouldn't*	6.12 6.10	(avoidable) obligation (*should* = past of *shall* only in rep. speech)	(avoidable) assumption
shall/shall not *shan't*	6.6	obligation/promise	prediction

will/will not won't 6.5	volition/insistence	strong prediction
would/would not wouldn't 6.9	sometimes past or tentative/hypothetical *will*	
must/must not mustn't 6.13 (+ need) 6.14	(unavoidable) necessity to act/not act	(unavoidable) deduction of truth
can't 6.3 (+ couldn't) 6.7	(necessity not to act) —————————	(unavoidable) deduction of impossibility of truth

The modals have a great variety of communicative functions, which sometimes appear unrelated. But broadly they can all be related to a scale ranging from possibility (*can*) to necessity (*must*). Within this scale there are two divisions: one concerned with possibility and necessity in terms of *freedom to act* (including ability, permission and duty), and the other concerned with the *theoretical possibility of propositions* being true or not true (including likelihood and certainty) — see table above. *Shall* is sometimes said not to fit into this scheme, but it is tentatively included here. The reference numbers are to the more detailed treatment in the later sections.

This chapter shows how the many apparently unrelated communicative uses can all be placed in a few broad categories on this two-fold scale. In fact, it will be seen that these categories (shown in **bold** letters on the left for each modal in sections 6.3-6.14) are not mutually exclusive, and individual usages frequently combine several meanings. For example: <You can catch the train if you hurry.> (6.3) is listed as opportunity, but also contains an element of ability.

6.3 *Can* — freedom to act/theoretical possibility

cannot, can't — **restriction on action / impossibility**

A	Permission	'Can I borrow your car, please?' [request] 'Of course you can' / 'No you can't.' We can't smoke in this theatre. You can say that again! [agreement] You can forget about it. [order/advice] This is awful work — you can do it again. [order] Can I help you? [offer]
B	Ability	'Can she speak Arabic?' 'Yes, she can.' I can see my cousin over there, but I can't see if he's alone. [Note: verb of sensation] Can you help me? [request] The sea can be very rough at times. It can't be helped. [resignation]
C	Opportunity	You can catch the 7.30 train if you hurry. I can telephone tomorrow if you like. [offer] Come early and we can have a picnic [suggestion] She can practise her Arabic with Abdullah next week.

D	**Theoretical (im)possibility**	'Can there be life on Mars?' 'There can't be.' What can the matter be? They can't be catching the 7.30 train. It's 7.29 already. You can't really mean that! [disbelief] 'Can that possibly be Tom on the phone?' 'It can hardly be Tom — he has only just left.'

Can means complete freedom and possibility, with permission and ability as variants of this. Can in general applies to now: permission, opportunity etc may exist now for the future. For past or future ability that does not exist now, we use be able to:

<She'll be able to scuba-dive when she's finished the course.>

For past ability — see 6.7.

A **Permission** Can/can't for permission/refusal of permission are more informal than may/may not. The idiomatic <'You can say that again!'> <'You can forget about it!'> both suggest an underlying 'you have my permission' — in one case because I agree; in the other, my permission is a disguised order.

B **Ability** is general ability now: <The sea can be rough — and sometimes is.> But can is used for actual achievement at this moment with verbs of sensation (see, hear etc), where the plain verb would apparently carry much the same meaning: <I see my cousin over there.>

Some other verbs, mainly stative (bear, remember, understand etc), also often follow the same usage.

C **Opportunity** Where there is a sense of opportunity, rather than ability, can is possible for future reference, even for a single occasion. Contrast:

<She can practise her Arabic when she meets Abdullah next week.> with the impossible <*She can speak Arabic better when she's had more lessons.> and <*The sea can be rough tomorrow.>

D **Theoretical possibility** Can implies general theoretical possibility. It is used in questions, but not in assertive statements unless qualified by a semi-negative (eg hardly). To answer <Can that be Tom on the phone?> we can say, <It may/could/might be>, but not <*Yes, it can be.>

Cannot/can't states complete impossibility, and not merely possibly not. (Contrast may not on the theoretical scale, which means possibly not and therefore possibly yes.) On the theoretical scale, cannot/can't implies the logical deduction of impossibility.

With action verbs, can't is sometimes ambiguous: <They can't catch the 7.30 train.> could mean either that it's too late (inability) or that permission has been refused. In practice, the context usually makes the meaning clear.

The progressive <They can't be catching the 7.30 train.> is almost certainly logical deduction eg [I am certain they are not catching the train — because they are having dinner with me].

6.4 *May* — permission/likelihood

may not (mayn't = very rare) — refusal of permission/likelihood-not

A	Permission	Only members *may buy* drinks at the bar. [club rule] Chairs *may not be removed* from the bar. '*May I borrow* your car?' [request] 'Of course *you may*.' ('No, you *may not*.') *May I help* you? [offer] That doesn't suit you, if I *may say* so. [polite formula]
B	Likelihood	Oh well, you *may be* right. [concession] You *may be* old — but that doesn't excuse you. [concession] She hasn't telephoned — she *may not know* the number. The sea *may be* rough with all this wind. [now or future] It *may well* rain. [*may well* = be very likely to] We *may have* a picnic tomorrow. [possible plan] They *may catch* the 7.30 train tomorrow. They *may be catching* the 7.30 train tomorrow.
	ADV	Do you think she *may be* away? [Note: Indirect question] We *may as well* go now. [unenthusiastic suggestion] *May you be* forgiven! [I pray you will be forgiven.]

May means permission and theoretical possibility — like *can*. But it does not mean ability, and the possibility is specific (not general) likelihood.

May-questions come under the general heading of permission (including offers). With likelihood, indirect questions are possible, but direct questions are old-fashioned. Negative questions are rare, even for permission. (Instead, *can't* and *couldn't* are preferred.)

For negation, contracted *mayn't* is rare — some people feel it is non-existent. With permission, the *not* negates the modal (as it does with *can't*). So *may-not* = permission not = permission refused: <You *may not*/can *not* (borrow the car) today.> But with likelihood, *not* negates the lexical verb, so the possibility of *may* itself is left open: <She *may* (*not* know the number) — but of course she may know it!>

A **Permission** *May/may not* implies the speaker's or listener's permission, — a club member to a non-member friend would probably say: <You *can't* buy drinks here — you're not a member.> because he is reporting an *external* rule.

Like *can*, *may* covers not only permission in the obvious sense, but also offers of help, where the two are interchangeable: <Can/may I help you?>

May cannot replace *can* in requests (*can* as ability): <Can you help me?> and not <*May you help me?>, nor where there is a strong implied command: <*This is awful — you may do it again.>

B **Likelihood** *May* is less general and more specific than *can*, and suggests some degree of actual probability. Contrast:

<We can have a picnic — but we may not.>, meaning 'We have the opportunity but probably won't take advantage of it' with <*We may have a picnic but we can't.>, which, if *may* implies likelihood and not permission, has the absurd meaning 'We'll probably have a picnic but it's impossible.'

Contrast also:

<The sea can be rough.> [And it sometimes is]
<The sea may be rough.> [Now or later]

May sometimes carries a feel of concession now, but without general possibility. Contrast:

<You may be right.> [I agree perhaps you are.] and

<You can be right and people still don't believe you.> [ie statement of fact].

May as well also relates to a specific occasion: <We may as well go now.> (For *might as well* see 6.8).

The formulaic use of *may* to express hopes and wishes for the future is somewhat formal and old-fashioned: <May you be forgiven.>

The progressive tense is almost certainly likelihood, not permission: <They may be catching the 7.30.> Compare *can't be*.

Note: *maybe* as one word is an adverb roughly meaning 'perhaps', so is closely connected with the likelihood scale:

<Maybe you're right.> [And maybe you aren't!]

<You may be right.> [But perhaps you aren't!]

6.5 *Will* — volition/prediction

will not/won't — refusal/prediction-not

A	**Volition**	
(a)	*willingness*	Susan *will* help. *I'll* help.
		If he *will just wait* a moment . . . [request]
		Will you help me, please? [request]
		Will/won't you have another drink? [invitation]
		Remember to write, *won't* you? [request]
		Don't forget to write, *will* you? [request]
		Hurry up, *will* you. [order]
		Will you do as you're told! [angry order]
		I *will accept* £5, not £50.
(b)	*insistence*	I *will* be obeyed.
	[Stress on	I *won't* go, and that's final.
	will/*won't*]	If you *will eat* so much, no wonder you're fat. [habit]
(c)	*intention*	*We'll come* about three o'clock, we *won't come* to lunch.
		I'll kill him for this!
		What *will* you *do* if you lose your job?
B	**Prediction**	
(a)	*'pure future'*	It *will* be generally dry tomorrow, but there *will* be occasional outbreaks of thundery rain in the south-west.
		I *won't get* the results until Tuesday.
		I'll be 21 next month.
		Will we ever *discover* the truth?
		Whatever *will be, will* be.
		What *will* you *be doing* this time next year?
		This time next week I *will* be *sunbathing* in Florida.
		You *will* be paid. [promise]
		You'll be sorry for this. [warning]
		You *will do* as I say. [order]
ADV (b)	*general deduction*	That *will* be Susan ringing now.
		That *won't* be Susan — she's away.
		If you eat so much, of course *you'll* be fat.
(c)	*habit and habit-power*	Children *will do* these things. [also = insistence]
		On holiday, *she'll often swim* before breakfast.
		This sack *will hold* 28lb of potatoes.
		6 into 5 *won't* go.
		This key *won't fit*.

The general meaning of *will* is near the necessity/certainty end of the modal scale. The underlying connection is close — if you are sufficiently determined to do something, that action can be confidently predicted!

A **Volition** includes willingness, insistence, intention. *Won't* = unwillingness, refusal. *Will* in the *if*-clause of a conditional sentence means volition/willingness. Question-forms (which can be analysed as enquiries about the hearer's willingness) function as requests, invitations, even orders. *Will/won't* tags tend to soften commands when they follow the normal tag pattern of reversal, but a positive tag with a positive imperative can sound annoyed.

B **Prediction** (a) *Will* — with *shall* — is the future tense of traditional grammar. But *will* is only sometimes a 'pure' future. Notice the present reference of insistence, general deduction, habit, power. The progressive *will be* DOING largely excludes volition and stresses general prediction (including futurity — see 5.16).

ADV (b) *General deductions* Predictions about the future and assumptions about now can be distinguished, but the basic meaning is much the same. *Will* is often used in the main clause of the so-called 'future conditional' and regarded as 'pure future'. However, *will* in this position does not always have to have a future interpretation as can be seen here, <. . . of course you'll be fat.> where the meaning seems to be present cause and effect.

(c) *Habit* Some people distinguish between 'persistent' habit: <Children will do these things.> and 'characteristic' habit: <She'll often swim . . .>. The real difference is that, if you disapprove, you can stress the *will* to emphasise the doer's pig-headed insistence on the course of action. (So that habit here combines volition and prediction). The examples given under *habit-power* are of a particular kind of characteristic habit. Some grammarians call this usage 'timeless prediction', which is an equally valid description.

Will is reducible to -'ll except in final position or where insistence is stressed. But contracted *won't* can be stressed and is common for refusal (ie negative insistence): <I won't do it — and that's final.>

6.6 *Shall* — obligation (promise)/prediction of future

shall not (shan't = rare) — prohibition/prediction-not

A Obligation	We *shall come* about 3; we *shan't come* to lunch. [promise] I *shall kill* him for this. [promise/threat] I *shall help*. [promise] These regulations *shall take* effect immediately. [order] Nobody *shall leave* the room during the exam. [order] You *shall* be paid. [promise] *Shall I help* you? [offer] *Shall we go* to the cinema? [suggestion] Let's go, *shall we*? [suggestion] What ever *shall we do*? [request for advice] *Shall he/they send* you a cheque? [request for instructions]
B Prediction '*pure future*' [*I/we* only]	I *shan't get* the results until Tuesday. I *shall be* 21 next month. *Shall we ever discover* the truth of this? *Shall I/we see* you next week? This time next week I *shall be sunbathing* in Florida.

Shall is more limited in meaning than the other modals, and is sometimes said not to fit into the possibility-necessity scale at all. However, a sense of obligation underlines some usages, while its strong sense of future is a form of prediction. In fact, it is alone among the modals in having exclusively future reference. *Shan't* is rare, especially in American English.

A **Obligation** With first person (*I/we*), *shall* is a sort of self-imposed obligation, and thus often a promise or threat. This explains why *shall* is here interchangeable with *will* (intention 6.5): announcing one's intention to do something (*will*) and promising to do it (*shall*) are similar. But with *I/we shall* questions, the speaker is — at a deep level — asking the person addressed to impose the obligation. The result may be offers, suggestions, requests for advice — and *will* is not possible. With second and third person, the speaker imposes the obligation and the result is usually orders. Again, *shall* here is not interchangeable with *will* except sometimes where *will* as prediction is similar to a promise:

<You *shall/will* be paid.>

B **Pure future** Here *shall* is only used in this meaning with *I/we* (and *shall* is roughly interchangeable with *will*.) With second and third person, the sense of speaker-imposed obligation or speaker's promise dominates so much that even a progressive tense cannot have a 'pure future' meaning. <This time next week you shall be sunbathing in Florida.> can only be interpreted as the speaker's promise.

Shall is never possible for the *will* of willingness, deduction or habit.

To sum up then on *shall/will*, it is misleading to suggest either that there is some 'future tense' in English using *shall* for *I/we* and *will* for second and third person (a rule of traditional grammar), or that, on the contrary, *shall* and *will* are interchangeable in modern English.

Shall and *will* have distinct meanings, but some of them sometimes overlap, as with *I/we* statements combining promise (*shall*) and intention (*will*). With *I/we* questions used as suggestions or as requests for advice, only *shall* is possible. In most other cases *will* is usable. Only *will* (never *shall*) carries meanings of general deduction, habit, or habit-power (6.5).

6.7 *Could* — freedom to act/theoretical possibility

could not/couldn't — restriction on action / impossibility

A	**PAST**	
1	**Permission**	I *could borrow* my father's car whenever I liked. [general]
		But I *couldn't have* it that particular day. [negative]
		Or rather, I *could only have* it for two hours. [qualified]
2	**Ability**	She *could speak* Spanish when she was six.
		I *could see* my cousin waving frantically. [single occasion]
		The dog *could always find* its own way home. [general]
		They *couldn't find* their way home that night. [negative]
		He *could hardly speak* — he was so upset.
		I *could only stutter* out my apologies.
		The sea *could be* very rough that winter.

	B	**NON-PAST**	
	1	*Permission*	*Could I borrow* your car next week?
			Could you hold the door open for me? [request]
			You *could type* this for me. [order/request]
	2	*Ability*	*I could see* my cousin over there, (if you got out of the way).
			I'm so angry, *I could scream.*
	3	*Opportunity*	You *could catch* the train — hurry!
			I could telephone you tomorrow. [offer]
			Come early and we *could have* a picnic. [suggestion]
			She *could practise* her Arabic with Abdullah next week. [suggestion]
ADV	4	*Theoretical (im)possibility*	The sea *could be* rough tomorrow.
			And it *could be raining.*
			There *could be* life on some of the planets.
			I could be wrong. [So don't quote me!]
			The house is shut up — there *couldn't be* anyone there. [deduction]
			He *couldn't mean* that — it's impossible.
ADV	5	*Hypothesis*	What marvellous weather for March — it *could be* July.
			I could be dead for all you care.
			If I were a bird, *I could fly.* [ability]

A PAST
Could replaces *can* in most usages in reported speech (11.46-48) but otherwise has limited past reference. Like *can*, *could* implies general possibility, rather than actual happening. So it is not surprising — though grammar books often remark on it — that *could* in the past implies general permission or ability, but not permission or achievement on a specific occasion, when we use *I had permission to*, *I was allowed to*, *I was able to* etc:

<The dog *was able to* find its way home that night despite the fog.>

Could is, however, possible for a single occasion when modified in some way (eg by *hardly, only, just*): <He *could hardly* speak.> etc.

Could is also usable for single events with verbs of sensation. This exactly parallels the usage with *can*: <I *could see* my cousin.>

Couldn't [negative] may be used for lack of ability, etc with reference to a single occasion: <I couldn't have the car that day.> but it often sounds a bit like reported speech (ie 'they said I couldn't have it.')

B NON-PAST
Could has many more usages with non-past reference than with past.
1 With **permission,** *could* is a tentative (and therefore sometimes politer) alternative to *can*.
2 & 3 Ability and opportunity The difference between these two meanings is perhaps less marked with *could* than with *can*. There is often also a sense of theoretical possibility with many uses of *could* - a sort of 'This could be so if . . .'

ADV **4 Theoretical (im)possibility** *Could* is not replaceable by *can* in positive statements. <The sea can be rough.> means 'It can be and is', which we have classified as 'ability'. <The sea *could be* rough.> of course includes an element of ability, but with present/future reference is predominantly theoretical.

ADV **5 Hypothesis (unreality)** Hypothesis is, of course, related to theoretical possibility. But in (5) we are hypothesising in ways we know to be totally false.

See also CONDITIONALS.

6.8 *Might* — permission/likelihood

might not / mightn't — likelihood-not

A	**NON-PAST**		*Might I borrow* your car?
1	***Permission***		*I don't like that, if I might give* an opinion.
	(Tentative)		*Might I remind* you of your promise?
			You *might type* this for me, please. [request/order]
2	***Likelihood/***		You *might be* right. [concession]
	possibility		She hasn't telephoned — she *might be* ill.
			She *might not know* your number.
			The sea *might be* rough. [now or future]
			We *might have* a picnic.
			They *might catch* the 7.30 train tomorrow.
			They *might be catching* the 7.30 train.
			Do you think she *might be* away?
			We *might as well go* now. [unenthusiastic]
			It *might be raining* now/tomorrow.
			There *might be* life on some planets.
			I *might be* wrong. [concession]
ADV	**3**	**Hypothesis**	It's warm for April — it *might be* summer.
			I *might as well be* dead for all you care.
ADV	**B**	**PAST** (RARE)	
	1	**Permission**	We weren't allowed to eat sweets in bed, but we *might* always *have* an apple. [fml]
	2	**Possibility**	Sometimes the dog *might find* his way home, but at other times we had to go and find him. [fml]
			Try as she might, she didn't manage to open the safe. [concession, fml]

A NON-PAST

1 & 2 Permission and likelihood *Might* is a more tentative alternative to *may*, and there is no great difference in many contexts. *Might*-questions (like *may*-questions) are mainly about permission, and very rarely about likelihood. To give or refuse permission tentatively might be confusing or impolite, so a probable answer to <Might I borrow your car?> is <Yes you *may/can*.> or <No you *may not/can't*.>, but not <*You might/mightn't*.>

Negative *mightn't* (like *may not*) leaves the possibility open (unlike *can't* or *couldn't*, which are deductions of impossibility):

<She *might* (not know) — but of course she might know.>

ADV **3 Hypothesis** Both *may/might* are more specific than *can/could*, suggesting there is a chance of something happening, not just a general theoretical possibility. Consequently, for a completely unreal hypothesis, *It might be summer* is a bit odd compared with *It could be summer*.

See also CONDITIONALS.

B PAST

Past usage of *might*, both for permission and likelihood, is rare, old-fashioned and formal, except when it replaces *may* in reported speech (11.46).

6.9 *Would* — volition/prediction

would not/wouldn't — refusal/prediction-not

	A	**PAST**	
	1	**Volition**	
		willingness	Susan *would always help* in those days. [+habit]
			He *would only accept* £5, though I offered him £50.
			All he *would do* was accept £5.
		insistence	He *would be obeyed*, and he *wouldn't listen* to advice.
			If she *would eat* so much, no wonder she was fat.
			They invited us for lunch, but we *wouldn't go* till later.
			You *would marry* him — we warned you not to.
ADV	**2**	**Prediction**	You *would do* a silly thing like that.
			On that holiday she'd *often swim* before breakfast. [+habit]
			It was a useful bag. It *would hold* 28lb. [+habit/power]
ADV	**3**	*'Future in the past'*	It was late in the year. Soon it *would be* Christmas.
			They were worried, because they *wouldn't know* the results until the following Friday.
	B	**NON-PAST**	
	1	**Volition**	If you *would just wait* a minute. [request]
			Would you help me please? [request]
			Would you do as you're told. [order]
			Hurry up, *would you*. [request]
ADV	**2**	**Prediction**	*Would that be* Susan ringing?
			Oh surely not. She'd *be* on the plane at the moment.
ADV	**3**	**Hypothesis**	I *wouldn't know*. [casual, rude]
			They *would like/prefer* . . .
			I *would say* / I *would think* . . . it's too expensive.

A PAST

Would can replace *will* in all its meanings in reported speech but otherwise has limited past reference, so that the categories of *will* (6.5) are not exactly paralleled.

1 Volition Like *could*, *would* is rarely used for single past actions. But — like *could* — it can be used for single past actions where the verb is modified (eg by *only*), or to convey strong insistence: <You would marry him.>

This is not surprising; volitional *will* (willingness, intention, insistence) does not confirm that a future action eventually happens, but if there was strong insistence in the past we infer that the action probably did happen. Where *would* implies more general past volition, there is often an overlap with habit:
<Susan would always help.> [She regularly did.]

ADV **2 Prediction** Since prediction by definition refers to the future, it may seem odd to include this heading under past usage. But there are certain parallels with *will*. *Will* as prediction includes deductions about single and habitual events in the present and future: <Children will do these things.> (6.5) means 'It is typical of them to . . .' Similarly, <You would do that.> means 'It was typical of you' (though notice that this refers to a single occasion).

ADV   **3 Future-in-the-past** The so-called future-in-the-past is of course 'pure future' transferred back in time, and *would* replaces *will* just as other past tenses replace other present tenses. It is like reported speech without reporting verbs:

(They knew) <It would soon be Christmas.>

B NON-PAST

1 *Would* is a tentative (usually politer) alternative to *will* in questions, requests, etc — but not in statements of willingness, insistence or intention, since it often has conditional undertones.

ADV   **2** *Would* is a less certain form of *will* for present prediction.

ADV   **3 Hypothesis** *Would* is more certain than *could* or *might*, which are often mere possibility. It can, however, be used as a sort of incomplete conditional sentence: <I wouldn't know.> [ie if you asked me]. <They would like . . .> [if they were asked]. Such tentativeness may be rude or polite. See also CONDITIONALS.

Would is reducible to -'*d* except (a) in final position, and (b) when volition is being emphasised.

6.10 *Should* — avoidable obligation/avoidable assumption

should not / shouldn't — obligation-not/assumption-not

NON-PAST		
1	**Obligation**	You *should* listen to your parents.
		Why *should* I? [rude]
		People *shouldn't* ill-treat animals.
		Shouldn't Tom be here soon? [Didn't he promise?]
		He *should* be here soon. [He promised . . .]
2	**Assumption**	Jane *should* be in New York soon/by now.
		This *shouldn't* cause any problem.
		We *should* know the results by Friday.
		How *should* I know? [rude]
		'Shouldn't Tom be here soon?' 'Yes, he *should*.'
3	**Hypothesis** [condition]	I/we *should* like/prefer . . .
		I *should* say/I *should* think it's too expensive.
		I *should* say nothing. [advice]
		Why *should* anyone steal my coat?

Should behaves differently from *could/might/would*. In limited ways, these three modals can be used in a simple sentence with past time reference. *Should* is not used in this way. It sometimes appears to be so, but this is always a sort of reported speech, with *should* for *shall*:

<He promised me the earth. I should have homes in Europe and America. I should travel. I should have everything I wanted.>

Should is also said to be different from *could/might/would* in not being a tentative equivalent of *shall* (as the others are of *can/may/will*). However, *should* is sometimes a weaker *shall*. Compare:

<Nobody *shall* leave the room during the examination.> [prohibition]
<Nobody *should* leave . . .> [prohibition weakened to advice]
<I *shall* arrive at 5 pm.> ['pure future' — near certain prediction]
<I *should* arrive . . .> [less certain assumption]

1 & 2 Obligation and assumption The meanings of *should* as obligation and assumption are closely connected — or would be in a perfect world. If it is right and proper to do something, it is reasonable to expect it to be done. Hence the ambiguity of many *should* sentences. This close connection explains why *should* for assumption usually assumes desirable things. (Stronger *will* and *must* can assume undesirable things.) Contrast: <The poor old lady will be/must be dead by now.> with <She should be dead by now.> which, although perfectly grammatical, is unlikely, or so we would hope!

3 Condition Some examples of *should* (like *would*) are perhaps concealed conditionals. With *I/we, should* and *would* are interchangeable in all the examples here. (But *should* cannot be used in *I/we would rather/sooner.*)

See also CONDITIONALS.

6.11 *Should* in subordinate clauses

ADV			
1 *Purpose* I telephoned	so that he	*shouldn't* worry. (*wouldn't* worry.)	
	in case he	*should* worry. (worried.)	
2 *Suggestion etc* They suggest (1)	that he	pays. (1)	
They suggested (2)		*should* pay. pay. [subjc]	(1,2)
		paid. (2)	
3 *Comment on theoretical possibility* It is/was advisable etc I am/was anxious etc	that he	*should* pay. pay. [subjc]	
I see no reason	why he	*shouldn't* pay.	
4 *Comment on presumed fact* It is a pity etc (1) I am sorry etc	that he	thinks so. (1)	
It was a pity etc (2) I was sorry etc		*should* think so. thought so.	(1,2)
I don't understand	why he	thinks/thought so. *should* think so.	
5 *Narrative intended to surprise* (. . . when who/what ...) We were just sitting there	when who *should* walk in but Jane.		

ADV   *Should* is widely used in subordinate clauses in ways that are very different from the other modals. The subordinate clauses may refer to past, present or future time.

In (1) purpose clauses, and the clauses of (2) and (3), *should* signifies proposed or anticipated (not actual) action, with *should* carrying a weak sense of obligation or assumption in most cases.

1 *Purpose* — see also 11.19.

2 *Suggest, etc* Other verbs in this pattern (note that subjunctive (4.28) and ordinary tenses are also possible) include:
agree, ask, command, demand, direct, order, propose, recommend, request, require, urge.

3 *Comment on theoretical possibility* Other adjectives in the pattern *It is advisable that . . .* include: *essential, important, necessary, unthinkable, vital.* Other adjectives in the pattern *I am anxious that* include: *adamant, determined, eager, keen.* Again the subjunctive (4.28) is an alternative.

4 *Comment on presumed fact* Here the *should*-verb is a presumed fact. Subjunctive is not possible, and the speaker is expressing emotional reaction. The effect of *should* is to stress this reaction by treating the event as an assumption rather than straight fact. There may also be a hint that there is/was a moral obligation for the event to be otherwise. Many other nouns and adjectives are possible:
    <It's *a disgrace, a relief, a scandal, a shame* . . .>
    <It's *absurd, disgraceful, odd, strange, praiseworthy* . . .>
    <I am *annoyed, delighted, glad, surprised* . . .> etc.

5 *Narrative intended to surprise* The meaning is: Jane did walk in, but you were not expected to guess this surprising fact.

For *should* in conditional clauses — see 6.22 and 6.26.

6.12 *Ought to* — avoidable obligation/avoidable assumption

ought not to/oughtn't to — obligation-not/assumption-not

A	**Obligation**	You *ought to listen* to your parents. Why *ought* I? People *oughtn't to ill-treat* animals. *Oughtn't* Tom to be here? He *ought to be* here soon.
B	**Assumption**	Jane *ought to be* in New York soon/by now. This *oughtn't to cause* any problems. We *ought to know* the results on Friday. *Oughtn't* Tom to be here soon? He *ought to be* here soon.

Ought to is usually interchangeable with *should* for meanings of obligation and assumption. In fact even question-tags can be mixed up:
    <People *oughtn't to ill-treat* animals, *should they?*>
    <Jane *ought to be* in New York by now, *shouldn't she?*>

Ought does not share the other uses of *should*. That is, *ought to* cannot replace *should* for hypothesis (6.10), nor in general for the meanings of 6.11.

In conditional sentences *ought to* carries the same meaning of obligation or assumption that it does elsewhere.

Ought to can have past reference only in reported speech.

6.13 *Must* — unavoidable necessity to act/ unavoidable deduction

must not/mustn't — unavoidable necessity not to act

A	Necessity to act	Dogs *must be carried.* [notice on escalator] I *must write* to my mother tonight. You *must listen* to me. I *must say* I think that's silly. [opinion] *Must you go* so soon? *Why must you make* so much noise? [complaint] People *must not ill-treat* children. [prohibition] You *must hurry* or you'll miss your train. [advice] She's terribly fat — she *mustn't eat* so much. [advice] You *must come* round for drinks. [casual invitation]
B	Unavoidable deduction	Jane *must be* in New York by now. She's terribly fat — she *must eat* too much. You *must be* tired after your journey. They *must be catching* a later train. You *must be* crazy. Why *must there be* a reason for her being overweight?

The basic meaning of *must* is necessity now or in the future. This covers both
(a) obligation/duty — a sort of moral necessity, and
(b) logical necessity — the unavoidable deduction that something must necessarily be so.

A **Necessity to act** This involves the speaker's authority, except in questions, where it invites the listener's. (Compare *may, should,* etc). The speaker is imposing an obligation, possibly on himself. However, the effect of speaker involvement may be neutralised when the speaker states some external rule with which he agrees. Notice that *must* can be used for what is objectively fairly weak necessity:
    <You *must* come round for drinks.>
    An obligation not to do something is expressed by *mustn't/must not*. Because *must* is speaker-imposed obligation, there is always an element of future reference for the activity that is necessary. But you cannot retrospectively lay an obligation. *Must* as past obligation therefore only occurs in reported speech. (6.1)

B **Deduction** *Must* as logical deduction is more likely to relate to present time than to some less certain future. We may make deductions about present states: <Jane must be there now.> or present habits: <She must eat too much.> But out-of-context statements about apparently single actions: <I must win.> <He must decide.> would usually be interpreted as obligation. Deductions about single future happenings are however possible: <The parcel must surely arrive soon.>
    Notice also how a progressive tense can suggest deduction rather than obligation. Compare *can't/may* etc: <They must be catching a later train.>
    For unavoidable deduction (or certainty) that something is not possible — see *cannot/can't* (6.3), *couldn't* (6.7).
    For *have to/ have got to* as obligation — see 4.14.

6.14 *Needn't/need not* — absence of necessity

(*need* — necessity)

A	**Absence of necessity to act**	(a) You *needn't write*, but please phone.
		He *needn't do* anything, need he?
	(a) *Modal*	You *needn't be* so rude. [complaint]
		Need you go so soon? You've only just come.
		Need I eat the fat?
		Need you see the doctor again? [Surely not!]
		Need I say more?
		I *need hardly say* how delighted I am.
		You *need only stay* a little while.
		I'm *not sure* whether we *need go* or not.
	(b) *Regular verb*	(b) He *doesn't need to* worry — he was born lucky.
		We *don't need to* book in advance, do we?
		Do you need to see a doctor? [possibly a suggestion]
		We *need to* go and book seats.
		You *need to* eat more.
		You *need to* be thinking about your career. [advice]
ADV	**B** **Absence of theoretical necessity**	Why *need there be* life on other planets?
		I agree. There *needn't be*.
		Well there *needn't be* — but there could be.

A Absence of necessity to act

(a) As explained in 4.25, *need* is both a modal and non-modal verb. The basic meaning of *need* is necessity now and in the future. But modal *need* is non-assertive, occurring mainly in the negative to express the absence of necessity, and in questions, where it hopes for the answer *No*, (ie it is seeking a denial of necessity). It only occurs positively if qualified in some semi-negative way: <I need *hardly* say . . .> or if subordinate to a non-assertive main clause: <I'm not sure whether we need go.>

(b) The regular (non-modal) verb *need* occurs positively, but the meaning is different from *must*. With *must*, the feeling of speaker-obligation is stronger. With *need* (though ultimately the words reflect the speaker's opinion) there can be an implication of internal necessity in the person/thing spoken about. Contrast:

[Mother to child] <You *must eat* your dinner.> [= I'm your mother and I say so.]

[Friend to friend] <You *need to eat* more — you're so thin.>
Must is possible in the second example, but would make the advice sound more speaker-related.

Both *needn't* and *don't need to* negate *need* and not the lexical verb that follows: ['There is *no* necessity to . . .']. This contrasts with *mustn't* which negates the following lexical verb (you must **not** DO). This explains why answers to both *must* and *need* questions can be the same:

<'Need/must I really do this again?' 'Yes, you must. / Well, no, you needn't.'>

With questions, modal <need I?> is often more intensely listener-related than regular verb <Do I need to?>. <Need I . . .?> is hoping for the answer 'No'. <Do I need to . . .?> is more concerned with the external facts of the situation. Compare:

<Need you see the doctor again?> [Surely not!]

<Do you need to see the doctor?> [Open question. Perhaps you need to.]

ADV **B** **Absence of theoretical necessity** This is a rarer meaning of *needn't* than absence of moral necessity to act.

Modals + perfect infinitive (eg *can HAVE DONE*)

6.15 Modals + perfect infinitives — time reference

These are not past tenses, as is sometimes stated, but are used to talk about past, present and future time. It is important to realise that the modal part normally has present/future, not past, reference. It is the 'have DONE' bit that indicates pre-achievement (in any period).

6.16 Present freedom to act

A **Promise/volition *now* for future**   I *shall have/will have repaid* everything I owe you by the end of the month.   We *shan't have/won't have forgotten* you so soon — don't worry.
B **Obligation *now* (or timeless obligation) for later**   You *must have read* this book before you start the course. [rare]
C **Lack of necessity *now* for past action**   You *needn't have brought* me flowers — how kind of you! [*oughtn't to/shouldn't have* are also possible here]   You *needn't have been* so rude. [complaint]

The 'present quality' of the perfect infinitive is clearly seen with *can have/may have/must have*, which are hardly usable on the freedom-to-act scale, since it is meaningless to give permission *now* or lay obligations *now* for actions to happen in the past.

A *Shall/will have* DONE are commonly used with future meaning with varying degrees of volition or promise.

B *Must (and shall) have* DONE are possible, but rare, with the implication that some prior achievement is an obligatory condition of something else happening: <You *must have read* this book before you start the course.> This sounds like an external precondition, and is different from the more usual <You *must read* this book . . .>, which sounds like advice or urging by the speaker.

131

C **_Needn't have_** DONE also clearly shows the present reference of the modal part of these tenses. The meaning is that no obligation exists _now_ for some action that in fact _has_ happened: <_They needn't have telephoned_> [but quite unnecessarily they _did_.] This explains why the meaning is quite different from <They didn't need to telephone.>, an ordinary past tense (negative) of the regular verb _need to_. This simply states that there _was_ an absence of need/necessity, and so leaves open the question of whether they _did_ or _did not_ telephone.

Notice that _needn't have_ DONE — like _needn't_ — can be used on the theoretical scale: <They _needn't (necessarily) have telephoned._> [What evidence do you have for assuming that they did?] But this is rarer.

6.17 Past freedom to act at some time

You _could_ have come yesterday/today/tomorrow. [You _had_ the opportunity to come, but you didn't take it.]
My brother _couldn't_ have come yesterday/today/tomorrow. [even if you had asked him]
You _could/might_ have typed this for me. [Criticism — why didn't you?]
I _could/might_ have been killed. [There was that chance.]
I _ought to/should_ have known you'd do a silly thing like that. [But I didn't know.]
She _ought to/should_ have gone to the dentist tomorrow. [But she has cancelled the appointment.]
Bill _would/might_ have bought a motor-bike last year/now/soon. [But he was in a bad crash last January.]

Only _could/might/would/should_ and _ought to_ + _have_ DONE have truly past meaning on the freedom-to-act scale. Here the opportunity/possibility etc of _could_, etc existed in the past, and by implication probably exists no longer. But the unrealised action of the _have_ DONE may relate to past, present or future time:
<He could have gone yesterday/today/tomorrow.>

6.18 Hypothetical (past) possibilities

It _could have/might have been_ summer. [But it was only April.]
I _could have/might have been talking_ to a brick wall. [My words had no effect.]
We _might as well have saved_ our breath. [Talking was a waste of time.]
We _might just as well not have gone._ [Going was a waste of time.]

I _wouldn't have thought/said_ that was a good idea. [If you had asked me.]
I _would have hoped_ you would learn/would have learnt from the experience.

Past missed opportunities mean that the events talked about did not in fact happen. This explains the use of modals + have DONE in the main clauses of past hypothetical conditions (6.24-25) and the reason why a feeling of hypothesis or condition often exists, even when these tenses are used without any conditional clause.

The common use of expressions like _I would have thought_ (social distancing for _I would think_ or _I think_) illustrates this. It hints at 'If I had been asked my opinion . . .' The opinion being expressed is of course a present one.

6.19 Theoretical assumptions *now* (about possibilities in past and future)

> Whatever *can have*/*could have* happened?
> They *should have*/*ought to have*/*would have* arrived by now. [If they had left in time.]
> There *may have*/*might have*/*could have*/*will have*/*must have* been an accident on the motorway. [not *can]
> They *couldn't have*/*won't have*/*can't have*/*shouldn't have*/*oughtn't to have*/*wouldn't have* taken the wrong road. [not *mustn't]
> We *shall have*/*will have*/*could have*/*may have*/*might have*/*ought to have*/*should have* heard something by this evening. [future]

With their theoretical meanings, all the modals can be used with the perfect infinitive, since it is perfectly possible to make assumptions *now* about the past, present or future. But they are (even with *could, might, should, would, ought to*) present assumptions, except in reported speech.

May can often be substituted for *might* on this theoretical scale with little change of meaning:

    <He *may*/*might* have been killed.> [Possible assumption now — we don't know.]

Notice how this contrasts with the freedom-to-act scale:

    <I/He *might* have been killed.> [There was a past chance of such an event — but we know I/he wasn't killed.]

So not <*I *may* have been killed.>

Can have DONE is restricted to non-assertive sentences (compare *can*):

    <What *can have* happened?>
    <Anything *can have* happened.>
    <Do you think something *can have* happened?>

But not <*Something can have happened.>

6.20 Ambiguities

Did he or didn't he? Will they or won't they?

	1 *Past* freedom to act at some time		2 Theoretical assumption *now* about possibilities at some time
A	He *could have gone* to the USA. [Missed opportunity. He said *No*. So he did *not* go, has *not* gone, is *not* going.]		He *could have gone* to the USA last week/by now/by next week. [Perhaps he *did, has, will* — we don't know his movements.]
B	He *might have telephoned* her. [He missed the opportunity for a past action. So he did *not*, has *not* telephone(d) her.]		He *might (may) have telephoned* her yesterday/by now/by tomorrow. [Perhaps he *did, has, will.*]
C	He *would have reached* New York . . . some time. [if some condition had existed; but he did *not*, has *not*, will *not*.]		He *would (will) have reached* New York last week/by now/by tomorrow. [We assume he *did, has, will.*]
D	He *ought to*/*should have gone* to the dentist. [But he did *not*, has *not*, will *not* — failed obligation.]		He *ought to*/*should have had* that tooth out last week/by now/by tomorrow. [We assume he *did, has, will.*]

Ambiguities can arise with [could/might/would/ought to/should + have DONE] because of the two different meanings and time contexts of this series as (1) past opportunity to act, etc and (2) present (or timeless) theoretical assumptions. Out of context, there are various interpretations of <He could have gone to the USA.> On the freedom-to-act scale (1) he turned down a past opportunity to go at some time so *could have gone* implies actual *not* going. This *could have* DONE, and similarly *might have* DONE are often used as criticism, just as *ought (not) to have* DONE and *should (not) have* DONE (D1) are.

On the theoretical scale (2) <He could have gone to the USA.> assumes the possibility of actual positive going at some time:

<He *could have gone* yesterday, for all I know.> [assumption about the past]

<He *could have arrived* by the time you get there.> [assumption about the future]

Negative assumptions about the future are possible with *might/would/ought to/should*:

<He *mightn't have left* New York by tomorrow night.>

But *couldn't have* DONE is the logical deduction of impossibility and such certainty is more likely to have past reference. Compare:

<He couldn't have left — he was still there a week later.>

<The house was shut up — there couldn't have been anyone there.>

Conditionals

6.21   A common simplification is to say that there are three types of conditional sentences, based on three ways of combining tenses in the *if*-clause and main clause — namely: **1** 'future': <If I see Tom, I will tell him.> **2** improbable/unreal: <If I saw him, I would tell him.> **3** 'unfulfilled past': <If I had seen him, I would have told him.> But this arbitrarily suggests that all other tense combinations are exceptions, which they are not.

Another way of looking at conditionals is to consider them in terms of:

Open (or real) condition (6.22) — open because the events described are a real possibility, already or in the future.

Hypothetical (or 'rejected') condition (6.24) where the condition is 'rejected' as unreal *now* — although in some cases they could happen later (see below).

6.22 Open conditions

A	Future possibilities [Main clauses refer to the *future*.]	Go, if *you've finished*.
		Go now, and I'll never speak to you again. [If . . .]
		Go now, or I'll never speak to you again. [Unless . . .]
		If you're *going* to watch TV, I'm going to bed.
		If you *won't tell* me, I'm leaving. [*won't* = refusal]
		If the trees *annoy* her, I'll cut them down.
		If it *will annoy* her, I'll cut them down. [*will* for later result]
		If you *should* see Henry, give him our love. [fml]
		If you *lost* your last camera, take care of this one.

B	Present and past habits	If my transistor *disturbs/disturbed* people, I turn/turned it down. If he *is/was* working, he always smokes/smoked.
C	Deductions	If he *can do* that, he can do anything. If you're *going* to the party, why haven't you brought a bottle? If I'm *leaving*, I ought to pack. If you *enjoyed* his last novel, you'll love this one. Why did he pay again, if he'd *already* paid?
D	Logical gap	If you're *going* to London, it's crowded in summer.

Open conditional sentences include:

A   *Future* possibilities (the traditional 'Type 1', plus some other patterns).
B   Conditions — present or past time — where one event *habitually* follows another:
   <If my transistor disturbs people, I turn it down.>
C   Conditions where a *deduction* is made:
   <If he can do that, and he can, he can do anything.>
D   Sentences where there is a '*logical gap*' between the condition and the main clause:
   <If you're going to London, (remember that) it's crowded in summer.>

6.23 Tenses in open conditions

When the main clause has future reference (6.22A), the *if*-clause can be any present tense (including the present perfect and *can* and *may*.) and even past tense:
   <If you lost your last camera . . .>
Will/won't is possible (a) meaning willingness etc, and (b) if, unusually, the condition event follows the main clause event chronologically: <If it will annoy her, I'll cut the trees down.> [I'll cut them down in order to annoy her.] *Should* (not *shall*) is possible, but it is formal and the condition seems less likely.

Imperatives are possible in the main clause. Imperatives are also possible as an alternative to the *if*-clause:
   <*Go now, and* I'll never speak to you again.> [If you go now, I'll never . . .]
   <*Go now or* I'll never . . .> [If you do not go now, I'll never . . .]
In conditions of habit and deduction (6.22 B and C) the *if*-clause implies fact:
   <If/when my transistor . . .>
   <If (as I believe) he can do that . . .> etc.
It is possible here to use the past perfect, which is usually said to be reserved for rejected past conditions (so-called Type 3). But in open conditionals the past perfect too implies fact:
   <If he *had already paid* (as we believe) why did he pay again?>
Modals in the main clause can result in ambiguity between a statement of habit and a hypothesis:
   <If I feel/felt tired I will/would go to bed.> [This may mean: 'Whenever I feel/felt tired, that's what I do/did.' or: 'Supposing I feel/felt tired, probably . . .']

6.24 Hypothetical conditions

A	**Unreal now or improbable future** (in conditional clause)	**1**	*now* If I owned a yacht If I had the money	I would I should I might I could	*some time* *(present or future)* be happy. buy another yacht.
		2	*future* If I won the lottery If you would lend me the money If you could lend me some If I were to win the lottery		
		3	*now* If I were rich $\longleftrightarrow$ If my father were alive $\longleftrightarrow$	I would $\longleftrightarrow$ he would $\longleftrightarrow$	*some time* have bought a yacht last year. have been 90 next year.
B	**Rejected past** (in conditional clause)	**1**	*then* If I had had the money If I had won the lottery If you could/would have lent me the money	I would I should I might I could	*some time* have bought a yacht last year/next year.
		2	*then* If I had bought a yacht	I would I should I might I could	*present* cruise every summer. be cruising in the Mediterranean now.

Hypothetical conditions include: **A** Unreality *now* (the traditional 'Type 2' conditional), and **B** the rejected past (traditional 'Type 3').

A **Unreal now** itself includes hypotheses about both now and the future:

<If I were a bird . . .>
<If I owned a yacht . . .>
<If I often visited the USA . . .>
<If I won the lottery . . .> [some time in the future]

Past tenses in the conditional clause denote, not past, but unreality. Contrary to a common rule, *could* and *would* are sometimes possible in the *if*-clause:

<If I could win . . .> = [If I were able to . . . If it were possible . . .]
<If you would lend . . .> = [If you were willing to lend . . .]

B **Rejected past** Here we normally have past perfect in the conditional clause:

<If I had won . . .>

Would have DONE and *could have* DONE are sometimes possible, but again only with meanings of willingness and possibility. Note that with a past perfect progressive tense the meaning may be a rejected condition for the future:

<If you had been coming tomorrow, you could have given Marian a lift.>

ADV *Would* DO — and *would have* DONE in *if*-clauses — carry the meaning of volition. They are only occasionally possible and *never*

● with stative verbs: <*If he would own a yacht, he would have a good time.>
● with undesirable possibilities: <*If I would lose all my money . . .>

- if the condition implies that the subject himself wishes it: <*If I would buy a yacht, I could have a good time.>

But:

<They say if I would buy a yacht . . .> [ie because they wish it]
<If he would buy one, he would have . . .> [We wish that he would]

See *wish* (6.27)

6.25 Tenses in hypothetical conditions

The common rule about hypothetical conditions, namely that we use <X would DO if Y DID> (for unreality now) and <X would have DONE if Y had DONE> (for the past) only applies if condition and consequence belong to the same time period. But they do not need to. We can also relate an unreal condition now to an unreal past or future consequence (A3) or a rejected past condition to its imagined present or future consequence (B2).

Subjunctive *were* can be used for all persons (instead of *was* and *were*) in hypothetical conditions: <If he were rich . . .>.

Another construction with *were to* is usable in unreal conditions with possible future realisation:

<If I were to buy a yacht, I would be so happy.>
It makes the condition more remote than *If I bought . . .*

6.26 Inversion of subject and verb

ADV Some conditional structures can take inversion of subject and operator and omit the *if*. The resulting structures are formal. They also suggest that the condition is unlikely to be met. The condition in 3 below is of course impossible.

1	If you (should) see Henry, give him our love.
	or *Should you see* Henry, give him our love.
2	If I were to buy a yacht, I would have a marvellous time.
	or *Were I to buy* a yacht, I would have a marvellous time.
3	If my bank had lent me the money, I would have bought a yacht.
	or *Had my bank lent* me the money, I would have bought a yacht.
4	It would be a wise move, if they only realised.
	or It would be a wise move, *did they only realise*.

Conditional clauses are a type of adverbial clause and can usually come first or second in a sentence. For conjunctions other than *if* see 11.20.

Wishing

6.27

I wish If only	[now]	I owned a yacht. [stative] I earned lots of money. [habit]	[now]
		I could win the lottery soon. you would lend me the money next year.	[future]
		I had had the money. we had bought a yacht. you had lent me the money.	[past]

Tenses after *wish* are similar to the tenses in the *if*-clauses of hypothetical conditions, but notice that:

1 wishing about the future requires *could* or *would*. <*I wish I won soon.>

2 you cannot wish about your own volition. <*I wish I would . . .> <*She wishes she would . . .>, etc.

6.28 Other hypothetical clauses

For other uses of past tenses for hypotheses, see 5.20.
Notice also the usage after *It's time*:
<It's time we went now/you weren't here.>
An infinitive is also possible:
<It's time (for us) to go now.>

7. VERB TYPES AND THE NON-FINITE VERB

Verb types — sentence patterns

7.1   Verbs can be classified by the way they relate to other parts of the sentence. A traditional division is into transitive verbs (those taking an object) and intransitive (without an object). A more modern approach, while not entirely dissimilar, refines on this. The basic distinction is between *linking* and *non-linking* verbs, or more accurately — since some verbs can be both — between linking and non-linking usage. All linking verbs are intransitive, but not all intransitive verbs are linking. Non-linking verbs are divided into intransitive verbs and those with various kinds of objects. We therefore have:

1 *Linking verbs* (sometimes called 'copula verbs') followed by a subject complement or an adverbial (7.2).
2 *Other intransitive verbs* (ie with no object) (7.3).
3 *Verbs with one object* (sometimes called monotransitives) (7.6).
4 *Verbs with two objects* (ditransitives) (7.7-11).
5 *Verbs with object plus complement* (7.14).
6 *Catenative verbs* (meaning chain-like).

Catenative verbs are verbs followed by another (non-finite) verb. They are sometimes analysed under (3) as verbs taking a kind of composite object, but they form a major category, which itself needs subdividing (7.25-54).

The distinctions between these six categories is not absolute, and some verbs fit into more than one, because of their different usages.

7.2 Linking verbs

A	BE	He *is* an engineer/so kind/at home.
B	**State**	*Keep* quiet/off.
		He *remained* a clerk.
C	**Result**	The meat has *gone* bad.
		He'll never *get* away.
		He *became* an engineer.

Linking verbs are intransitive. They do not in themselves have much meaning, but they serve to link the subject to the main predication. This predicate is usually an adjective or noun acting as a 'subject complement', although it may be an adverbial. When it is a noun, the subject and the predicative noun refer to the same person or thing in

the 'real world'. This is not the case with non-linking verbs. Compare:
<*He* became *an engineer.*> [linking verb — same person] and <*He*
liked *the engineer.*> [non-linking verb — different people].

BE can take many more types of complement than other linking verbs
— for example an infinitive:

<His ambition was *to retire* at fifty.>

Linking verbs include:

A	BE
B	*appear, feel, keep, look, prove, remain, seem, smell, sound, stay, taste* [all indicating the same state or place]
C	*become, come, fall, get, go, grow, turn* [resulting state or different place]

7.3 Intransitive verbs

A	'Pure' intransitive	Summer has *arrived* at last.
B	Intransitive or linking	The food has all *gone.*
		It's *gone* bad.
C	Occasionally transitive	Please don't *talk.*
		Don't *talk* shop.
D	With cognate object	The bride *smiled* (a radiant smile).
E	Similar meaning to transitive	Have you *eaten?*
		Has Tom *written?*
F	Adverbial needed	She *lives* in London.
		I'm going to *lie down.*

A There are very few verbs that are purely intransitive, as most have other, transitive uses. Purely intransitive include *arrive, disappear* — and usually *go, come.*

B Some intransitive verbs are also linking verbs with a slight shift of meaning: <to *come* clean, to *go* bad, to *appear* happy, to *remain* convinced> etc.

C Verbs that are basically intransitive have a restricted range of objects when used transitively: <run a race, run a mile, talk 'shop', walk the dog> etc.

D Some intransitive verbs can take cognate objects: <*smile* a radiant *smile*, *live* a wretched *life*>. That these really are intransitive is shown by the fact that they are odd if turned into the passive:
<*A radiant smile was smiled by the bride.>

E Some basically transitive verbs are often used intransitively, but there is a latent or 'understood' object. Compare also: <That child never washes (himself).> <Do you smoke (cigarettes)?> <He's reading.> <She can't write.>

F Although intransitive, *live* and *lie* [= be at rest] normally need some kind of adverbial:
<She *lives* in London / from hand to mouth.> but not <*She lives.>
<He is *lying* down/in bed/on the floor.> but not <*He is lying.>
Compare also *get* [manage to reach/leave] as in <get away/get home>.

7.4 Related intransitive/transitive sets

Intransitive	Tom has *fallen* in love again.
Transitive	He hasn't *felled* that tree yet.

A few irregular intransitive verbs have related transitive verbs, so here we can clearly say that one set is always intransitive and the other transitive.

Irregular intransitive			Regular transitive	
fall	fell	fallen [*down*]	fell	felled [*trees*]
lie(lying)	lay	lain [*down*]	lay(laying)	laid [*eggs, tables*]
rise	rose	risen [*early*]	raise	raised [*hands, salaries*]

7.5 Subject of intransitive as object of transitive

Subject + intransitive	My feet *hurt.*
Transitive (+ object)	These shoes *hurt* my feet.
	These shoes *hurt.*

Some verbs can occur intransitively: <My feet *hurt.*> and also transitively with the subject now the object: <These shoes *hurt my feet.*> There is sometimes also a third possibility: <These shoes *hurt.*>

This is different from some other verbs that can be used transitively and intransitively (7.3E):

> <John has eaten his dinner.>
> <John has eaten.>

But <*His dinner has eaten.>

Verbs like *hurt* include:
begin, blow up, boil, burn, close, cook, fly, grow, move, open, ring, sell, shut, stop

7.6 Verb + direct object

A	Straight transitive	Nobody *uses* that library.
B	Phrasal transitive	Someone could *look* these words *up.*
C	Prepositional transitive	Does anyone ever *look at* this magazine?
D	Reflexive	I *cut* myself on a rusty nail.
E	Adverbial needed	*Put* that book *down/on* the shelf.

Transitive verbs taking a single object constitute a very large class of verbs too big to list. True transitive verbs can occur in the passive. This is also true of so-called phrasal and prepositional transitive verbs (but not reflexive verbs):

A <That library *isn't used.*>
B <These words could *be looked up.*>
C <Is this magazine ever *looked at?*>
(See also 10.21)

D Reflexive pronouns are a kind of direct object, and verbs using them may be called reflexive verbs. But few English verbs are only reflexive (perhaps to *pride oneself.*)

Some verbs are used reflexively or intransitively with little change of meaning: <to *wash*/to *wash oneself.*> But in other cases the meaning is entirely different:

> <I can't stand.> [I must sit down.]
> <I can't stand myself like this.> [I don't like myself.]

E *Put* is an unusual transitive verb in that it must have both an object and an adverbial. Other verbs like this are *place*; also *stand* and *treat* with certain meanings:

<He *stood* the boxes *on top of each other.*>
<They *treated* the dog *well/badly.*>

Notice that many transitive verbs do not allow the suppression of an object as mentioned in 7.3E <*He uses.> <*We make.> <*I don't like.>

7.7 Verb + 2 objects (pattern A)

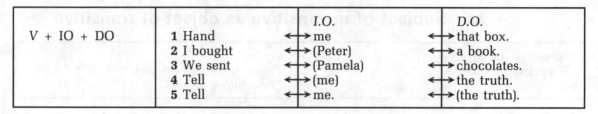

		I.O.	D.O.
V + IO + DO	**1** Hand	←→ me	←→ that box.
	2 I bought	←→ (Peter)	←→ a book.
	3 We sent	←→ (Pamela)	←→ chocolates.
	4 Tell	←→ (me)	←→ the truth.
	5 Tell	←→ me.	←→ (the truth).

Verbs that can take two objects include: general verbs in the pattern *verb + indirect object + direct object* (pattern A), and many reporting and thinking verbs in the same pattern, often with a clause as the direct object. (see 7.10).

7.8 Alternative pattern with to/for (pattern B)

Verbs in pattern A can usually but not always take the alternative [V + DO + *to/for* + IO] (pattern B).

For example: (1) Hand that box *to me.*
(2) I bought a book *for Peter.*
(3) We sent chocolates *to Pamela.*

Ask and *cost* are the commonest verbs that do not normally convert to this pattern (though *ask a favour of someone* is possible):

<I asked them the time.>   <*I asked the time to/for them.>
<It cost me a fortune.>   <*It cost a fortune to/for me.>

(a) *To* and *for* are not usually interchangeable, but depend on the verb. Indirect objects are usually animate in some way: <I handed *the bank* a letter.> but not necessarily human: <I gave *the dog* its dinner.>

With *give,* completely inanimate indirect objects are possible: <I gave *the car* a wash.> <I gave *the door* a coat of paint.> The alternative pattern B is not possible here.

(b) Stylistically, pattern A is preferred when the indirect object is short and/or known, and pattern B when the indirect object is long and/or new. Contrast:

<He always takes *her* a present.> [short and known]
<You'd better take a present *to those people next door.*> [long and new information]

(c) *Pronoun objects*
When both IO and DO are personal pronouns, the B pattern [DO + *to* IO] is always possible:

<He posted it to me.>
<I'll send them to her.>

The pattern IO + DO is used less, but occurs:

<He gave me it.>
<I'll lend you them.>

(d) Common verbs taking both pattern A <I sent her chocolates.> and B <I sent chocolates to her.> include:

book (for), bring (to), buy (for), call (for), cash (for), choose (for), cook (for), do (for), fetch (to/for), find (for)†, get (for), give (to), hand (to), keep (for), leave (to/for), lend (to), make (for), offer (to), owe (to), pass (to), pay (to), post (to), promise (to)†, read (to)†, save (for), sell (to), send (to), show (to)†, take (to), teach (to)†, tell (to)†, throw (to), write (to)†
† = also take that-clauses

7.9 Omission of one object

The indirect object (but not the direct object) can usually be omitted with these verbs without fundamentally changing the meaning:
<I bought a book.> (7.7.2) <*I bought Peter.>
<We sent chocolates.> (7.7.3) <*We sent Pamela.>
Some verbs must however have two objects:
<Hand me that box.> (7.7.1).
<Hand that box to me.> <*Hand me.> <*Hand that box.>
A few verbs can omit either the indirect or the direct object (see 7.7.4 and 7.7.5). They include: ask, pay, promise, show, teach, tell.
<Tell the truth.>
<Tell me.>

7.10 Reporting and thinking verbs

		IO	DO
compulsory IO	He assured	them them	(that) he would support them. of his support.
optional IO	He admitted	(to me) —	(that) he was wrong. his mistake (to me).

Most verbs followed by clauses are, broadly speaking, verbs of reporting and thinking. Modern grammarians often analyse [verb + finite clause] as [verb + object] and similarly [verb + indirect object + finite clause] as [verb + two objects].

7.11 Compulsory indirect object

Some reporting verbs are two-object verbs; that is, they must take an indirect object before a clause <*He assured that he would pay.> An alternative pattern is with [of + noun] instead of the clause — see examples with assure (7.10). Most of these verbs (but not assure) also occur in the non-reporting pattern <He convinced them.>.

Verbs with compulsory indirect object include: assure, convince, inform, notify, persuade, remind. Also: tell must normally have an indirect object when followed by a that-clause. This contrasts with say (11.44).

7.12 Optional to + indirect object

For another group of verbs, the indirect object is optional. But when there is one, it must be preceded by to whatever position it occupies and even if the direct object is only a noun, and not a clause. See examples with admit (7.10), and note never <*He admitted me that . . .> <*He admitted me his mistake.>

For other thinking verbs taking *that*-clauses, see verbs with † listed under catenative verbs (7.25-54). And see nominal clauses and reported speech (11.38, 11.41).

7.13 Other verbs with two objects

ADV   A number of non-reporting verbs can also relate a subject to two other people/things:

<I congratulated *them* on *their engagement*.>
<We cannot keep *pace* with *inflation*.>
<He took *charge* of *the proceedings*.>

Some grammarians include such verbs under the heading 'verbs with two objects', but the terms direct and indirect objects do not apply. It should be noticed that many of these verbs form part of a fixed phrase consisting of [verb + noun + preposition] where few, if any, variations are possible. You can only congratulate someone *on* something; you keep pace (or in step) *with* something. Notice here the resemblance to phrasal or prepositional verbs with one object: <Keep up *with* something.>

7.14 Verb + object + complement

ADV

	Type of complement			Object	Complement
A	Nominal complement	They ←→	made ←→	her ←→	group-leader.
B	Adjectival — state	We ←→	found ←→	the place ←→	quiet.
C	Adjectival — result	They ←→	painted ←→	the town ←→	red.
D	Introductory *it* as object	We ←→	think ←→	it ←→	a shame that . . ./ sad to . . .

Complements in this pattern may be nominal or adjectival. Notice (D) where the introductory *it* stands for the object, which follows later as a finite or non-finite clause. Catenatives in the pattern [V + O + -en] (7.53) could be included here: <We found it deserted.> So, too, on a different analysis, could a verb like *put* that must have an adverbial complement: <Put the book on the table.>

Notice also the relationship between: <She considered herself lucky.> [V + O + C] and <She considered herself to be lucky.> (7.36).

Non-finite verbs: forms and functions

7.15 Simple forms

The non-finite parts of the verb (4.5) are:

base:	bare infinitive (*write*)
base:	*to*-infinitive (*to write*)
-ing form:	'present participle' (*writing*)
-en form:	'past participle' (*written*)

The past participle is often called the '-*ed* form', which it is in regular verbs, but it is more convenient to keep the term '-*ed* form' for the past tense and '-*en* form' for the past participle. The names present and past participle are somewhat misleading if one considers the use of these words in the formation of complex tenses (chapter 5). When used alone as simple participles, the present participle is usually active in meaning and the past participle is usually passive.

7.16 Complex infinitives and participles

Following the rules for the formation of complex tenses (BE + -ing, HAVE + -en etc) it is possible to make complex infinitives and participles.

	Active		Passive	
Infinitives Standard	Standard *to write*	Progressive *to be writing*	Standard *to be written*	Progressive *to be being written*†
Perfect	*to have written*	*to have been writing*	*to have been written*	*to have been being written*†
Participles Standard	*writing*		*written*	*being written*
Perfect	*having written*	*having been writing*	*having been written*	*having been being written*†

Some people deny forms marked † exist. They are avoided by careful speakers and writers.

Complex forms are used in much the same way as simple ones:

<She seemed *to be listening*.> [progressive]
<He denies *having told* anyone.> [perfect]
<*To be notified* in advance would be helpful.> [passive]

The perfect infinitive can have the same sort of unreal/unachieved meaning as the past perfect tense:

<I would like *to have been invited*.>
<They were *to have telephoned* us.>

7.17 Negative infinitives and participles

ADV   Infinitives and participles are made negative by putting *not* in front of them:
<He pretended *not to understand.*>
<It was unkind *not telephoning us.*>
<*Not to have warned us* was unforgivable.>

7.18 Split infinitive

ADV   It is often considered bad grammar to 'split' an infinitive by putting a word between *to* and the base word. However it is sometimes acceptable:
(a) <The United Nations is expected *to strongly condemn* (country X's) action in sending armed fighter planes over the territory of another independent sovereign state.>
(b) <Could I ask you *to kindly ring* my secretary?>
In (a), *is expected strongly* would hopelessly alter the meaning; *to condemn strongly* is possible but breaks another 'rule' about not separating a verb from its object. In (b) *kindly* cannot be moved.

7.19 Functions of non-finite forms

ADV   The non-finite parts of the verb have many functions.
(a) They form parts of complex finite verbal groups (ie after catenative verbs — see 7.25-54).
(b) They can function alone in their own clauses (11.7-8, 11.12).
(c) Participles can function as adjectives (8.29, 8.31).
(d) *To*-infinitives can 'complement' adjectives (8.16): <difficult to understand>, and can postmodify nouns (2.37): <a book to read> <a house to let>.
(e) *To*-infinitives and *-ing* form also have many nominal functions. Theoretically, these forms could be analysed as non-finite noun clauses (chapter 11), but the parallel with clauses is not always very apparent, *-ing* forms in particular being often much more like simple nouns. Some differences between the *to*-infinitive and *-ing* are discussed below.

7.20 *To*-infinitive and *-ing* form

Subject	*To know all is to forgive all.* [+ *complement*] It isn't very nice *to gossip about one's friends.* *For him to have gossiped like that* was disgraceful. *Seeing is believing.* [+ *complement*] *Gossiping about friends* is not very nice. It's no use/no good *crying over spilt milk.*
Apposition	His ambition, *to win the men's singles at Wimbledon,* was understandable. His great success, *winning the men's singles,* was well deserved.
Complement	His ambition was (for his son) *to win the men's singles.* The poor weather was *to blame* for the low attendance. His great success was *winning the men's singles.*

Both *to*-infinitives and *ing*-forms can function as subjects of sentences, in apposition to nouns, and as complements of subjects. When a *to*-infinitive is the logical subject, modern English on the whole prefers an introductory *it* as grammatical subject. Introductory *it* is also used with the set phrases *It is no use/no good* DOING. Compare also *It's not worth* DOING, though there the *-ing* phrase is analysed as following a preposition — (10.4).

In complement position after BE, the *to*-infinitive may be noun-like or adjective-like. Contrast the noun-like *to win the men's singles* which can also appear in apposition, with <The poor weather was *to blame*.>, where the *to*-infinitive is adjectival. Non-finite forms in 'object' position are dealt with under Catenatives 7.25-7.53.

7.21 The meaning of non-finites

Sometimes it seems as though the choice of different non-finite forms in a structure — as subject of a sentence, or after catenative verbs, for example — is arbitrary. But there are connections between form and meaning.

A **To-infinitive** The *to*-infinitive (not, of course, the perfect infinitive — 7.16) frequently carries a general meaning of the future. Notice:
1 Auxiliaries that must be followed by a *to*-infinitive usually have a strong element of future. This is particularly true of *have to* and *be to*:
    <I *have to go* to the office tomorrow.>
    <We *are to meet* his father at the weekend.>
    <He *was never to see* his native land again.>
2 *To*-infinitive as a non-finite adverbial clause often means purpose:
    <*To open*, cut along the dotted line.>
3 *To*-infinitive postmodifying in a noun phrase can also mean purpose:
    <Is there any salt *to put on the potatoes*?>
4 Predicative adjective + *to*-infinitive often looks to some future action:
    <He is keen *to go* / certain *to come*.>
5 Future plus consequence is found in some *to*-infinitive clauses:
    <I arrived *to find* (that) the bird had flown.>
6 In catenative + *to*-infinitive, the second verb usually refers to an action later in time than the first:
    <I would like *to play* tennis.>
7 For nominals, if there is a strong feeling of future, a *to*-infinitive may be essential (and an *-ing* form impossible):
    <His ambition was *to win the men's singles*.>

B **-ing form** The *-ing* form looks backward, not forward. It suggests actions or states already existing or achieved.
1 *Nominal*
    <*Winning the men's singles* brought some useful prize money.>
(The *to*-infinitive is impossible here.)
2 *Catenative + -ing* Generally speaking the first (finite) verb looks back to an earlier action/state — or to a generalised (timeless) action:
    <I enjoy *playing* tennis.>

C **-en form** Basically this is a mixture of achievement (hence the name 'past' participle) and passive:
    <I must get my suit *cleaned*.>

7.22 The *-ing* form — gerund or participle?

A distinction is often made between gerunds ('verbal nouns') and participles, which are more like verbs or adjectives. In fact the *-ing* form cannot be quite so neatly divided.
1 At one extreme are words derived from verbs that are completely nominal. They take articles and adjectives and plural *-s* (eg *a meeting/meetings, a booking/bookings.*) When used like this, such words are unable to have their own subjects or objects as they could if they were verbal.

147

2 Other -*ing* forms, while having noun-like functions in the sentence (eg as subjects or objects) have varying degrees of verbalness. Some -*ing* forms are rather like an uncountable noun (eg *singing*). They may be preceded by determiners and adjectives, and possibly followed by an *of*-phrase representing the object:

<The *choir's brilliant singing of Messiah*>.

Sometimes an -*ing* form is more verb-like, taking a direct object and perhaps adverbs, but not determiners or adjectives:

<*Singing Messiah well* is not easy.>.

At other times, there is an even greater fusion of both noun-like and verb-like characteristics:

<*Edward's singing hymns loudly* annoys me.>

Here the possessive *Edward's* suggests that *singing* is a noun, but *singing* has its own object and adverb. Further along the scale we have <I heard *Edward singing in the bath*.> where *Edward's* is not possible and *singing* is more verbal (7.46). But <I dislike *Edward singing/ Edward's singing*.> are both equally possible; there is no clear-cut classification.

7.23 Infinitive as main verb

ADV   Occasionally — contrary to all the rules — the infinitive is used as a main verb (ie, the verb of a main clause):

Why (not) DO <Why bother, if you don't like it?>
        <Why not forget it?> [Why don't you forget it?]
To think . . . <To think that we wasted our time and money!>
        <To think he never told us!> [It is amazing to think . . .]

7.24 Non-finite forms as other word classes

Some participle forms, derived from verbs, are firmly established as other parts of speech. They include:

A **Conjunctions** *considering (that), providing (that), seeing (that), supposing (that), granted (that), provided (that)*:

<*Granted that* he's kind, I still don't like him.>
<*Seeing that* you're so clever, why did you get it wrong?>

B **Prepositions** *concerning, excepting, including, regarding*:

<The report says nothing *regarding* costs.> [about]

These conjunctions and prepositions may also have verbal uses. Contrast:

1 (a) <*Supposing* they don't come, what will you do?> [If . . .]
    (b) <*Supposing* him to be a burglar, she hit him on the head.> [Imagining that . . .]
2 (a) <I *was including* VAT in the cost.> [progressive tense]
    (b) <The price *including* VAT is £10.75p.>

In (2), it is easy to see how one word class can merge with another. Is *including* VAT in (2b) a reduced relative clause (meaning 'the price that includes . . .') or is it the equivalent of 'with VAT' and therefore like a prepositional phrase?

C **Nouns** For -*ing*-forms as nouns (gerunds) — see 7.22.
For participles as semi-nouns — see 8.28.

ADV **D** **Adverbials** Occasionally a participle form is used like an adverb:
<*boiling* hot, *hopping* mad [angry], *raving* mad [crazy]>.

Catenative verbs

7.25

1	Verb + bare infin	Please let		go.
2	Verb + **to**-infin	I want		to sleep.
3	Verb + **-ing**	She dislikes		dancing.
4	Verb + **-en**	He got		paid.
1a	Verb + object + bare infin	Please let	me	go.
2a	Verb + object + **to**-infin	I want	everyone	to sleep.
3a	Verb + object + **-ing**	She hates	the children	dancing.
4a	Verb + object + **-en**	He got	the money	paid.

Ordinary verbs (ie not auxiliaries or modals) that can be followed by another ordinary verb are called *catenatives*. They are grouped into four main types according to which non-finite form the second verb takes. And which form (bare infinitive, *to*-infinitive, *-ing* or *-en*) comes second in these complex groups depends on the meaning of the catenative.

Some catenatives also occur in similar patterns but with an intervening noun or pronoun. Whereas in 1-4 the subject of the sentence is also the subject or 'doer' of the second verb, in 1a — 4a we find that the grammatical object of the first verb is the 'subject' of the second verb:

<Please let *me* go.> [I will go.]

Some catenatives can be used in only one, and some in more than one, pattern. Catenatives that can also be followed by a finite clause beginning with *that* are marked † in the following sections.

7.26 Verb + bare infinitive

A	They	⟷	make do	⟷	with very little money.
	Don't	⟷	let go	⟷	of the ladder.
B	Please	⟷	help wash up	⟷	the dishes.

A *make believe/make do*
hear say/hear tell
let fall/let fly/let go/let slip
B *help*

The main use of the bare infinitive is after modals (see chapter 6). Otherwise is has very limited use in verb groups.

A Phrases with *make*, *hear*, and *let* (as above) are virtually a closed set. (rare except *make do* and *let go*.)

B *Help* is the only verb that combines freely with other verbs in this pattern, and *help to* is an alternative. (For *can/can't help* + *-ing* — see 7.45).

Passives with any of these verbs are rare or impossible.

7.27 Verb + object + bare infinitive

A	We heard	Tom	say (that) there was a good programme on TV tonight.
Passive:	Tom	was heard	*to say* . . .
B	Please help ←→ me I've known ←→ it I've never known ←→ Tom Let ←→ 's/us Please let ←→ me Never let ←→ it		←→ wash up the dishes. ←→ snow there in the summer. ←→ forget his mother's birthday. ←→ go. ←→ go home now. ←→ be said that . . .
Passive:	I was ←→ made Tom has never ←→ been known		←→ to feel foolish. ←→ to forget . . .

A *feel†, hear†, notice†, observe†, perceive†, see†, smell†, watch†.*
B *bid* (old-fashioned), *have, help, let, make, (have) know(n).*

7.28 Verbs of perception with object + bare infinitive (7.27A)

These imply a single complete action. Contrast these same verbs with verb + object + -ing (7.46).

Passive is possible with *feel, hear, observe, see,* but using a *to-*infinitive.

When the meaning is mental, not physical, perception, then a *that-*clause is used:

<*I hear (that) he has got a new job.*> but not <**I hear him to have got . . .*>

For a few of these verbs in V + O + -en — see 7.53.

7.29 Miscellaneous (7.27B)

For *have* in this structure (meaning to cause or to experience something) see 4.15. *Know* in this pattern is usually in the perfect (*I've known . . .*). *Let's,* which functions as a suggestion (rather like *Why don't we . . .?*), is grammatically *Let us.* Only the full form *Let us . . .* can be used when the meaning is 'Permit us/Allow us . . .' Passives are possible with *bid, help, make, know,* but they take a *to-*infinitive in the passive. *Let* can occur in the passive — without *to*: <*It was let go of.*> but this is rare. A more normal passive equivalent of <*They let me go home.*> would be: <*I was allowed to go home.*>

7.30 Verb + to-infinitive

A	He *agreed* ←→ to come on holiday with us. She *has promised* ←→ (not) to go. They *claim* ←→ to have found the answer (7.31) I wouldn't *care* ←→ to live near the sea. Can you *afford* ←→ (not) to live in London?
B 1	I *happen* ←→ to believe this. He doesn't *seem* ←→ to be enjoying himself. It *appears* ←→ (not) to have mattered. The letter *turned out* ←→ (not) to have been sent by air.

B	**2**	I *came*	←→ to realise my mistake.
		Some people *tend*	←→ (not) to be noticed.
C		He *said*	to come. [infml]
		I didn't *think*	to tell you. [infml]

A large group of verbs occur in the pattern verb + *to*-infinitive but *never* in verb + object + *to*-infinitive and never in verb + *-ing* form.

A Future/Purpose etc: *afford, agree†, aim†, apply, arrange†, care, claim†, condescend, consent, contract, contrive†, decide†, decline, demand†, deserve, determine†, endeavour, fail, hasten, hesitate, hope†, long, manage, offer, prepare, pretend†, profess†, promise†, refuse, resolve†, seek, strive, struggle, swear†, threaten†, undertake†, volunteer* [† = can take a nominal *that*-clause]
B **1** *appear to, chance to, happen to, seem to, turn out to*
   2 *come to, fail to, proceed to, tend to.*
C *say, think* [infml]

7.31 Future/purpose etc (7.30A)

In the majority of verbs taking this pattern (7.30 A), the verb looks forward to the second verb (in the *to*-infinitive), so the infinitive has a feeling of future. The subject of the first verb is also the doer of the infinitive. These verbs all broadly concern the subject's purposes, aims, decisions about his own future actions.

Claim is an exception to this. It is often used with a perfect infinitive to refer to prior action.

Other verbs in this group may be used with a perfect infinitive in a sort of 'future perfect' sense: <I hope *to have finished* it by tomorrow night.> Progressive and passive infinitives are also possible: <He pretended *to be working*.>

Promise is often used with a noun/pronoun after the verb: <I promised him to go.> but this is nevertheless this pattern and not to be confused with [verb + object + *to*-infinitive]. The *him* is an indirect object, and the subject of the *to*-infinitive is the same as the subject of the main verb: 'I promised him that I would go'.

Afford is often used with *can*, rather than by itself: <I can afford to . . .> and not <*I afford to . . .>

Care + *to*-infinitive is used mainly in non-assertive forms (ie questions and negatives).

7.32 Alternative: verb + *that*-clause

He decided (not) to go.	*But* He decided (that) } It was decided (that) }	neither of them would go. [different subject]
He agreed to lend her some money.	*But* He agreed (that) } It was agreed (that) }	he had already lent her money. [prior action]

Verbs marked with † in 7.30 can take a *that*-clause, and must do so if the subject of the infinitive is different from the subject of the first verb. <*He decided them to go.>, or if the reference is to action prior to the first verb <*He agreed to have lent . . .>. Most verbs taking a *that*-clause can be used passively, with *it*: <It was decided . . .>.

7.33 *Happen to* etc (7.30 B)

Appear, happen, seem and a few other verbs fit into a slightly different category. In addition to appearing in this pattern, they are used in the pattern: [*It* + verb + *that*-clause]:

<It appears that the letter was not sent.>

Although they cannot be made passive which some of the Group A verbs can in different patterns: <The terms were agreed.>   <It was decided that . . .>, they can take a passive, as well as an active, infinitive:

<The letter turned out *not to have been sent.*>

Tend to etc (7.30 B2): Another small group of verbs found in this pattern cannot take [*It* + *Verb* + *that*-clause] <*It tends that . . .*> but can take a passive infinitive: <Some people tend *not to be noticed.*>

7.34 *Say, think* (7.30 C)

These usages with *say* and *think* are very colloquial:

<He said to come> [He said we should come/could come, etc]
<I didn't think to go.> [I didn't think of going.]

For more normal patterns with *say* — see 11.44

Think usually takes *that*-clauses, or is used with a preposition: *think about, think of* etc.

7.35 Negation

With many of the verbs in 7.30, either the main verb or the infinitive can be negated, or both. But the meaning may be different:

<She *hasn't agreed* to go.> [The possibility of her going is open.]
<She has agreed *not to go.*> [She won't go.]
<She *hasn't agreed not to go.*> [Someone thinks or hopes that she won't go, but the possibility is open.]

For other verbs that can take verb + *to*-infinitive and also verb + object + *to*-infinitive — see 7.43. For verbs taking *to*-infinitive or (object) + *-ing* — see 7.47.

7.36 Verb + object + *to*-infinitive

A			
They don't allow	←→	you	←→ to stop on the motorway.
The government compels	←→	everyone	←→ to wear seat belts.
Seat belts could cause	←→	people	←→ to crash!
Passive: You	←→ are not allowed		←→ to stop on the motorway.
Everyone	←→ is compelled		←→ to wear a seat belt.
B 1 We assumed	←→	him	←→ to be a careful driver.
He considers	←→	himself	←→ (to be) unlucky.
They now believe	←→	the accident	←→ to have been due to human error.
We supposed	←→	him	←→ to be a qualified instructor.
I imagine	←→	it	←→ to have been an accident.
Passive: He	←→ is known		←→ to be a careful driver.
The accident is now believed			←→ to have been due to human error.
B 2 He		is said	to be very upset.
C We rely on		you	to help us.

152

A (7.37-38) assist, beseech†, bribe, cause, caution†, challenge, charge†, command†, compel, condemn, defy, direct†, drive, empower, enable, encourage, entitle, entreat†, forbid, force, get [cause], incite, induce, impel, implore†, instruct†, invite, lead, leave, oblige, order†, persuade†, press, remind†, request†, sentence, teach†, tell†, tempt, trust†, urge†, warn†

B **1** (7.39) assume†, believe†, consider†, declare†, discover†, fancy†, feel†, find†, imagine†, judge†, know†, observe†, presume [assume]†, proclaim†, prove†, report†, represent†, reveal†, show†, see [mental]†, suppose†, think† (see note), understand†

    2 (7.40) repute, rumour†, say†

C (7.41) count on, depend on, rely on

7.37 Imposing one's will (7.36A)

Verbs in this pattern, with an obligatory object between the two verbs, have the general meaning of imposing one's wishes upon other people. So again the infinitive has a sense of future and purpose. The verbs range from beseeching or inviting at one end of the scale to forcing or impelling at the other.

Two sub-classes can be made in terms of meaning, on the basis of the function of the central noun/pronoun:

(a) The noun is the object of the main verb and the 'subject' of the infinitive:

    <I assisted him to come.> [I assisted him. He came.]

(b) The whole infinitive phrase, rather than just the noun, is the object of the main verb:

    <I caused (him to come).> [*I caused him.]

But this distinction is not always clear-cut.

Passive Most of these verbs can be used in the passive — often with the agent unexpressed:

    <You are not allowed to stop on the motorway.>

Another passive pattern that is sometimes possible is [active verb + object + *to be* DONE]:

    <He ordered seat belts to be fitted.>

7.38 Ambiguity

Ambiguity may sometimes arise when the same 'surface structure' can stand for two different underlying structures:

    <She left him to go on holiday alone.>

This could be either (a) catenative group, where passive is possible, meaning 'He was left to go alone' (he presumably had to go alone) or (b) 'She left him' (not catenative) + purpose clause (ie in order to/so that she could go on holiday).

7.39 Assumptions and opinions (7.36B)

Verbs in 7.36B are 'mental-state' verbs and all commonly occur with *that*-clauses.

    <We assumed that he was a careful driver.>

When these verbs occur in this [verb + object + *to*-infinitive] pattern, the only possible infinitive in many cases is BE.

Often, but not always, an alternative pattern is possible omitting BE — in other words with a noun or adjective complement:

    <He considers himself a careful driver.>

Passive Many of these verbs can take passive in two ways:

(a) <He is assumed to be a careful driver.>

(b) <It is assumed (that) he is a careful driver.>

7.40 Passive only (7.36B2)

A few verbs of assumption do not appear at all in the active pattern
<*They repute him to be . . .> But they can appear in the passive:
<He is *reputed/rumoured/said* to be a millionaire.>: Note — only:
<It is rumoured/said that . . .> and not <* It is reputed . . .>.

7.41 Prepositional verbs (7.36C)

A number of prepositional verbs take [verb + object + *to*-infinitive]
and can sometimes be used in the passive.
For some V + O + *to*-infinitive verbs in other patterns, see 7.45, 7.46
and 7.52.

7.42 Verb + *for* + object + *to*-infinitive

I have arranged *for the bank to send* you the money.

In terms of meaning this pattern is similar to [verb + object + *to*-infinitive], since the middle noun (*the bank*) is the doer of the infinitive verb. But grammatically it is different, because the middle noun (*the bank*) cannot be considered an object of the verb. Instead, we can analyse the whole phrase (*for the bank to send you the money*) as a non-finite noun clause — which could, in fact, appear in other nominal positions: <For the bank to send you the money would be a great help.>

Verbs taking this pattern include several verbs listed under [verb + *to*-infinitive] (7.30). Since such verbs *never* take [verb + object + *to*-infinitive], this [verb + *for* object + *to*-infinitive] is for them the obligatory alternative.

Verbs using this pattern include: *agree, aim, apply, arrange, care, contract, contrive, long, strive, undertake.* Also *wait*.

7.43 Verb + (optional object) + *to*-infinitive

A	I would love We can't bear	(you) (him)	to go camping this summer. not to come too.
B	Bill has asked He has asked He intends He means Tom probably won't bother	←→(them) ←→ ←→(Joanna)←→ ←→ ←→(her) ←→ ←→(them) ←→	to come with us. to join us. to enjoy himself. to have a good time too. to come.
	Passive: Joanna has been asked		to join us.

A | *can + bear (non-assr), hate, like, love, prefer, need, want, wish†*
B | *ask, beg†, bother, choose, dare, expect†, help, intend†, mean†, require, trouble*

A and B both contain verbs that can be used with or without an
object — ie they belong with verbs like *agree* (7.30) and *command* (7.36).
They are mainly concerned with the likes and wishes of the subject.

Without an intervening object they concern the wishes of the subject about his own future actions etc. When there is an object, they relate to wishes about another person's actions. Notice that *dislike* does not occur in this pattern (7.45).

A-verbs do not normally have corresponding passive sentences, but B-verbs can.

With both groups, it is usually the whole [noun phrase + to-infinitive], and not the noun alone which can be regarded as the object of the first verb:

<We can't bear (you not to come).>

This does not mean 'We can't bear you.' But notice

<Can I bother you (to pass the salt)?>

For *wish* + *that* — clauses — see 6.27.
Notice that *want* never takes a *that*-clause <*I want that I/you . . .>
For verbs in this pattern and in
[verb + (object) + -ing] — see 7.47.
[verb + object + -en] — see 7.53.

7.44 Verb + *-ing* (without object)

A	Charles *admitted*	⟷ borrowing my car without permission.
	I *deferred*	⟷ writing to his father.
B	I must *give up*	⟷ worrying.
	Why does he *keep on*	⟷ borrowing my things?
C	I am *going*	⟷ swimming.
	Will you *come*	⟷ swimming with us?
	Giles *came*	⟷ laughing down the road.
	Rachel *spent* the day	⟷ lying on the beach.
	The day *was spent*	⟷ lying on the beach.
	Fred *stood/lay/sat*	⟷ looking straight ahead.
	Sheila *burst out*	⟷ crying.

A	*admit†, avoid, defer, deny†, escape, finish, postpone, practise, report†*
B	*carry on, give up, keep on, put off,* etc.
C	*come, go* (and see examples)

The general meaning of the -ing form is either (a) an action or state prior to the action of the main verb:

<He *admitted borrowing* my car.>

or (b) the general idea of activity:

<I *deferred writing*>, often contrasted with a single, perhaps future, action as implied by the *to*-infinitive <I decided to write.>

'Without object' means patterns without an object between the two verbs (7.25). Some of these verbs can take ordinary noun objects:

<Charles admitted his mistake.>

A Other verbs that are followed by -ing form can also take an intervening object (7.45). Words listed here normally do not, and are mainly concerned with the subject's own actions.

B Phrasal verb catenatives are always followed by the -ing form, and never by the *to*-infinitive (10.26).

C This group is a problem! The -ing forms partly resemble reduced relative or adverbial clauses. (Once again the language refuses to fit into neat pigeon-holes.) *Go/come* are followed by -ing forms of various sporting activities (*dancing, jogging* etc) and also *shopping*. *Spend* + TIME is an odd construction, because it is incomplete without a following phrase, which is therefore a sort of complement. But the complement may, of course, be an adverbial: <She spent the day there.>

For verbs in this pattern that can also take the *to*-infinitive or 'objects' — see 7.47-52.

7.45 Verb + (object or genitive) + *-ing*

A	I dislike	⟷	(Tom)	⟷ watching television.
	We would not contemplate	⟷		⟷ going alone.
	Just imagine	⟷	(Tom's)	⟷ sitting through that old programme again.
	I can't help	⟷	(him)	⟷ wanting to see it.
	That will save	⟷		⟷ wasting time.
	They have suggested	⟷	(his)	⟷ going to the theatre.
B	Please forgive		me/my	asking.
C	That would entail		(them/their)	buying a new set.
D	Tom insists on He is looking forward to		(us/our)	buying a new set.

A *advocate†, anticipate†, appreciate†, begrudge, (can) face, can help (non-assr), can stand (non-assr), contemplate, consider†, detest, dislike, enjoy, fancy†, favour, imagine†, justify, mention†, mind†, prevent, report†, resent, resist, risk, save, suggest†, stop, tolerate*
B *excuse, forgive, pardon*
C *(It) entail, involve, necessitate*
D *(dis)approve of, be/get used to, insist on, look forward to, object to, resign oneself to*

A Verbs in this group can take three patterns:
<I dislike watching television.>
<I dislike him/Tom watching. . .>
<I dislike his/Tom's watching. . .>
The pattern with an object (*him/Tom*) is more informal than the genitive (*his/Tom's*) and disapproved of by some people, though a common feature of English. The presence of either an object or genitive usually introduces a different subject for the action of the -ing form from the subject of the main verb (though *us/our* are possible). But this does not mean that if there is no object or genitive the doer of the -ing form is the same as that of the main verb. Whether it is or is not depends on the meaning of the main verb. In:
<Tom advocates waiting patiently.>
Tom may or may not be involved in the waiting, but other people definitely are. But if
<Tom resents having to wait.> then Tom does the waiting.
Notice particularly that *dislike, suggest* and *stop* are among the verbs here. They never take *to*-infinitive, either with or without an object:
<* I suggest (you) to go.>

Contrast also:

    <I can't help DOING something.> [I can't stop myself]

    <I can't help you (to) DO something.> [I am unable to assist you.]

B Unlike all the other verbs in this section, which can occur without either object or genitive, these verbs must have one or the other because two different subjects or doers are always involved.

    <Please forgive me/my asking.>

    <Surely he will forgive them/their saying so.>

C This is a small group of impersonal verbs — with *it* or *that* as subject:

    <It entails (them/their) buying a new set.>

D Prepositional verbs (10.20-24) can only be followed by the *-ing* form of a verb, never the *to*-infinitive, even when the preposition is *to*. Notice especially *look forward to* and *be/get used to*.

7.46 Verb + object + *-ing* (participle)

A	I heard	←→ the orchestra	←→ playing beautifully.
	Have you seen	←→ Nureyev	←→ dancing?
	We watched	←→ the audience	←→ streaming out of the theatre.
B	We consider	←→ him	←→ lacking in common sense.
	We discovered	←→ Tom	←→ drinking in the bar.
	We found	←→ the others	←→ waiting outside the theatre.
	No one had imagined	←→ Tom	←→ arriving early.
C	I caught	←→ someone	←→ trying to take my drink.
	Don't keep	←→ people	←→ waiting.
	That kind of thing leaves	←→ me	←→ gasping.
	It set	←→ me	←→ thinking.

A	*feel†, hear†, notice†, observe†, perceive†, see†, smell†, watch†*
B	*consider†, discover†, find†, picture†, represent†, reveal†, show†*
C	*catch, keep, leave, send, set*

The *-ing* form in this structure is definitely more a participle than a nominal. Hence, the genitive is not an alternative to the object. For this reason also, ambiguity can arise between this pattern and the same surface structure of [subject + verb + object with *-ing* postmodification]:

    <I didn't see the child helping at the party.>

Does this mean <I didn't see that child actually helping.> (this pattern) or <I didn't see the child that was helping.> (reduced relative)?

A This is the same group of perception verbs that can also take [object + bare infinitive] (7.28). The *-ing* form often implies action in progress, contrasted with a single action where the duration is not important. Contrast:

    <We arrived late and could hear the orchestra already playing.>

    <We heard them play three pieces that evening.>

B Some, but only some, verbs of assumption and opinion (7.39) can also fit into this [verb + object + *-ing*] pattern, but with this *-ing* pattern the meaning tends to be of physical rather than mental perception. Contrast:

    <We found them to be very clever children.>

    <We found them waiting outside the theatre.>

C With this small group of verbs, the -ing form is very verbal in feeling. Send in this pattern is mainly used in a few set phrases <send someone/something flying/packing> etc.
For *get/have* in this pattern — see 4.15.
Most of the verbs in this section can be used in the passive.

7.47 Verbs taking *to*-infinitive or *-ing*

A I remember (2nd event)	←→ (them/their) ←→	writing down their telephone number. (1st event)
I didn't remember (1st)	←→	to phone them last Saturday (2nd)
I shall never forget (2nd)	←→ (my/our) ←→	meeting them in New York last year. (1st)
Don't forget (1st)	←→	to send them a Christmas card. (2nd)
I do so regret (2nd)	←→	upsetting them. (1st)
I regret (1st)	←→	to say she's a fool. (2nd)
He went on and on (2nd)	←→	complaining. (1st)
But finally he went on (1st)	←→	to talk about something else. (2nd)
I have tried [experimented]	←→	eating nothing but bananas.
I try so hard [make an effort] (1st) ←→		to lose weight. (2nd)
B Paul hates/can't bear	←→ (you) ←→	to jog in the evening.
He really loves/prefers	←→ (you/your) ←→	jogging before breakfast.
I would like/love/prefer	←→ (you) ←→	to go with him.
We can't bear/hate/don't like	←→ (you/your) ←→	going alone.
C This suit needs/wants	←→	cleaning.
This problem needs/wants/ requires/deserves/doesn't bear	←→	thinking about.
They require/need/want	←→ him	←→ to pay in advance.
We need/want	←→ them	←→ sitting in their seats by 2.15 pm.
He deserves	←→	to win.
D I began/started	←→	jogging last winter.
The weather has begun/started	←→	to get warmer at last.
This will start	←→ the ball	←→ rolling.
E 1 He advised	←→ me	←→ to play tennis.
They didn't advise	←→ (our)	←→ jogging.
2 He dreads	←→ (you/your)	←→ telling her.
I dread	←→	to tell her.
3 He intends/means	←→ (us)	←→ to go to Athens by bus.
I intend/shan't bother	←→	going next month.
It means [necessitates]	←→ (us/our)	←→ sleeping on the bus three nights.
4 I understood	←→ Tom	←→ to say he was coming.
We can understand	←→ (him/his)	←→ wanting to come.

A (7.48) *forget†, regret†, remember†, go on, try*
B (7.49) *can bear (non-assr), hate, like, love, prefer*
C (7.50) *bear, deserve, need, require, want*
D (7.51) *begin, cease, commence, continue, start*
E (7.52) **1** *advise†, allow, encourage, forbid, permit, recommend†, urge†*
     2 *dread†, fear†, neglect, omit, plan†, propose†*
     3 *bother, trouble, intend†, mean†*
     4 *understand†*

A number of verbs can take both the *to*-infinitive and the *-ing* form. The tables above indicate where 'objects' are also possible.

7.48 Future or prior action? (*forget* etc 7.47A)

The basic difference here is between the *to*-infinitive as future, subsequent to the main verb — and the *-ing* form for prior activity.
(a) With *forget*, the *-ing* form is normally only possible with phrases like <I'll never forget DOING> <He's never forgotten DOING> <* I forget DOING>.
No intervening objects are possible with [V + *to*-infinitive], but *forget, regret, remember* can take [V + O /gen + ing.]
(b) *Go on to* DO something means to proceed to do something different; *go on* DOING = continue doing the same thing. *Stop* is sometimes included in text books as a verb parallel to *go on*, but [*stop* + *to*-infinitive] is *stop* plus a separate infinitive of purpose: <He stopped (DOING something or other, in order) to talk to me.>
(c) [*Try* + *to*-infinitive] has the common infinitive meaning of future and purpose, plus *try*'s basic meaning of 'make an effort'. With [*try* + *-ing*], the *ing* form has a more noun-like value of activity, and *try* means something like experiment with or test. (Compare [*try* + NP]. <He tried a different approach.> <Try this new cheese.>

7.49 Verbs of liking and not liking (7.47B)

These versatile verbs (7.47B) can take:
[V + *to*-infin] (7.43) <I'd love to come.>
[V + O + *to*-infin] (7.43) <I'd love you to come.>
[V + *-ing*] <I love watching television.>
[V + O/gen + *-ing*] <I don't like you/your watching television.>
[V + O + *-en*] (7.53) <I prefer the sound turned down.>
The infinitive patterns (7.43) suggest active choice and/or single events and therefore the future in relation to the main verb. The *-ing* forms here suggest an activity already in progress, or an activity seen as an existing general 'thing'. So, as with the verbs in 7.47A, the infinitive has future meaning and the *-ing* points backwards.

7.50 *-ing* with 'passive' meaning (7.47C)

The *-ing* form following the verbs of 7.47C often has a sort of passive meaning, while the *to*-infinitive (7.43) has active meaning. Contrast:
<Your suit *needs* cleaning.> [Your suit needs *to be cleaned*.]
<You *need to/want to* look after your clothes.> [You should . . .]
Notice that *bear* in the pattern [inanimate subject + *doesn't/won't* etc + *bear* + *-ing*] has a passive meaning:
<This problem doesn't *bear* thinking about.> [It's too awful to be contemplated.]
But an [animate subject + *can't/couldn't bear* + *ing*] (as in 7.47B) is active:
<I can't bear [I hate] thinking about this problem.>
With *can/could bear* (non-assr) a *to*-infinitive, also with active meaning, is common (7.43), but *doesn't/won't bear* etc are not used in this way.
Unlike the verbs in 7.47 A and B, these verbs do not take a genitive, since the *-ing* form is more like a participle than a gerund:
<We need/want *them* sitting . . .> <*. . . *their* sitting . . .>.

7.51 *Begin, start* (7.47D)

With these verbs there is little difference in meaning between a following *to*-infinitive and an *-ing* form. Objects are not normal, except in *start something/someone* DOING *something*:

<This will start the ball rolling.>

When the second (following) verb is a stative verb (eg a verb of perception) that does not normally take progressive tense anyway, the *to*-infinitive is, of course, usual:

<I began to understand his point of view.>

Begin + *-ing* form is sometimes said to be more deliberate than *begin* + *to*-infinitive. Contrast:

<I began jogging last winter> rather than <I began to jog . . .>

<The weather has begun to get warmer at last.> not

<*begun getting . . .>. But this is not a hard-and-fast rule.

7.52 A rather mixed bag! (7.47E)

1 Verbs like *advise* use object + infinitive when another person is specifically mentioned:

<He advised me to play . . .>

but the *-ing* form for more general activity. Notice how the *to*-infinitive has future meaning in relation to the main verb.

2 These verbs (*dread* etc) do not usually take an object (*dread* itself is rather an exception here). *To*-infinitives are probably more usual, but *-ing* forms are common.

3 *Bother, trouble, intend* are used in the patterns

<I intend to go>,

<I intend going>, and

<I intend you to go.>

Mean is used in the patterns

<I mean to go>, and

<I mean them to go>

but *mean* DOING is mainly used with an impersonal subject (roughly with the meaning of 'It involves DOING'.

4 *Understand* is used like *forgive* (7.45B) and *assume* (7.36B).

7.53 Verb + object + *-en*

A	I *can't bear*	my steak	overcooked.
	I *want*	it	underdone.
B	I *heard*	←→ my name	←→ called.
	We *saw*	←→ our team	←→ beaten.
	He *felt*	←→ himself	←→ cheated.
C	We *found*	←→ the poor dog	←→ chained up.
	Photographs *showed*	←→ it	←→ tied to a post.
	We must *leave*	←→ no stone	←→ unturned.
	I shall *make*	←→ my views	←→ known.

A	*can bear* (non-assr) *hate, like, love, need, prefer†, want*
B	*feel†, hear†, see†*
C	*discover†, fancy†, find†, imagine†, keep, leave, make, picture†, report†, show†*

160

A This is the same versatile group of verbs that can also take [optional object + *to*-infinitive] (7.43) and [object/genitive + *-ing*] (7.47).

B Only some verbs of perception (as listed here) are at all usual in this pattern (see also 7.27).

C Again, there is some overlap with the verbs that also take [verb + object + *-ing*] (participle) (7.46).

For *get/have* in this pattern <I had my car resprayed/stolen.> — see 4.15

7.54 Verb + *-en* (without object)

Get lost! [rude]
Henry got injured.
I can't get started.

Get is the only verb that regularly and productively appears in this rare pattern.

Have occurs in the old-fashioned *Have done.* [Stop! Consider it finished!]

Notice also *get* + *-ing* in
<Get moving!>
<We'll never get going at this rate!>

8. ADJECTIVES
What are adjectives?

8.1   A traditional definition of an adjective is that it says what somebody or something is like. Modern grammar prefers to define adjectives — like other major word-classes — by (a) position/function and (b) form and inflection. We can, however, say that many adjectives denote qualities. In other words, they often have a sort of descriptive meaning.

8.2 Position/function — attributive

The typical, most characteristic position for an adjective is between a determiner and a noun:

Determiners	Adjectives	Nouns
All those three	?	houses
Several more	?	people

This pre-noun position is called *attributive*, because the adjective attributes a quality or characteristic to the noun.

Determiners	Adjectives	Nouns
All those three	old attractive	houses
Several more	charming distinguished	people

8.3 Adjectivals

When other parts of speech occur in this position and function in this way, they are called *adjectivals*; for example, *boat* in *boat people*. (Contrast this with *boathouse, greenhouse, outhouse* where two words have fused to form a compound.) 'Adjectival' is a general term often used to include real adjectives, plus other words and also phrases when functioning attributively. Some adjectivals can also occur in predicative position.

Attributive:
<a *love/hate* relationship, a *never-to-be-forgotten* day, a *have-a-go* girl, the *then* president>.

Predicative:
<You're being *holier-than-thou.*>, <Don't be so *down-to-earth.*> etc.

8.4 Position/function — predicative

Subject	BE *or linking verb*	Predicative adjective (complement of subject)	
The people Some houses	are seem appeared	very	old. attractive. charming. distinguished. but *boat

The second major position for adjectives is following BE or other
linking verbs in the *predicative* position of a sentence. We put *very*
into this frame, because otherwise the slot following some linking
verbs and particularly BE may be occupied by other word classes eg
nouns, as in *The people are farmers.*

8.5 Predicative complement of object

ADV

Subject	Verb	Object	Predicative adjective (complement of object)
The news	made	them	happy.
I	consider	what he did	outrageous.
She	pushed	the door	shut.
They	painted	the town	red.

Predicative adjectives also act as complements to objects.

8.6 Form and inflection

Many adjectives have no characteristic forms, but there are some
which have. Typical adjective endings include: *-able/-ible (desirable,
contemptible), -ish/-like (childish, childlike), -full/-less (hopeful, hopeless),
-ous (dangerous, delicious), -y (pretty, dirty).* See 9.7 and 9.8 for adjectives
ending in *-ly.*

Adjectives are distinguished by two inflections for *degree: -er* for
comparative and *-est* for superlative. The base is sometimes called
positive degree. But not all adjectives take these inflections and some
words that do are classed as adverbs (chapter 9) or as
determiners/pronouns (eg *few*). English adjectives do not 'agree' with
nouns (for plural or gender) as they do in some languages.

8.7 Central and marginal adjectives

Words that fit all the positions described and that can also be
inflected are central or 'core' adjectives (eg *small, large, wet, dry*).
Others, that fit only one position or cannot be compared (*utter, afloat*),
are more marginal.

Meaning

8.8 Stative or dynamic?

Most adjectives (like nouns) are stative — they describe fairly
permanent inherent qualities. This is particularly so when they occur
in attributive position, as part of the noun phrase:
    <my old blue jacket>.
But even in predicative position most adjectives remain stative, which
is why it is usually odd to use progressive (temporary) tenses with
adjectives. Stative adjectives need stative verbs: <*My jacket is being
old and blue.> <*She is being beautiful.> Some adjectives, however,
can be used predicatively to suggest a temporary state or a result:
    <She is deliberately being difficult.>
    <He is getting/looking stronger.>

8.9 Gradability

The reason why some adjectives do not have inflected forms, and are not preceded by *very*, is connected with gradability. This is a distinction based on meaning. Most adjectives can be seen on a scale of intensity:

old, older, oldest; quite/very/extremely old

Other adjectives cannot be so graded. Ungradable adjectives include:
(a) attributive-only adjectives (*former, outright, chemical*, etc)
(b) nationality adjectives (*English, Scottish, French* etc) in their primary sense. But <He is more Welsh than the Welsh.> [He behaves in a Welsh way.]
(c) adjectives with an absolute meaning (*alternative, average, equal, extra, hourly*, etc). Hence the irony of Orwell's famous line in Animal Farm:

<All animals are equal, but some are more equal than others.>

8.10 Defining and non-defining

ADV The concept of defining and non-defining relative (adjectival) clauses is well-known. (11.27-30). Less obviously, the distinction also applies to adjectives:

<I'd like to marry a tall, dark, handsome man.> [defining]
<How's your tall, dark, handsome husband?> [presumably non-defining].

Most adjectives are defining, but adjectives applied to proper names (ie 'unique' people and places) are normally non-defining:

<sunny Eastbourne, beautiful Bath, Lucky Jim.>

8.11 Marked and unmarked

Many common adjectives can be grouped in pairs with opposite meanings. In each pair, one word is the unmarked term.
In *how*-questions, for example, we ask — quite neutrally — *How old/big/heavy/long/wide/deep/tall* . . .?

<How old is your grandfather?>
<How old is the new baby?>

But the corresponding terms for opposite qualities (*How young/small/light* etc) would have marked implications:

<They say your grandmother's very young: how young is she?>
See also 8.24 and compare also unmarked pronouns, determiners, adverbs in: *How much/many/often/far* . . .

8.12 Meaning and position

Most 'descriptive' adjectives can be used in both attributive position, defining a noun by some fairly permanent inherent quality <a kind person>, and in predicative position, where the quality is 'predicated' as new information <She is kind>, <That is kind of you.> But some adjectives can only be used in one of these positions. Why?

In general, adjectives that appear only in attributive position are less adjective-like than descriptive adjectives.
(a) Some relate the noun to someone/something else (*former*);
(b) Some are like intensifying or limiting adverbs (*utter, chief*).
(c) Some are noun-related (*chemical, coastal*).
(d) Some overlap with adverbs (*indoor; indoors* adv). See 8.13

Note: Attributive-only does not mean that the adjective cannot occur in a noun phrase in the predication of a sentence:

<What you say is utter nonsense.>

What it does mean is that such adjectives cannot stand without a noun: <* This nonsense is utter.>

Adjectives restricted to predicative position — the dynamic, verbal position in a sentence — are, by contrast, more verbal and/or they refer to a more temporary state (*asleep, alight*). See 8.14.

Some adjectives have a descriptive meaning that can be both attributive and predicative, plus an attributive-only intensifying or limiting meaning:

<a *strong* man>, <He is *strong*.>

But

<a *strong* possibility> [attributive only]. See 8.15.

8.13 Attributive only

ADV	**A** **Relationship: -er**	
	former, latter, inner, outer, upper, elder etc	In *former* times people lit their homes by gas, not electricity. [past, not recent] The *latter* is considered safer. [last-mentioned] Let's buy tickets for the *upper* circle. My *elder* sister. Who's the *elder*?
	B **Intensifying**	
	mere, merest, utter, very [extreme], *outright, out-and-out*	The *mere* mention of fire alarmed him. [the mention by itself] I've only got the *merest* idea. [the smallest idea] It's *utter* nonsense. My *very* own. What happened at the *very* end? It's an *outright/out-and-out* lie.
	C **Limiting**	
	joint, lone, only, sole, chief, main, principal, very [exact, that and no other]	Many couples have *joint* bank accounts. Tom is an *only* child and the *sole* heir. The *chief/main/principal* reason is . . . A holiday is the *very* thing you need.
	D **Noun-related**	
	chemical, coastal, earthen, maritime, nuclear, solar etc	a *chemical* formula, *coastal* defences, an *earthen* pot, *maritime* law, a *nuclear* submarine, *solar* energy
	E **Alternative past participles**	
	drunken, sunken	a *sunken* garden 'What shall we do with the *drunken* sailor?' [song]
	F **Miscellaneous**	
	indoor, outdoor, inside, outside; downtown, uptown [Am Eng]	an *indoor/outdoor* swimming pool an *inside/outside* wall a *downtown* restaurant/an *uptown* area

A **Relationship**

(a) Certain words in -er indicate relationships of contrast, not degree, as true comparatives do. So we cannot say <* former than>. They only take attributive position. There are superlative forms related to

165

these adjectives: (*foremost, inmost/innermost*) but the meanings do not correspond in any very regular way.

Some adjectives that are compared regularly (eg *fine, finer, finest*) can also be used to show relationship rather than degree. Contrast:

    <I did not understand the finer points of his argument . . .> [relationship]

    <The more expensive ring was the finer.> [comparative]

(b) *former, latter* are formal.

As adjectives (*former* meaning past/earlier and *latter* (rare) meaning recent), these words are attributive only. With singular count nouns, *a* or *the* is possible: <a/the former president>.

Preceded by *the*, and usually with no following noun, these words are often used in written English to refer to the first mentioned and the last mentioned of two things in the text. So, in the example at A in the table, *the latter* stands for 'electricity'. In this usage they are rather like pronouns.

(c) *elder* Again *the* is required when there is no following noun. We cannot say <* I am elder (than) you> or <* Who's elder?>

See also 8.19.

B Intensifying

Intensifying is a general label that includes intensifying upwards (*very*) and downwards (*mere*).

(a) Although *mere* [simple, only] and *merest* [smallest, least] occur, there is no *merer*.

(b) *very* (extreme). Compare this usage with *very* as an adverb (9.22), and as a limiting adjective in C.

(c) *outright*, like *very*, can also be an adverb, and *out-and-out* is adverbial in form though not in use.

(d) Other intensifying adjectives (which with other meanings can be both attributive and predicative) include: *absolute, certain* [undoubted], *clear, close, complete, definite, firm, great, perfect, pure, real, strong, sure, thorough*.

C Limiting

Like A and B, limiting adjectives are not concerned with inherent characteristics.

(a) *Lone* means 'without a companion' rather than 'lonely': <a lone detective/tourist/yachtsman>. Predicative equivalent is *alone*.

(b) *Only* — again, a word usually functioning as an adverb.

(c) Other limiting adjectives (which with other meanings can be both attributive and predicative) include: *certain* [particular], *exact, particular, precise, principal, same, specific*.

D Noun-related

Many noun-related adjectives can and do occur in predicative position, and not everyone will agree with the examples given here. However

(a) actual nouns in attributive position usually occur immediately before the head noun and are felt to be so much a part of the head that they cannot be separated off to occur in predicative position. (For adjective order — see 8.27.)

(b) noun-related adjectives also have a tendency to be interpreted in the same way, and are often felt to be like noun compounds: <* The defences were coastal.>

E Alternative past participles

Some verbs that have two alternative past participles use their old irregular past participle only in attributive position. Compare also verbs that

(a) use the old form adjectivally, <a clean-shaven man>, <He is clean-shaven> but the regular form for the verb <He has shaved.>, or

(b) only use the old form adjectivally <a swollen neck>, <My neck is swollen.>, but use either for the verb <My neck has swollen/swelled up.>

F Miscellaneous

The close relationship between adjectives and adverbs is further shown by *indoor, outdoor, inside, outside, downtown, uptown*. In predicative position all six (two with added *-s*) are felt to be adverbs: <He was indoors/outdoors/inside/outside/downtown/uptown.>

8.14 Predicative only

A ***a*-series**	**Examples**
afloat, afraid (that/of/about), aghast, agog, akin (to), alert, alight, alike, alive, alone, aloof, amenable (to), amiss, asleep, ashamed (of/to/that), averse (to), awake, aware (of/that), awash	Try to keep *afloat*. [Contrast — *floating* debris] The child is *afraid* of the dark. [Contrast — a *frightened* child] They look so *alike*, you'd think they were twins. Is the fire *alight*? They were pulled out *alive* from the wreckage. [Contrast — *live* animals, *living* creatures] Are you *alone*, or is there someone else there? You should be *ashamed* of yourself.
B Health adjectives faint, fine, ill, poorly, well, unwell (+ better)	I feel faint/fine/ill/poorly/well/unwell/better
ADV **C Adjectives and past participles with usually obligatory complementation** answerable (to/for), bound (to + *infinitive*/for), conducive (to), content (to + *infinitive*/that) devoid (of), indebted (to), inclined (to), liable (to/for/to + *infinitive*), loath (to + *infinitive*), opposed (to), prone (to), subject (to), tantamount (to)	I'm not *answerable* to you! He's *bound* to lose his money — he always does. We were *bound* for New Zealand via Singapore. I am perfectly *content* (to stay at home.) The road is *liable* to get muddy in the winter. You'll be *liable* (to a fine for parking there.) I am *loath* to make any comment.

A *a*-series

All the words in this series can fit into the slot after linking verbs, but some are more adjective-like and some more adverb-like than others. (For words in the *a*-series classed as adverbs — see 9.11.) *Ashamed* is unusual because it is participle-like in form (it is connected with the verb *to shame*) but yet it is only an adjective (we are ashamed *of*, not *by* something). Some *a*-words (*akin, averse*) must take complementation and could therefore also be listed under C. (For *alone* as focusing adverb — see 9.21)

It is not always possible to find an attributive equivalent to these adjectives, for the obvious reason that attributive and predicative positions to some extent have their own meaning. For example, *alone* is usually emotionally neutral — referring to an action or temporary state (without other people, by oneself). The nearest attributive adjective is the limiting *lone*. Related adjectives that can appear in both positions suggest a more inherent characteristic — *lonely* (and unhappy) or *solitary* (deliberately avoiding company).

B **Health adjectives**

Strictly speaking, these words should not be included in this table, as, with the exception of *poorly*, they can all appear attributively — at least in American English. But as attributive adjectives in British English, <a fine man> <a better person>, they do not refer to health. Usage is complicated:

(a) In British English all these words refer to a possibly temporary condition of health and are only predicative. To make a comment on someone's more long-term health we could say: <He's a sick man/a healthy/unhealthy person.> or <He's (un-) healthy.>

In American English, *ill/well* are used attributively: <an ill/well woman.>

(b) Predicative *sick* means different things in British and American English.

<He was sick yesterday.> <I've been sick.>

In American English these are unspecific about the nature of the ill-health. In British English they suggest vomiting. So British English prefers:

<He was ill/wasn't well.> <I've been unwell.>, etc.

Sick in attributive use has the more general meaning of illness — <a sick man, sick leave, a sick room.>

ADV **C** **Adjectives with complementation**

On the whole, adjectives with complementation do not precede a noun, so any adjective that obligatorily takes complementation is likely to be predicative only. (Or possibly in post-position).

Content is perhaps the commonest of those adjectives that do not have to take complementation, but which are nevertheless predicative only. (The attributive equivalent is *contented*.)

8.15 Adjectives with different meanings in attributive and predicative position

ADV	Attributive only	Attributive and predicative
	A Intensifying	**Descriptive**
	He/It is an *absolute/complete/perfect/ proper/pure/real/sheer/thorough/total* — villain/disgrace	*absolute* trust. His trust in them was *absolute*.
		proper behaviour. His behaviour was quite *proper*.
	an *absolute/complete/real/total* — beginner/stranger	*pure* water. Is the water *pure*?
	a *big* eater/spender	*real* antiques. They're not *real*.
	a *firm/great/strong* believer in discipline	a *big* man. He's *big*.
	We are *firm/good/great/old* — friends	*firm* ground. The chair's not *firm to stand on*.

a *good/poor* reader/walker a *good* tennis-player *Poor old* Charles! *Poor* you! a *strong* candidate a *close friend*; *close* relations [by birth] a *sure* sign [definite]	*good* ideas/plans/food/news. The food/news etc was *good*. Stella's *good* at games. *a poor* man [= pathetic or lacking money.] He's *poor*. [= lacking money] a *strong* man/*strong* tea. He/It is *strong*. a *close* result. The result was *close*. The weather's *close*. [= stifling] We are *sure* that . . . It is *sure* to be.
B Limiting A *certain* person is always borrowing money from me. [not named but we all know who!] There's a *certain* satisfaction in being right. [some] In this *particular* instance . . . [this and no other] It's of no *particular* interest. [special]	**Descriptive: mainly predicative** We are *certain*. [free from doubt] The train's *certain* to be late. They are most *particular* about it. [fastidious, fussy]
C More permanent quality *ready* cash/money [available easily] a *ready* answer [quick] a *late* breakfast/train/holiday [deliberately timed to be late in the day etc] the *late* President [recently dead]	**More temporary quality** We are *ready* to go. Dinner's *ready*. [prepared and waiting] My brother/The train is *late*. [not on time, later than expected.]

ADV **A** **Intensifying** (a) Many adjectives are used in both positions with general descriptive meanings, and in attributive-only position as intensifying adjectives. Many common adjectives, when attached to people-nouns, do not denote a characteristic of the person, but are more like an adverb, saying how that person behaves in the capacity named. For example, <a big eater> is not necessarily a big person (though perhaps he should watch out!) but someone who eats a lot. <Poor old Charles> may deserve our pity but we do not mean 'He is poor and old'. It should also be noted that some adjectives can be used predicatively to refer to non-inherent characteristics:

<These members are new.> <That player is good.>

So it is a rather grey area of English grammar.

(b) *Close* in predicative position is sometimes adjectival:

<The weather's close.>

<He's close.> [mean with his money, infml]

and sometimes more adverbial:

<My sister and I are very close.> [ie emotionally close]

B **Limiting** *Certain* and *particular* almost always have limiting meaning in attributive position. When they refer to mental attitudes they tend to be predicative only. Thus: <Certain people never hesitate over making a decision.> would be understood to mean 'some people' (contrasted with others). If we mean 'self-confident, convinced people', we would say <People who are certain never hesitate . . .> Similarly with *sure* (A above): <We are sure that . . .> <*Sure people . . .*>. But if these words are qualified, attributive use with mental meaning is just possible:

<Such particular people are tiresome.>

<I admire such very certain people.>

C *ready/late* These illustrate clearly how attributive position can mean a more inherent characteristic (*ready money* is that kind of money), while the same adjectives used predicatively have a more dynamic and temporary meaning (*ready/late* at a particular moment).

Adjective complementation

8.16 Predicative

<table>
<tr><td>**A**</td><td>**Adjective + preposition**</td><td>I was *amazed at* your news.
He is *good at* games/*for* nothing!
          to his mother/*with* children.
Henry's very *different from* his brother.
Who's *interested in* archaeology?
Why are you *afraid/fond/jealous of* these people?
He's too *dependent on* his parents.
You'll be *liable to* a fine *for* parking here.
I am *due for* a rise.
These mistakes are *due to* carelessness.
This is *similar to* mine.
Your explanation is not *consistent with* your earlier remarks.
I am not *used to/accustomed to* living like this.</td></tr>
<tr><td>**B**</td><td>**Adjective + *to*-infinitive**</td><td>1 She was *hard to leave.*
2 The food was *delicious to eat.*
3 He was *stupid (not) to leave her.*
4 I should be *thrilled to see her again.*
5 He was *reluctant to leave her.*
6 She was *quick to take offence.*
7 He is *certain/likely/to leave her.*
8 He is *apt/bound/to forget.*</td></tr>
<tr><td>**C**</td><td>**Adjective + noun clause**</td><td>I'm *sure (that)* you'll understand.
We are *uncertain if/whether* Henry can help.
We are *delighted (that)* you've won the Premium Bond prize.</td></tr>
<tr><td>**D**</td><td>**Adjective + wh-word + *to*-infinitive**</td><td>We are *uncertain/not sure*   *how/when/where to go.*
                               what/which/who to choose.</td></tr>
</table>

ADV

There are four main types of adjective complementation — that is, a following phrase that complements or completes the sense of the adjective in predicative position.

A **Prepositional phrase** (a) Many adjectives take optional complementation of this kind. A few (eg *averse*) must do so. See 8.14. Some adjectives always take the same preposition (eg *fond of*); others take a variety of prepositions according to meaning (*good at/for/to/with*). Consult a good dictionary.
(b) *Different from* is standard English; *different than* is American English; *different to* is popular usage.
(c) *Be/get accustomed to* and *be/get used to* take a noun or gerund. Do not confuse with *used to* DO (4.26).

ADV **B**   ***To-infinitive*** This particular 'surface structure' is notorious for concealing several different underlying relationships. The *to*-infinitive in fact functions here as a kind of reduced clause — and the variety of meanings can be seen by the different ways it can be expanded.
1 The grammatical subject of the sentence (She) is the understood object of the *to*-infinitive. Compare: <It was hard for him to leave her.> Also in this pattern: *easy, difficult, impossible.*
2 Again, the subject of the sentence (the food) is the understood object of the infinitive. But here we cannot transform the sentence into <* It was delicious for him . . .>. On the other hand omission of the infinitive would not greatly change the meaning: <The food was delicious.> Contrast: <She was hard.> [heartless]. Many adjectives and infinitives are used in this pattern.
3 Here the subject of the sentence is also the (non-) doer of the action in the infinitive. Compare: <It was stupid of him (not) to leave her.> Other adjectives — all ascribing moral or mental qualities to the doer — are *brave, clever, cruel, foolish, good* [kind], *generous, horrible, intelligent, (un-)kind, mean, polite, practical, rude, selfish, sensible, silly, right, wrong, unworthy.*
4 This structure is comparable to an adverb clause — <thrilled if I saw her.> Adjectives include: *glad, grateful, happy, (un-)lucky, proud, sad, sorry* and many *-en* participles.
5 The combination of an adjective of volition plus a *to*-infinitive has the common meaning of futurity (ie the feeling in the adjective precedes the action, which may not happen). Other adjectives: *afraid, anxious, eager, impatient, keen, loath, ready, reluctant, willing* and *-en* participles (eg *determined*).
6 This is a smallish group where the adjective has a related adverb: <She took offence quickly.>
7 The adjective relates to the speaker's (not the subject's) opinion. Adjectives are *certain, likely, unlikely. Compare:* <It is certain that he . . .>
8 Again, the adjective relates to the speaker's opinion. Adjectives include *apt, liable, prone* (suggesting habit), and *bound, sure* (indicating prediction) but <*It is liable that . . .> etc is not possible.

C   **Noun clause** Adjectives referring to reactions and opinions (*certain, sure, uncertain,* etc) are followed by *that-* clauses (statements) and *wh-* clauses (indirect questions).
Structures in B and C must not be confused with the use of some of these adjectives in sentences with introductory *it*, where the *to*-infinitive or the clause does not complete the adjective but is the postponed subject of the sentence:
   <It was hard *to leave her.*>
   <It is certain (that) *he'll go.*>
Compare also <It was advisable *to leave her.*>, never <* He was advisable . . .>.

D   Indirect questions can be reported in reduced form after some adjectives with a *wh*-word (not *why*) plus *to*-infinitive.

ADV   *Note:* A common expression, though structurally unusual, is [busy + verb *-ing*], as in [He was busy working.]

8.17 'Split' complementation

		det	adj	n	adj complementation
A	**+ Preposition**	a	hopeless	child	at games
		a an	good unsuitable	place	for a factory for a holiday
		a	different	person	from his brother
		—	lovely	weather	for ducks
		a	good	pen	for drawing with
		a	calm	person	in emergencies
		a	similar	camera	to mine
B	**+ to-infinitive**	a	hard	story	to swallow
		an	easy/easier impossible	puzzle	to solve
		a an	cheap expensive	car	to buy to run
		a	useful	pot	to put things in
		a	good better	person	to go on holiday with
C	**'General ordinal' +** **prepositional phrase** **or + to-infinitive**	the	first second third etc best next last another	thing ←→ item ←→ person ←→ one ←→ person ←→ matter ←→	to say/to be said on the agenda to ask in the queue to know about it for consideration

Adjective complementation can occur in attributive use (ie before nouns). But the normal pattern here is 'split' around the noun, eg

A <a *good* place *for a holiday*> = [adj + n + PP]
B <an *easy* puzzle *to solve*> = [adj + n + *to* -infin]

'Split' patterns also occur in comparative and superlative patterns followed by *as/than/of/in* (8.21):

<a *keener* boy *than him*>
<the *keenest* boys *in the school*>.

Notice that, in terms of meaning, patterns with *different* and *similar*, included here, could be considered with comparison:

<a *different* person *from his brother*> = 'He is not as . . . as his brother.'

<a *similar* camera *to mine*> = 'It is (almost) the same as mine.'

A   + Preposition

Split complementation is common with many prepositions, but does not occur with *of* — perhaps because [noun + *of* + noun] is so often a single noun phrase: <a packet of cigarettes>. So <* He is a *proud* person *of his achievements*.> The seemingly contrary <He is the proud father of twins.> is explained as 'the proud (*father of twins*)'.

172

B   **+ *to*-infinitive**

The way in which an adjective may be 'incomplete' until its complementation is added after the noun is clearly shown by an example like

    <This is a cheap model, but it is *an expensive* car *to run*.>

Normally it is odd (except in advertising language) to put the complementation before the noun: <an expensive to run car>, but sometimes this order is used because the split order is impossible:

    <Plaque is a *hard-to-see* film which forms constantly on the teeth and gums.>

Here <* a hard film to see> is impossible. Why? Perhaps because *film* is new and probably surprising information, and needs emphasising, whereas <a hard film to see> would imply we already know it is a film. Compare, using the word *film* in its more usual sense, the acceptable:

    <This is easy film to develop.>

C   **'General ordinals'**

Are *first* and *next* determiners or adjectives? Whichever they are — and notice how like superlatives they are — they can take the same sort of split patterns that ordinary adjectives do.

For patterns with *too/enough* — see 9.24.

Comparison

8.18   Regular inflection of adjectives

A	**One-syllable words**			
	Regular with -er/-est	kind	kinder	kindest
		big	bigger	biggest
		dry	drier	driest
		long	longer	longest
	Exceptions — using more/most			
	participles	bored	more bored	most bored
	nationality words	(see 8.9)		
B	**Two-syllable words**			
1	**with -er/-est**			
	ending -y	pretty	prettier	prettiest
		(un-)happy	(un-)happier	(un-)happiest
		silly	sillier	silliest
	ending -er	clever	cleverer	cleverest
2	**with -er/-est or more/most**			
	ending -le :	able	abler/more able, ablest/most able	
		gentle	gentler/more gentle, gentlest/most gentle	
		simple	simpler/more simple, simplest/most simple	
	ending -ow :	narrow	narrower/more narrow, narrowest/most narrow	
	other :	polite	politer/more polite, politest/most polite	

Similarly: *common, cruel, handsome, obscure, pleasant, quiet, remote, sincere, solid, stupid*

3 with _more_/_most_ only			
predicative _a_-series:	afraid	more afraid	most afraid
participles:	worried	more worried	most worried
	pleasing	more pleasing	most pleasing
other:	ancient	more ancient	most ancient

Similarly: _antique, careful, careless, certain, complex, content, fertile, foolish, frequent, hostile, modern, modest, public, private_

C Three-syllable words
(and longer)

Regular with _more_/_most_	beautiful	more beautiful	most beautiful
	intelligent	more intelligent	most intelligent

Similarly: _practical, proficient_ and _all_ adjectives with three or more syllables.

Comparison of adjectives is effected either by:
(a) adding -_er_ for comparison and -_est_ for superlative, subject to the usual spelling rules, or
(b) using the adverbs _more_ and _most_ before the adjective.

A One-syllable words normally take the inflected forms. Spelling exceptions are: _shy/shyer/shyest._ Similarly _sly._ Exceptions to the inflection rule, and taking _more_/_most_ instead are:
(a) past participles (eg _bored, pleased_):
    <I was more bored than usual.>
(b) ungradable adjectives, which of course take no form of comparison, though notice the colloquial:
    <You couldn't be more right/wrong.>

B Two-syllable words
1 Adjectives ending in -_y_ normally inflect, and can do so even when prefixed by _un_-, thus becoming three-syllable adjectives, eg _unhappy, unhappier._ Adjectives ending in -_er_ also commonly inflect, eg _clever(er)._
2 Grammarians disagree about adjectives ending in -_le_ and -_ow_, eg _narrow._ Some list them with _pretty_ etc as normally taking inflection. Others consider they are just as likely to use _more_ and _most._ For _little_ — see 8.18. A number of other two-syllable adjectives use both ways of making comparison. The _a_-series and participles normally use _more_/_most_ only (though _tireder_ is certainly possible.) The safest 'rule' when in doubt is to use _more_ and _most._

C Three-syllable words
Words with three or more syllables almost always use _more_ and _most_ only.

When two or more adjectives are used together, even a one-syllable adjective may use _more_/_most_:
    <She is more kind and gentle than her mother.>
    <A more kind and gentle person you couldn't hope to meet.>
(or _kinder and gentler_).

8.19 Irregular inflection of adjectives and adverbs

	Adjective	Adverb	Comparative and superlative (of adjectives and adverbs)	
A Adjective only	old	—	older elder	oldest eldest
B Adjectives and adverbs	good well	well	better	best
	bad	badly	worse	worst
	far		farther further	farthest furthest
	late		later latter [adj only]	latest last
C Adjectives and adverbs, overlapping with pronouns and determiners	little		lesser less [adv, pro & det]	least
		much	more	most

There are very few irregular comparative and superlative forms, but some overlapping with other classes, particularly adverbs. *Much* (although not an adjective) is included here for convenience.

A *older/oldest* are the regular comparative and superlative forms.
Elder/eldest are used with reference to family relationships, but only in attributive position:
    <my elder sister> <their eldest child>.
In predicative position, when *than* can follow, use *older*:
    <My sister is older than me.> and not <* My sister is elder . . .>

B *Good* is an adjective with wide meaning: *well* is a predicative 'health' adjective (8.14). Contrast:
    <I feel *good*.> [confident, pleased etc]
    <She is *good*.> [virtuous, good at something etc]
    <I am/feel *well*.> [fit, in good health]
Far is mainly non-assertive. <It's far away.> is acceptable, but not
<* It's far.> (See also 9.10)
Farther/further and *farthest/furthest*: the alternative spelling forms are interchangeable when the meaning relates to distance:
    <I can't walk any *farther/further*.>
    <Tom always walks (the) *farthest/furthest*.>
    <The *farthest/furthest* house is theirs.>
But *further* can also mean 'extra/more':
    <If there are no *further* questions, I declare the meeting closed.>
Late/later/latest is regular when referring to time:
    <Is there a *late/later* train?>
    <I always get up *late*.>
    <I'd rather go *later* than earlier.>
    <The *latest* train I can get without having to change is the 10.06.>

Latest (as an adjective only) also means most recent, up-to-date:

    <Have you heard the *latest* news?>

    <What is the *latest* craze?>

Last (adjective and adverb) is commonly contrasted with *first* or *next*:

    <Tom was *the last* to arrive. Who was *the first*?> [adj]

    <Tom arrived *last*. But who arrived *first*?> [adv]

    <When did we *last* meet? When shall we meet *next*?> [adv]

Latter is an adjective only. It can contrast with *first*:

    <The *first/latter* half of the nineteenth century>.

For *latter* vs *former* — see 8.13.

C   Here adjectives overlap not only with adverbs, but with pronouns and determiners. Determiners were traditionally regarded as a kind of adjective, but *much/many/few/little* are the only determiners and pronouns that take comparative and superlative forms (3.19).

Little is the only word belonging to all four classes. As an adjective with its ordinary size meaning, it does not take comparative and superlative, and it has emotional overtones: <a dear little boy> <*a dear small boy>.

Lesser is an adjective, except in compounds (8.20). It is rare and formal.

    <That's true of many people to a greater or *lesser* extent.> [smaller]

    <A *lesser* man than Churchill might have given up.> [of lower quality]

Least when used as an adjective, also refers to quality rather than simple size:

    <She complains at the *least* thing.> [the merest, most trivial]

8.20 Adjective compounds

good-looking	better-looking	best-looking
good-humoured	more good-humoured	
bad-tempered	more bad-tempered	
badly-off	worse off	worst off
well-off	better off	
well known	better known	best known
little known	lesser known	least known
farsighted	more farsighted	most . . .
farfetched	more farfetched	
shortsighted	more shortsighted	
hardwearing	harder wearing	
able-bodied	more able-bodied	

Some adjective compounds containing a short, usually irregular adjective or adverb followed by a participle or the word *off*, inflect the first part for comparative and superlative, while others use *more/most*. There appears to be no clear rule, but *more/most* are possible in the majority of cases. (For the use or omission of the hyphen with compounds of this sort, see F T Wood: *Current English Usage*.)

8.21 Comparison: usage and meaning

Structure in both predicative and attributive use is basically

Equality: as . . .   as . . .

Comparative: $\left\{ \begin{array}{l} \text{adj } + \text{ -er} \\ \text{more } + \text{ adj} \end{array} \right\}$ than . . .

Superlative: the $\left\{ \begin{array}{l} \text{adj } + \text{ est} \\ \text{most } + \text{ adj} \end{array} \right\}$ in/of . . .

It is sometimes said that the comparative must be used when comparing only two things, and the superlative for three or more. Hence the 'rule' that it is incorrect English to say:

<My eldest son is 16.> if you only have two sons, or

<Shall I get beef or lamb? — which do you think is the best?>

It is true that formally one can say: <My elder son> or <Which is (the) better?> But the essential difference between comparative and superlative is that in comparison one or more *people/things* is separate from the others, whereas with the superlative, the *person/thing* being compared is within the same group, not outside.

<My son is younger than the other boys.> [He is not one of the others.]

<He is the youngest in this road.> [He is one of them.]

So the first examples, where the two *people/things* being compared are together in a group, ie my two sons, two kinds of meat, may not be wrong after all!

The superlative normally requires *the* (unless replaced by *this* etc or by a possessive determiner, eg *my*) because the meaning is a form of definiteness. It is followed by *in* for place and *of* with words denoting the group of which the *person/thing* is a member <in this road>, <of all the boys>.

A Predicative use (ie without nouns)			
Bill is	as not as not so	keen afraid as forgetful	Patrick. I am.
You seem		keener more afraid than less forgetful	me. before.
	the	keenest most intelligent	in the class. in the world.
		least forgetful	of us all. of the boys.

B Predicative — with incomplete comparison		
You are He seems Which one is	as	keen.
	(the)	keener. keenest. less/more intelligent. least forgetful.
	the	most intelligent.

A   In predicative use where comparison is made in full (ie with following, *as, than* or *in/of*) *the* is essential with superlative, but articles are not used elsewhere. The comparative may sometimes involve only one *person/thing*, but at different times.

B   If the comparison is not completed, then *the* is optional with both the comparative and the superlative, except that *the most* is preferable to *most* (which can mean *very* with no sense of comparison). See 8.25. The difference between <You are cleverer.> and <You are the cleverer.> [fml] is that the first implies *than* some other person(s), and the second implies *of the* (definite) *two*. (Compare: superlative *the*.)

8.22 Comparison within the noun phrase

A 1 Noun phrase including comparison

Boys / A boy	as	keen		Bill	should join the team.
As keen a boy [fml]	as			him	would get in.
Keener boys / A keener boy	than			he is	will be chosen.
The keener / The keenest boy(s)	of . . . / in . . .				

2 Noun phrase — incomplete comparison

He is	as keen	a boy. [fml]
	a/the	keener boy.
They are	(the)	keener boys.
He is/They are	the	keenest boy(s).

B 1 Comparison with such

It isn't / Is it	such	a good game / good fun [mass]	as	basketball.
They aren't / Are they	such	keen boys	as	the others.

2 Such	a good team / enthusiasm	(as this)	deserve(s)	support.
	keen boys	(as these)	should not be ignored.	

A 1 When adjectives are used with nouns (ie as part of the noun phrase) the adjective usually comes after the noun in comparisons of equality:

    <Boys/A boy as keen as . . .>

and similarly with mass nouns:

    <Enthusiasm as great as this . . .>.

The alternative order

    <As keen a boy as . . .>

is much more formal, and is virtually impossible with plural or mass <* as keen boys as . . ./as great enthusiasm as . . .>. Contrast such . . . as in the noun phrase, where the order is [such (+adj) + n] — see B. With comparative and superlative, 'split' patterns [adj + n + than/of/in] are normal.

2 Comparative and superlative forms sometimes occur in a noun phrase without a following as/than phrase etc. But obviously in the wider context the full comparison is implied:

    <'Tom's keen, but James isn't.' 'Oh, I disagree. James is every bit as keen a boy.'>

The is essential with the superlative in these 'incomplete' noun phrases, whether with singular or plural subject.

B Comparisons of equality are sometimes made with *such*. If the whole comparison forms part of the noun phrase it can occur in positive sentences:

    <*Such a good team as this* deserves support.>

But when the comparison itself constitutes part of the predicate, and additionally there is an *as*-phrase <as basketball> or an *as*- clause <as basketball is> then *such* is only used in non-assertive contexts: <* It is such a good game as basketball.>

8.23 *the same as*

Basketball is (not)	the same as	netball.
Bill feels		me. I do.

Some grammarians analyse the phrase *the same (as)* as a complex determiner/pronoun. Others say it is [*the* + adjective]. It functions rather like *as . . .as* in a comparison of equality. *The* is essential in this structure.

For comparison clauses (and *than me*) — see 11.23-11.24.

For *such* (determiner/pronoun) — see 3.36.

For *so/such* in purpose & result clauses — see 11.19 and 11.25.

8.24 The effect of negation on comparison of equality

The comparison of equality, expressed predicatively by *as* + adj . . . *as*, can be negated, but the resulting statements of inequality may not always mean the same as related comparative statements.

1 Bill is	older taller	than	Susan.
2 Susan is	not as old not as tall	as	Bill.
3 Susan is	shorter younger	than	Bill.
4 Bill is	not as short not as young	as	Susan.

If we think of meaning, statements (1) and (2), using unmarked adjectives (8.11) mean roughly the same. They are all, in fact, neutral as to whether Susan and Bill are old or young, tall or short, compared with other people. Statements (3) and (4), using marked terms, are different. Statement (3) is possibly still neutral; at least, Susan could be old, though some people might feel — out of any context — that she is perhaps on the short side. But (4) is by no means neutral. Susan is definitely short and young; and Bill is almost certainly short and young too.

8.25 Comparative forms indicating contrast

Like the attributive-only adjectives ending in *-er* — eg *utter* (8.13), a number of words ending in *-or* also have no positive or superlative forms.

Exterior/interior, inferior/superior, junior/senior, major/minor indicate contrast, but not degree:

<Money is only *a minor* problem; the *major* worry is where to go.>

Junior/senior can be compared with *more/most,* and take complementation:

<He's *the most senior man* in the department.>

<He's *senior to* Mr Bloggs.>

Some regular adjectives can also be used in their comparative forms to express contrast rather than actual comparison:

<The *older* generation often only wants peace and quiet.>

8.26 Other uses of *more/most*

A	**Predicative**
1	He was *more* silly than wicked.
2	You are *more* than kind/*most* kind.
B	**Attributive**
	A/The most extraordinary thing happened to me on the way to the bank.
	The Dolmetsch family are *most* accomplished musicians.
	He started on the project with *the keenest* intentions.

A **1** *More* is essential here, and the inflected *-er* is impossible. The meaning is roughly — 'He was silly: wicked is the wrong word.' If we mean that he was both we would have to say:

<He was even more silly than he was wicked.>

Similarly: <He was not so much wicked as silly> is not a true comparison of equality, but again means 'He was silly (not really wicked).'

2 Again, inflected forms are impossible here. The meaning of both is roughly the same: 'You are very kind.'

B [*Most* + adjective] can also be used attributively with the sense of *very*

<a most extraordinary thing> = [a very extraordinary thing].

[Adjective + *-est*] is sometimes possible in this position: <the keenest intentions> = [very keen intentions].

For *more/most* — see also 3.19 and 9.27.

For [the . . . the . . .] — see 11.24.

For more about comparison clauses — see 11.23.

Adjective order

8.27

Determiners	1 Subjective opinion	2 Size, shape, etc + participles	3 Proper adj	4 Noun or made of	5 Purpose? relating to? consisting of?	Head noun
all of these	lavishly [adv]	bound		Agatha Christie		thrillers
a	super de luxe			solid copper		oil lamp
this	classic	sparkling	French			wine
a	super	seven-piece matching			towel	set
a	wonderful			duckfeather & down	continental	quilt
a	huge impressive				private	reference library
a	good old-fashioned			beech-framed	rocking	chair
a	beautifully [adv]	carved		bronzed aluminium		frame
a	delightful	pink and blue	Indian	cotton		dress
an	attractive	mature semi-detached				bungalow

(a) When several adjectives are used together attributively in a noun phrase, there are various constraints on the order in which they appear. Grammarians differ about the details, and completely foolproof rules do not exist. However, in general the order is:

1 Adjectives denoting subjective opinions come first, furthest from the noun.

2 Next adjectives of more general description, including size, shape, age and colour. There is no general agreement about the order, although size often precedes shape: <a large oblong box> and age usually precedes colour: <an old blue box>.
Participle adjectives also come here, possibly preceded by an adverb of subjective opinion: <lavishly bound>.

3 Proper-name adjectives showing where something came from (eg *Indian*).

4 Noun attributes — especially showing what something is made of.

5 Other nouns including gerunds (not participles) come here, and sometimes adjectives of a close-to-noun kind ending in (-al) — eg *continental*.

In other words, adjectives that most closely belong to the noun come nearest to it, while the speaker's opinions are furthest away. The table is only a guide. Normally one does not expect so many adjectives in one noun phrase, except in advertising jargon (from which most of these examples are taken).

ADV (b) In some cases the obvious word order may be departed from for reasons of style. Another factor influencing the order may be how far a particular combination of [adjective + head noun] is considered to be a compound.

Sometimes an unusual order is used to avoid possible ambiguity:

<. . . *the American former holder* of the world high-jump record>.
Here we would expect *former* as a kind of determiner to precede a proper adjective, but the writer wants to avoid the suggestion that the holder was formerly American (and is not now). Similar considerations doubtless influenced the word order in <*a male would-be graduate*>. Notice also how a participle may itself modify another:

<a suspected broken arm> [ie an arm that is suspected of being broken]

(c) *And* is not normally used in *attributive* position. But it must be used if two or more colours, or attributes of the same kind, are used:

<pink and blue, duckfeather and down, red, white and blue>.
This also applies in predicative position. *And* is sometimes also used between the last two general adjectives of a series:

<a huge and impressive private reference library>.
But notice <*a huge, impressive and private reference library> and <*a huge, impressive, private and reference library>.
In predicative position *and* is normally used between the last two descriptive adjectives:

<This reference library is huge and impressive.>
But <*This towel set is super, seven-piece and matching.> because noun-type attribution and words felt almost to form a compound with the noun head cannot be used predicatively.

Adjectives as nominals

8.28

| A People — plural | 1981 was the Year of *the Disabled*.
'The alternative is to revert to a kind of barbarism where *the unfit*, *the eugenically unsound*, *the helpless* and *the unwanted* are slaughtered.'
'. . . make a donation to Help *the Aged's* work — towards a day centre for *the lonely*, medical treatment . . . for *the old*, or help for *the housebound*.'
To *the pure* all things are impure!
'*The city's poor* have built shacks for themselves on the hillside.' '*What poor*? There aren't *any poor* in my country.'
Old and *young* should help each other.
You really shouldn't confuse *the Chinese* and *the Japanese*. |

B	**People — singular**	*The Almighty* [God] *The accused* pleaded 'Not guilty'. [also plural] *The deceased* was the victim of a bomb attack. No impresario wants to risk big money on *an unknown*. Tom is always *the first* to arrive and *the last* to leave. Alexander *the Great*. Jude *the Obscure*.
C	**Abstractions and things**	*The unthinkable* has happened. The Theatre of *the Absurd* was developed by Beckett, Ionesco and Genet. Are you interested in *the occult*? I'll do *my best*. I thought *the worst* was over, but *worse* was to follow. Which will you have, *red or white*? Sebastian was aiming for *a gold*. *Obtainables* — we can obtain the *unobtainable* [Advertisement]

A People — plural

1 [*The* + adjective], including -ing and -en participles, can be used to mean a category of people as a whole. 'Whole' here does not have to mean 'throughout the world' but a total group in a particular context. The adjective does not take -s but plural verb is required and the meaning is plural. We cannot say <*a/the handicapped *is* . . .>. Common adjectives used in this way include:
rich/poor; old/elderly/young; deaf/blind; sick/injured/disabled; innocent/guilty/wicked; brave/strong; homeless/unemployed; bereaved/living/dead. Also: some *nationality* nouns (2.22).
Not all adjectives can be used in this way — it would be odd to speak of <*the eager, the fond> but, as the examples show, given the right context some improbable adjectives are possible.
2 The definite article is sometimes omitted in double structures:
    <*Old and young* should help each other.> and *the* is also sometimes replaced by other determiners:
    <*What poor*? There aren't *any poor* in my country!>
3 Exceptionally, *young* can refer to animals:
    <The giant turtle lays her eggs in the sand, then returns to the sea and never sees *her young*.>

B People — singular

Although [*the* + adjective or participle] with reference to people normally stands for plural, there are exceptions:
1 *The accused* has both singular and plural reference. *The deceased* (old-fashioned) usually means the dead person (ie singular).
2 *The first/last* and superlatives generally can mean person [sing] or people [pl] according to context:
    <Tom and Jane were the first . . .>.
3 [*The* + adjective] following a name is also commonly singular:
    <Alexander the Great>.
4 [*A/an* + adjective] is said by most grammar books to be impossible, but exceptionally occurs: <an unknown>.
However in general one cannot say <*an aged> <*a poor> etc.

183

Adjectives and nouns — Note
A distinction may be made between adjectives that do not have noun homonyms (*aged, poor, sick* etc) and those that do (*black, bankrupt, dear, innocent, national, neutral, savage,* etc). In the latter case, both singular nouns <*a/the savage*> and plural <*(the) savages*> are available, and therefore *the savage* as an adjective for plural people is less likely. However both plurals may be possible in some cases. Compare:

<*The innocent* were thrown into prison with *the guilty*>

<*The Innocents* Abroad> [book by Mark Twain about some naive travellers].

C **Abstractions and things**

1 [*The* + abstract adjective] (taking singular verb) can stand for an abstract idea or quality in general: <the unthinkable> <the occult>.

2 Some cases of adjectives without nouns are perhaps to be explained as ellipsis (12.2). Either the noun has been previously mentioned, or it is obvious from the context (perhaps of situation). If you are offered *red* or *white* at a dinner party, you know it is wine. *English* or *continental* refers to breakfast. But these are still felt to be adjectives.

3 On the other hand, some uses of adjectives without nouns seem to be not so much ellipsis as the process at work of an adjective becoming a noun. *A gold* is a gold medal for athletes, and feels noun-like. Some words that started life as adjectives with following nouns have achieved full noun status; eg *a pub* comes from *a public house; a private* comes from *a private soldier*. Both these (and others like them) are 100% nouns and can take plural *-s.*

4 Sometimes — unusually — a word that is still an adjective, not a noun, is used with plural *-s* to denote things. *Obtainables/ unobtainables* refer to tickets for theatre and sporting events.

Adjectives or verbs?

8.29

---

amazing/amusing/annoying/astonishing/boring/calculating/charming/disappointing/ disturbing/embarrassing/encouraging/exciting/frightening/interesting/insulting/loving/ pleasing/puzzling/satisfying/shocking/staggering/surprising/terrifying/tiring/worrying

---

amazed/amused/annoyed/bored/concerned/disappointed/disturbed/embarrassed/excited/ frightened/interested/involved/pleased/puzzled/satisfied/shocked/surprised/terrified/tired/ worried

---

A Some verb participles have acquired complete adjectival status. They can:

(a) be preceded by *very* (not possible with verbs):

<That's a very interesting story.>

(b) be compared with *more* and *most* (like adjectives):

<I felt more tired than ever.>

(c) be attributive, predicative or in post-position.

The commonest are given above.

B In predicative position, there is usually no difficulty in understanding whether adjective or verb is meant, since most of these forms are from transitive verbs, and as verbs they take objects:

<This noise annoys me/*is annoying me.*> [verb]

<This noise is (very) *annoying.*> [adj]

In the passive, fully verbal meanings can take [by + agent], whereas -en forms as adjectives take a variety of prepositions: *amazed/amused at; disappointed at/with; frightened about/of; interested in*, etc.
But sometimes there is a mixture of adjectival and verbal use:

<I felt *very exhausted by* all the work.>

Very exhausted — like an adjective; *by the work* — verbal. Ambiguity can arise with participles of intransitive verbs:

<Elspeth is trying.>

Is she trying hard to do something [verb] or is she a trying (= annoying) person?

ADV **C** *Pseudo-participles* A number of adjectives (and adjective compounds) are participles in form but there is no corresponding verb. For instance,

1 [noun +-en]: *diseased, leisured, monied*
2 [word (or prefix) + noun +-en]: *middle-aged, open-ended, twin-bedded, underprivileged, unprecedented, well-intentioned*
3 [word (or prefix) + participle]: *discontented, unexplored, uninvited, heart-broken/breaking, unconvinced/-ing, unthinking*
4 [adverb + participle]: *outspoken†, overdressed, well-read†, oncoming* (traffic), *outgoing, well-meaning*
(† Note the active meaning — an *outspoken* person speaks out, a *well-read* person has read a lot.)

D *Active vs passive* Several intransitive verbs (ie that cannot be passive) use their -en participle with past but active meaning:

<a *departed* friend [a friend who has died]: an *escaped* prisoner, a *grown* woman, a *retired* bank manager>.

8.30 Verbal forms in attributive position

1 Most non-adjectival participles cannot appear in attributive (ie adjectival) position, although they are possible in post-position, where they can be interpreted as part of a reduced relative clause — ie they are still verbal and dynamic (compare 8.31):

<Two teenagers were among the 14 people *arrested*.> [post-position] <*the 14 *arrested* people> [attributive]

<People *objecting* must lodge a formal complaint.> <*objecting* people>

<Who is that man *waving* over there?> <*Who is that *waving* man?>

<Look at that girl *reading* in the corner.> <*that *reading* girl>

But sometimes we do find participles before a noun, even though they are not fully adjectival:

<a *helping* hand, a *rampaging* mob, a *sleeping* child>
<He was hurt by *flying* bricks.>

But not <*The hand is helping.> and the participles are verbal only in <The mob is rampaging.> <The child is sleeping.> and <Bricks were flying.>

2 Some participles that are not adjectival, and that cannot take attributive position alone, can do so if qualified:

<a *much-needed* reform†, a *greatly loved* aunt, an *often repeated* phrase, a *soul-destroying* job> etc.

† *much* (not *very*) because these forms are verbal, not adjectival.

Post-position and 'reduced' relative clauses

8.31

ADV	Adjective in attributive position	Post-position adjective as (part of) reduced relative
	A Adjectives The *present* staff include an ex-prizefighter. [staff employed now] Let's drink to *absent friends*. We must talk to *a responsible person*. [reliable/in authority] Please put all the *available chairs* into the hall.	The *staff present* (on Saturday) enjoyed the show. *Staff absent* from the meeting are asked to explain their non-attendance. We must talk to the *person responsible*. [ie for this] Are there any *more chairs available?*
	B Fully adjectival participles *Concerned parents* have protested. [anxious, worried] It's a long, *involved story*. [complicated] A naughty child is *a bored child*. I met *some very interesting people*.	The *people concerned/involved* are invited to a meeting. [affected] A child *bored by having nothing to do* often gets naughty. I never meet *anyone interesting*.
	C Verbal participles Try the *left luggage* office. The men were hit by *flying bricks*.	What shall we do with the *three days left*? *Bricks flying in all directions* were a considerable hazard.

Adjectives (including predicative-only such as *alone*, but not attributive-only) can occur after the noun. This position is the same as relative clause position. So adjectives here function as a kind of *reduced* relative clause. A relative pronoun and part of the verb BE could be supplied:

<A woman alone> = [a woman *who is* alone]
<The staff present> = [The staff *who were* present]
<Anyone interesting> = [anyone *who is* interesting]

The -*ing* form in this position does not necessarily imply progressive tense and even stative verbs can take it:

<Anyone wishing to attend should . . .> = anyone who wishes . . .

But the -*ing* form does imply action at about the same time as the main verb, so preferably not <*Staff missing yesterday's meeting are asked . . .>, but <Staff who missed . . .>.

Nor are 'perfect' participles used in reduced relative clauses: So not <*Staff having missed the meeting are asked . . .>.

For reduced adverbial clauses — see chapter 11.

A **Adjectives** The tendency of attributive position to suggest a more permanent characteristic and post-position to suggest a more temporary meaning is particularly clear with *present*. *Absent* is not strictly comparable, and is less likely in post-position without further post-modification.

A few adjectives in *-ible* and *-able* occur in post-position with temporary meaning, eg *available, bookable, conceivable, feasible, possible, responsible, suitable*. Post-position is particularly likely in patterns like [*Are there any* n + adj?] or [*The only* n + adj]:

<Are there any chairs available?>

<The only seats bookable in advance . . .>.

B **Fully adjectival participles** Note the different meanings of *concerned* and *involved*. In predicative position, *concerned* out of context <I am concerned> would almost certainly mean 'anxious' (about/over the poor state of the school, etc), though the more verbal meaning is possible if spelt out: <We were all *concerned in* the successful effort to raise money.>

<As far as I'm concerned> means 'as far as it affects me'.

C **Verbal participles** The possibility of non-adjectival participles in attributive position is discussed in 8.30. *Left* (from *leave*) is possibly only used attributively in what is a virtual compound: *left luggage*.

ADV **D** Both adjectives and participles in post-position may be defining or non-defining (like relative clauses) and are similarly punctuated (11.27):

<I couldn't bear to live in a house *haunted by a murdered child.*> [defining]

<The house, *decaying and haunted,* had stood empty for months.> [non-defining]

<The case should never have come to court, said Mr X, *defending.*> [non-defining]

<The next day Ovett, *recovered from his toothache,* was in Milan.> [non-defining, note active meaning (8.29)].

8.32 Post-position only

There are few adjectives that have to take post-position.

A *Proper* as in: <*The Festival proper* only lasts a week, but there are other activities going on throughout the month.> [the festival accurately defined] Contrast:

<a *proper* villain> [utter], <*proper* behaviour> [correct].

B *Deep, high, etc* in phrases of measurement always follow, never precede, their nouns: <ten metres high>.

Note the difference between:

<10 feet square> = 10 feet x 10 feet, square in shape

<10 square feet> = 10 x 1 square foot in area, any shape

		deep high
six ten twenty a hundred	inches feet metres	long square tall wide
	years	old

C Set compounds/phrases

Most noun phrases in the unusual pattern [noun + adjective] (eg *heir-apparent*) are derived from French. They are rather fossilised and formal (but menu language does produce new English and American forms):

    <the chairman/president elect, the attorney-general, a court-martial, the heir-apparent, the postmaster-general>

    <Apple Charlotte, Peach Melba, Chicken Maryland, whisky sour>.

D Indefinite pronouns (and adverbs) in the *any*-series can only be followed, never preceded, by adjectives. But this is explainable in terms of 'reduced relatives'. This is also the position for *else* (usually classed as an adverb):

    <Can't we do *something different*?>

    <There's *nowhere nice* round here.>

    <What *else* is there to do?>

any-	body	different
every-	one	nice
no-	thing	else
some-	where	

9. ADVERBS

What are adverbs?

Adverbs have been described as 'the least satisfactory of the traditional parts of speech'. In fact, this word class is rather a rag-bag for words that will not fit anywhere else.

There are, however, some characteristics shared by many adverbs.

9.1 Form

The derivational ending *-ly* characterises what we may call obvious or central adverbs. The ending is derivational, not inflectional, because this type of adverb is derived by adding the ending to an adjective.

This is the open class among single-word adverbs — the class that can easily acquire new words (eg *hopeful/hopefully*). But many adverbs do not have any characteristic forms.

Some adverbs are inflected for comparative and superlative, like adjectives (9.12).

9.2 Position/function

There are three main positions for adverbs. They are:

front — before the subject of the sentence:
mid — between the subject and the verb (9.13 for details);
end — after an intransitive verb, or after an object or complement:

    <*Now* we are going to consider adverbs.>
    <We are *always* considering adverbs.>
    <We are going to discuss adverbs *thoroughly*.>

Traditional grammar says that adverbs 'modify' verbs — hence the name — and also adjectives <*extremely* kind> and other adverbs <*extremely* badly>. In fact they may modify the whole sentence <*Obviously*, I don't know everything.>, and many other parts of speech, for example <*rather* a muddle>   <the river *below*> [nouns]; <*nearly* everybody>   <*almost* nothing> [pronouns].

9.3 Adverbials

As well as adverbs themselves, many phrases and clauses can (a) occupy an adverb's position in a clause or sentence, (b) have the same sort of meaning as a single adverb. The term 'adverbial' is used to cover such phrases and clauses, plus single-word adverbs:

    <I met Bill *last night*.> [noun phrase as adverbial of time]
    <We went *to a pub*.> [prepositional phrase as adverbial of place]
    <*To be honest*, I didn't enjoy it.> [non-finite clause as sentence adverbial]
    <*Although the beer's good*, the place has no atmosphere.> [finite adverbial clause]
    <*When drunk*, Bill gets excited.> [verbless time clause]

This chapter is primarily concerned with single word adverbs — but some common adverb categories (particularly place) include many prepositional phrases, and these are to some extent dealt with here. For non-finite, finite and verbless adverbial clauses — see chapter 11.

9.4 Meaning

Modern grammar follows traditional grammar in using meaning as a basis of adverb classification. But, since adverbs as a whole are so complicated, there is no consensus as to what the broad categories should be, beyond a general agreement that 1 *Manner*, 2 *Place*, and 3 *Time* form separate categories. Most modern grammarians like to divide up the old vague *Degree* category into more manageable sections, but although this is helpful, it has led to a bewildering proliferation of labels. Here — to avoid further confusion by inventing still more labels — we adopt two major labels in current use, but avoid most of the sub-categories. Instead of the old Degree, we therefore have — 4 *Focusing*, which mainly consists of limiting adverbs, and 5 *Intensifiers* — a term which means words that intensify both upwards (*enormously*) and downwards (*almost, barely*). (Compare limiting and intensifying adjectives).

9.5 Adjuncts, disjuncts and conjuncts

One important classification, which was not made explicitly in much traditional grammar, is a broad three-fold division into:
1 adjuncts — adverbs (and adverbials) that are fully integrated into clause structure;
2 disjuncts — where the adverbial does not relate to any individual element of the sentence, but states the speaker's or writer's position;
3 conjuncts — which often function to connect a new sentence with something that has preceded:

    <He spoke fully and *honestly*.> [adjunct]
    <*Honestly*, what's going to happen next?> [disjunct]
    <We *still* don't know anything.> [adjunct]
    <*Still*, it was a good meeting.> [conjunct]

Both 2 and 3 are sometimes referred to as sentence adverbials. In this book, disjuncts are called *sentence adverbs* 6 and conjuncts are dealt with as *connecters* 7.

Form — and comparison

9.6 Formation of adverbs from adjectives — with *-ly*

A	**Regular general:**	Add *-ly* to adjective, including those with the endings shown.		
		cold/coldly	quick/quickly	
	consonant + *-e* :	nice/nicely	wise/wisely	
	vowel + *-le* :	sole/solely	pale/palely	but whole/wholly
	vowel + *l* :	oral/orally	careful/carefully	cool/coolly
				but *notice* full/fully

B	**Other words ending with -e**			
	consonant + *-le* :	Drop -e and add -y only.		
		able/ably	regrettable/ regrettably	single/singly
	vowel + *-e* :	Drop -e and add *-ly*		
		due/duly	true/truly	

C	Words ending with -y :	Change -y to -i and add -ly.		
		happy/happily	lazy/lazily	pretty/prettily
		dry/drily	gay/gaily	
	but	shy/shyly	sly/slyly	
D	Words ending -ic :	Add -ally.		
		cryptic/cryptically	ethnic/ethnically	
	but	public/publicly		

Many adverbs are formed by adding -ly to adjectives, with spelling rules as above. Not all related adjectives have strictly corresponding meanings.

<Our *present* problems.> [now,current]
<We'll be there *presently*.> [soon]
<They are *presently* living in Washington.> [Am Eng = now, currently]

9.7 -ly words — adjectives only

A	from nouns & verbs:	*beastly, beggarly, costly, cowardly, friendly, leisurely, likely, lovely, masterly, miserly, worldly* etc
B	from adjectives:	*deadly, elderly, lively, lonely, lowly, sickly*
C	other:	*silly, ugly*

Some common words ending in -ly are in fact adjectives only. They cannot be used as adverbs, and if an adverb is needed a phrase must be used:

<He acted *in a cowardly way*.>   <* He acted cowardly.>
<They greeted us *in a friendly manner*.>   <*friendlily>
Note also: <*deadly* poison> [adj] but <*fatally* injured> [adv].

9.8 -ly words — same form for adjectives and adverbs

hourly, daily, nightly, weekly, fortnightly, monthly, yearly, early. But *annual* [adj] and *annually* [adv].

Some common words in -ly are both adjectives and adverbs:
<What's the point of having *daily* papers delivered *weekly*?>
Note also *kindly* [adverb and old-fashioned adjective], though current adjective is *kind*.

9.9 Adjectives and adverbs with same form (without -*ly*) plus a second -*ly* adverb

adjective	adverb	-*ly* adverb
clear glass/writing, etc	Stand *clear* of the doors.	Speak *clearly*. You're *clearly* right.
close encounters	Come *close*.	a *closely* guarded secret.
a *direct* train	We drove *direct* to Leeds.	It doesn't *directly* concern me.
It's not *easy*.	Take it *easy* — there's no hurry.	You'll pass the exam *easily*.
fine hair/weather	He's doing *fine* now.	*finely* chopped onion
high hopes/a *high* roof	Jump as *high* as you can.	We think *highly* of you.
a *slow* train	The workforce is going *slow*.	The train was going very *slowly*.
Sorry. *Wrong* number.	You've done it all *wrong*.	I *wrongly* imagined that she loved me.

A number of words have two adverb forms — one, the same base form as the corresponding adjective, and the other with -*ly*. In many cases the -*ly* form is used in general adverbial positions, while the base-form adverb is used in a complement position:

    <Stand *clear* of the doors.>
    <You've done it all *wrong*.>

This is clearly on the borderline with adjectives, though the fact that these are nevertheless adverbs is shown by substituting other adjective/adverb pairs:

    <You've done it *well/badly*.> Not <*You've done it good/bad.>

Other similar adjective/adverb pairs include *deep(-ly)*, *firm(-ly)*, *late(-ly)*, *loud(-ly)*, *right(-ly)*, *short(-ly)*, *tight(-ly)*, *wide(-ly)*.

Note also: *even(-ly)*, *fair(-ly)*, *hard(-ly)*, *just(-ly)* and *near(-ly)*, where *even*, *just*, *fairly*, *hardly*, *nearly* have special adverbial meanings. Compare also: expressions like *sound asleep*, *wide awake*, where the first word is adverbial, though *soundly* and *widely* are common adverbs.

9.10 Adjectives and adverbs with no -*ly* form

A number of words have the same form (without -*ly*) for adjectives and adverbs, including: *dead*, *far* (rare as adj); *long*, *straight*, *still*. Compare <Bang-bang! You're *dead*.> [adjective] and <You're *dead* right.> <*dead slow*> [adverbs].

In modern English *far* is non-assertive:

    <'How *far* is it?' 'It isn't *far*.'>

It is also used in the phrases *too far*, *as (so) far as*, etc. But in positive statements about distance we prefer <It's a *long way*.>.

9.11 *a*-series adverbs

aboard, abreast, abroad, ahead, aloud, apart, ashore, aside, astride
Adjective or adverb: *afloat, afoot, aloof, alone, amiss, astray*

The *a*-series of adverbs should be compared with the *a*-series of adjectives. These adverbs commonly occupy end-position, which is like the predicative position occupied by *a*-adjectives. Some words are entered in dictionaries as both parts of speech and some also as prepositions.

9.12 Comparison

The comparison of adverbs is similar to the comparison of adjectives, though not identical.

For irregular inflections see 8.19. Notice that although *much* (like *more* and *most*) is adverb, pronoun and determiner, *many* is pronoun and determiner only.

'Rules' for the regular comparison of adverbs are:

(a) Add *-er*/*-est* to one-syllable words, including those that are also adjectives. This rule also applies to *early* (which is both adj and adv):

fast/faster/fastest   *late/later/latest*
soon/sooner/soonest   *early/earlier/earliest*

(b) Use *more* and *most* with all other words, even with two-syllable words ending in *-ly*:

slowly/more slowly/most slowly;   *quietly/more quietly/most quietly*

Exceptionally, with a few words, both types of comparison are possible:

often/more often/most often or *oftener/oftenest*
quickly/more quickly/most quickly or *quicker/quickest* (ie the adjectival forms).

Mid-position

9.13

A   With single verbs (including HAVE and DO)

They	⟷ still	⟷ know nothing.
She	⟷ only	⟷ plays squash at weekends.
He	⟷ already	⟷ has two houses.
We	⟷ usually	⟷ have kippers for breakfast.
She	⟷ hardly	⟷ does a thing!
You	⟷ always	⟷ must!

(Do you ever read The Sun?)	I sometimes	do.
(Will you tomorrow?)	I probably	will.

B   Mid-position in longer verbal groups

	subject	1st aux (op)	adv	2nd aux	3rd aux	lexical verb etc
BE	She	is	⟷ never	⟷		at home.
	They	were	⟷ always	⟷		making errors.
	He	was	⟷ definitely	⟷		warned.
	It	wasn't	⟷ actually	⟷ being ⟷		packed then.
	Is [op]	she [S]	⟷ merely	⟷		waiting?
HAVE (aux)	I	have	⟷ already	⟷		waited an hour.
	She	has	⟷ only	⟷ been ⟷		waiting an hour.
	He	had	⟷ certainly	⟷ been		told.
	I	have	⟷ simply	⟷ been	⟷ being	⟷ massaged.
	They	haven't	⟷ yet	⟷ been	⟷ (fully)	⟷ informed. [pasv]
	Haven't [op]	you [S]	⟷ ever	⟷		thought about it?

193

MODALS	It	will ↔ probably ↔ be ↔ (completely)			finished now. [passive]
	They	may ↔ perhaps ↔ be ↔			leaving.
	She	can ↔ hardly ↔ have ↔ been ↔			listening.
	They	must ↔ surely ↔ have ↔ been ↔			told.
	He	might ↔ actually ↔ have ↔			realised by now.
	They	need ↔ never ↔			know.
	You	mustn't ↔ ever ↔			tell anyone.
	Could [op]	you [S] ↔ possibly ↔			wait?
DO (aux)	Do [op]	you [S] ↔ really ↔			mind?
	Did [op]	they [S] ↔ eventually ↔			telephone?

A Mid-position means before a simple lexical verb (ie a one-word affirmative present or past tense, with no auxiliary or modal). This includes HAVE and DO as lexical verbs (but not BE). It also applies to auxiliaries and modals when they are used on their own in ellipsis.

B When the verb is a one-word form of BE (am, is, are, was, were) the adverb follows. Similarly, when there is a verb group of two or more words, the adverb comes immediately after the operator (ie after a finite part of BE/DO/HAVE or a modal). However, modals do not keep this 'rule' so closely as the other auxiliaries. There is particular flexibility with need/used to/ought to and have to (= must). Mid-position adverbs sometimes come before the first auxiliary for emphasis:

<She never is at home.>
<You never can tell.>

With passives, manner adverbs often come immediately before the lexical verb:

<They haven't been fully informed.>

Classification by meaning and position

9.14

		Mainly modifying	Usual position
1 Manner (9.15)		Verbs	End (but mid if value judgement)
2 Place (9.16)		Verbs	End
3 Time (9.17-20)	(a) Definite	Verbs	End
	(b) Frequency (indefinite)	Verbs	Mid
	(c) Relationship	Verbs	Mid usually possible but often front or end.

194

4 *Focusing (or limiting)* (9.21)	Various word classes	(a) Mid for verbs (b) Before other word(s) receiving focus or intensification
5 *Intensifying* (9.22-33)		
6 *Sentence adverbs* (9.34)	Sentences	Front
7 *Connecters* (9.35-36)	Joining two sentences	Front

As outlined in 9.4 and 9.5, we classify adverbs into seven categories on a combined basis of meaning and function. And since position is related to these, we find, not surprisingly, that each category favours one of the three main positions. These seven types of adverbs are summarised here and dealt with more fully in the sections indicated. For a more detailed discussion on the relationship between position and meaning, see 9.37.

9.15 Manner

			Adverbs
You	⟷ should treat	⟷ your dog ⟷	more *gently*.
Please	⟷ speak	⟷	*slowly*.
I	⟷ can't run	⟷	*fast*.
(I'm not a thief and) you	⟷ should not treat	⟷ me	⟷ *so*.
She	behaves		*Prep Phrases* { like her mother. in her own inimitable way.
They	arrived	⟷	*Prep phrases* by taxi [means].
	Open	⟷ it	⟷ with a tin-opener. [instrument]
He	writes	⟷	*Adverbs* well/carefully.
The book	is	⟷	well/carefully written. [passive]

Form This category includes *so* (some uses only); the irregular *well*; also *hard, fast* etc and many single words ending in *-ly*. eg *badly, beautifully, carefully, daringly, frankly, generously, hurriedly, ingeniously, loudly, openly, politely, quietly, quickly, sensibly, violently, willingly*.

Other manner adverbials consist of *prepositional phrases*, eg <like her mother> <with great insight>. [by + noun] is used to express means and [with + noun] to express instrument.

Function Manner adverbials answer the question *How?* They show how the action of the verb is carried out. Manner adverbs are normally used with dynamic, not stative, verbs.

Position End-position is usual, though in the passive, single-word adverbs often precede the past participle. Front-position is sometimes possible:

    <Hurriedly, he banged the door.>

Many manner adverbs can be used to make some sort of value-judgement, eg *carelessly, foolishly, greedily, politely, sensibly.* When they are, mid-position is common — and may be essential to avoid ambiguity. Contrast <He smiled foolishly.> with <He foolishly smiled.> and see 9.37.

9.16 Place

Tom is working *downstairs.* [location]
I'll just run *upstairs* and tell him lunch is ready. [direction]
Your change is *here.* [location]
Come *here.* [direction]
We live *in a small house in London.* [2 locations]
The river lay *down below.* [location]
The giant stumped *away.* [direction]

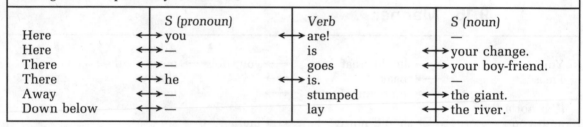

	S (pronoun)	Verb	S (noun)
Here	you	are!	—
Here	—	is	your change.
There	—	goes	your boy-friend.
There	he	is.	—
Away	—	stumped	the giant.
Down below	—	lay	the river.

Form Single-word adverbs of place have no special recognisable form, though they include (a) words ending in *-wards* (usually *-ward* in American English) and (b) the series *-where.* They also include many short words that also function as prepositions.

Single-word adverbs of place constitute a closed class. Prepositional phrases of place are obviously open class, eg <to the shops> <in the shop>.

Single-word adverbs of place include:
here, there, where, anywhere, elsewhere; backwards, forwards, downwards, upwards; abroad, away, back, downstairs, east (etc), far, indoors; about, above, behind, down, in, on, off, (See also prepositions, chapter 10.)

Function Place adverbials answer the question *Where?* and, like manner adverbs, they relate to the action/event of the verb. A semantic distinction can be made between location (plain *where?*) and direction (*where to?*).

Position End is usual. If two adverbials of location come together, the smaller (in the real world) can usually come first. So preferably not <We live in London in a small house.>

Place adverbs sometimes take front-position. This is normal — and quite informal — with *here* and *there.* But with other adverbials this structure can seem rather formal, especially as with nouns (though not pronouns) subject-verb inversion is needed. But note that this does not require an operator: <*Down below did lie . . .>. Contrast negative inversion (9.39).

9.17 Time

A 1	**Definite points periods** (end-position)	<We're going to the theatre *tomorrow*.> *today/tomorrow/tonight/yesterday/now/ then* [at that time] *this morning/last week/six years ago* [noun phrases] *at five o'clock/on Saturday* [prepositional phrases]
A 2	**Definite frequency** (end-position)	<I pay my newspaper bill *monthly*.> *hourly/daily/nightly/weekly/fortnightly monthly/bi-monthly/quarterly/annually/once, twice a week/four times a year*
B	**Frequency** indefinite time (mid-position)	<I *never* go to the theatre.> *always/ever/often/never/rarely/seldom/sometimes* *hardly ever/scarcely ever* *frequently/generally/occasionally/regularly/usually*
C	**Relationships** indefinite time (often in mid-position)	<I had *just* paid my newspaper bill.> *already/just/still* *since/yet* *afterwards/earlier/later/soon* [+ front or end] *again/first/then* [next] *last* [+ front. And see Connecters] *eventually/finally/formerly/lately/previously/ recently* [+ front or end] *once* [some time in past] [+ front] *early/late/before* [usually end]

Form Single-word time adverbs are a fairly closed class, but time adverbials also include words and phrases that belong to other classes. Eg nouns (*today, last night*), adjectives or determiners (*first, next*), prepositions and conjunctions (*after, since*).

Function and position Time adverbs answer the question *When?* But this simple statement conceals a variety of types, occupying front-, mid- and end-positions.

Various semantic sub-categories have been suggested, mostly related to position, but there is no single obviously right solution. A further complication is that some words have several meanings and belong to several categories. The scheme adopted here is inevitably a compromise and a simplification.

The positions indicated are guidelines only. Many adverbs can be fronted for emphasis. Other factors, such as the other constituents of the sentence or style generally, also affect what positions are acceptable.

Adverbial phrases, including prepositional phrases meaning duration-from — eg <for six years> <since 1980> — usually occupy end-positions. Front is possible.

A   Definite time Both definite points and periods of time and definite frequency normally take end-position (A1 and 2). Notice *ago* and *once*. *Ago* is unlike all other adverbs because it cannot stand alone, but must have a preceding word — eg <ages ago/an hour ago/long ago>. *Ago*-phrases usually need past tenses (not perfect).

Once meaning a single time (ie not *twice*) is normally in end-position. It is definite frequency, answering the question: *How often?* But when it means 'on some occasion' in the past, it is usually mid or front (9.18): *once* as a conjunction is, of course, front: <*Once* [as soon as] I'd read it, I understood.>

B **Frequency-indefinite time** Mid-position is normal. *Ever* is mainly non-assertive. It cannot take front-position. *Never/rarely/seldom* (and *hardly ever/scarcely ever*) have negative implications and do not take negated verbs. For inversion with front-position — see 9.39.

Indefinite frequency adverbs are sometimes used to convey the same sort of meaning as indefinite determiners:
    <Planes sometimes crash.>
means 'Some planes crash.' (not — All planes do this sometimes!)

C **Relationships — indefinite time** Most of the adverbs in this group can occupy mid-position. But most of them can also occupy front or end, with varying implications. Some of these words can act as connecters (9.35) when in front-position.

(a) *Already/just/still* almost always take mid-position (9.19). *Already* and *still* are normally used in affirmative statements and questions. Non-assertive *yet* is used for negatives and questions (c below).
With action verbs, *already* and *yet* need a perfect tense: <She has/had *already* told us.>
But with stative verbs, a simple tense is possible: <I *already* know/knew.> <I don't know *yet*.>
Still can precede or follow negation (see 9.38 for the different implications). It also often takes end-position.
(b) *Just* As a time adverb, *just* takes mid-position. It takes a perfect tense (rather than past) in British English, but in American English often takes past:
    <We are *just* leaving.> [= at the moment]
    <Tim has *just* left.> [= very recently]
    <Tim *just* left.> [Am. Eng.]
Compare also *just* — focusing adverbs (9.21) <He *just* left without saying goodbye.> and intensifying (9.30) <I *just* adore him.>
(c) *Since* can be an adverb on its own, as well as part of a prepositional phrase (see chapter 10) functioning as an adverbial. Both *since* and *yet* normally take end-position, though mid is sometimes used:
    <'Has Mike arrived *yet*?' 'Not *yet*.'>
    <He hasn't arrived *yet*.>
    <Have you seen him *since*?>
    <We saw him last week, but we haven't seen him *since*.>
    <We have *since* seen his mother, though.> [fml]
(d) *Last* Notice the different meanings conveyed by *last* in different positions:
    <I saw Tim *last*.> [Tim was the last of a series of people seen by me. Or possibly — I was the last person to see Tim.]
    <I *last* saw Tim . . .> [The last time I saw him was . . .]
(e) *Early/late* usually take end-position.

9.18 Frequency — indefinite or definite time

Subject	Mid-position indefinite frequency	V + O or C	End-position definite time
They ←→		held their meeting	←→ yesterday.
The firm ←→		publishes the accounts	←→ annually.
They ←→	usually	come out	←→ in January.
People ←→		used to walk more	←→ years ago.
I ←→		rang the bell	←→ once/twice.
I ←→	once [at one time]	thought of becoming a doctor.	
She ←→	occasionally	goes skiing.	
They ←→		arrived	←→ at 5 o'clock on Saturday morning.

The table shows how indefinite frequency (9.17B) takes mid-position, but definite frequency, like all definite time, favours the end (9.17A).

9.19 Relationships — indefinite time

Subject	Op	Mid-position	Lexical verb etc	End-position
She ←→	has ←→	already/just ←→	told us the news.	
I ←→		already	←→ know/knew the answer.	
We ←→	are ←→	already/just →	leaving.	
We ←→		still	←→ want to see you.	
He ←→	has/had not ←→	(yet) ←→	visited them	←→ since/yet/lately.
We ←→	must ←→	(soon) ←→	leave home	←→ earlier/later/soon.
We ←→	should ←→	(first) ←→	wash the car	←→ first/next.
I ←→	will ←→		telephone Tim	←→ last.
We ←→		last	←→ saw Tim	←→ at Beryl's party.
We ←→		formerly/previously	←→ lived in Norfolk.	←→ (formerly/previously).
I ←→	have ←→	recently ←→	been ill.	←→ (recently).
They ←→	have ←→	finally ←→	bought a new car.	
They ←→		eventually	←→ sold the old one.	←→ (eventually).
We ←→			knew this	←→ before.
You ←→	must		←→ go there	←→ early/late.

The table shows the usual positions for some common time-relationship adverbs (9.17C). Brackets show alternative positions.

9.20 Adverbs of manner, place and definite time in end-position

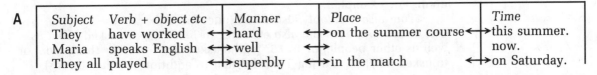

	Subject	Verb + object etc	Manner	Place	Time
A	They	have worked	←→ hard	←→ on the summer course ←→	this summer.
	Maria	speaks English ←→	well	←→	now.
	They all	played	←→ superbly	←→ in the match	←→ on Saturday.

199

B

Subject	Verb of motion	Place (direction)	Manner	Time
He	arrived	←→home	←→by taxi	←→yesterday.
We	are going	←→to Brighton	←→by train	←→on Sunday.
She	ran	←→down the road		
			←→quickly.	

A If manner, place and time adverbials occur together in end-position, they often occur in that order. But questions of style, emphasis and the length of the adverbial can lead to a different order.

B With verbs of motion, adverbs of direction usually follow the verb (before a manner phrase.)

9.21 Focusing

Who *exactly* do you want?
What *exactly* are you saying?
I am not paying £50 *just/merely* for bed and breakfast.
'I *just/merely/simply* want to enjoy myself.' 'Me too.'
Harry *alone/Only* Harry can afford that sort of money.
I'm *only* here for the beer.
At least the place is warm.
I *don't* care for it *either*.
Even the bars in this hotel are not very good.
You can't do that — *even in Las Vegas.*
Tom *also/even/only/just* asked Juliet for £5.
Tom asked Juliet for £5 *too/as well*.

Form Most focusing adverbs are single words, including some *-ly* forms, but a few prepositional phrases also belong here. Focusing adverbials include:

alone, just, only; exactly, merely, purely, simply, solely, chiefly, especially, mainly, mostly, particularly, primarily, principally; at least, in particular; either, neither, nor (see note following); *also, even, too, as well.*

Function/position/meaning Focusing adverbs are so-called because they focus attention on a limited part of the sentence, often one word. In general, the adverb comes immediately before the word or phrase being focused on.

(a) *Alone* usually focuses on a noun or pronoun and must follow it. (Compare *alone* as adjective).

Exactly is common with *wh*-words and often follows.

Merely/purely/simply almost always precede the word or phrase focused upon.

(b) *Just/only/even* can precede the focused-upon word, but like *also* they often take mid-position. This may lead to ambiguity, since it is not always clear whether part or all of the predicate is being focused upon. For example:

<Tom *also/even/only/just* asked Juliet for £5.>

Out of context, does the *also* etc refer to *Juliet*? (eg he asked Juliet as well as other people) or to *£5*? (eg he asked her for other things too) or to *asked Juliet for £5*? (eg Tom did that in addition to other things).

In spoken English, the ambiguity can be resolved by stressing the relevant word(s). For written English, prescriptive grammarians demand shifting the adverb, or rewriting the whole sentence. But the fact is that this is a favourite position for these words and context often makes the meaning clear. Notice the difference between focusing *only* (as here) and *only* as a concessive connecter: <I can ask her. *Only*, I'd rather not.>

For *just* see also 9.17 and 9.30.

(c) *Either/too/as well* *Either* must come at the end of a clause, and is used after negative statements (9.39). *Too/as well* follow positive words or clauses. *Too/as well* in clause-final position can lead to the same ambiguity as *also/even* etc above. For example:

<Tom asked Juliet for £5 *too/as well*.>

Here the focus could not be on the whole predication, but it could certainly be on *Juliet* or on £5.

(d) *Neither/nor*:

<This place is *neither* cheap *nor* cheerful.>
<*Neither* Vanessa *nor* Tim like(s) it.>

Some grammarians classify *neither* and *nor* here both as focusing adverbs and as correlative conjunctions! This just shows the overlap of word classes. Notice also that *neither* and *either* (but not *nor*) also belong to determiners and pronouns.

9.22 Intensifiers

A	*absolutely, completely, decidedly, deeply, enormously, entirely, fully, greatly, heartily, highly, incredibly, intensely, perfectly, positively, really, simply, strongly, thoroughly, totally, utterly* etc
B	*awfully, badly, terribly, pretty* [infml]
C	*too, very* [never with verbs], *just, well, indeed,* *far, much, more, most, a lot, lots, how, so;* *quite, rather, fairly, enough;* *kind of, sort of* [infml]; *somewhat, a bit, a little, less, least;* *barely, hardly, little, scarcely; at all* [non-assertive] *almost, nearly, practically, virtually*

Form Many *-ly* adverbs fall into this category, but it also includes some short common words of multiple meaning. There is also an overlap with determiners/pronouns (*much, more, most, enough, a bit, a little*).

Function Intensifying adverbs can intensify verbs, adjectives and other adverbs. Some also modify indefinite pronouns, cardinal numbers and *all* and *half*: <hardly anyone, barely three, almost all/half>. All adverbs modifying other adverbs are intensifiers by definition.

Position When modifying a verb, most of these adverbs occupy mid-position, but end-position is often possible. When modifying an adverb or adjective, intensifiers usually immediately precede that word, except *enough*, which follows (9.24).

A These *-ly* words have the general meaning of intensifying upwards: <absolutely marvellous, deeply in love, incredibly lucky>. Notice how some of them correspond to intensifying adjectives (eg *absolute, perfect, utter*).

B *Awfully/pretty/terribly* are used as intensifiers in informal English. *Pretty* here means *rather* or *almost*. *Pretty well* as a compound means 'very nearly':
> <He was *awfully/pretty/terribly* upset.>
> <They are working *awfully/pretty/terribly* hard.>
> <I've *pretty well* finished now.>

Badly (meaning 'very much') is mainly used with *want* and *need*:
> <I *badly* want/need a new car.>
> <I want/need a new car *badly*.>

C Words in this group are dealt with separately below (9.23-32).

9.23 *Too* and *very* — with adjectives and adverbs (positive degree), and determiners/pronouns

With 1,2,3
 	
Too
Very
 	
Far
Rather } too
Somewhat
 	
With 1,2 only
 	
Much
A bit } too
A little
	1 *adj and adv*
	    positive degree
	    cheap(ly)
	    quick(ly)
		The music is *rather too quick*.
		I sold it *much too cheaply*.
		That was *a bit too cheap*.
		a *very cheap* holiday

	2 *det + mass noun*
	    much money
	    little time
		far too little money
		much too much money
		not very much time
		very little

	3 *det + count pl*
	    many people
	    few books
		rather too many people
		somewhat too many books
		very few books
		not very many

(a) *Too* and *very* modify adjectives and adverbs — but *never* verbs. As a matter of style, *too* is best avoided within the noun phrase, as such structures tend to be formal <too cheap a holiday> or awkward <? too cheap holidays>. Both words normally take positive degree only (1), and they are never used with comparative forms (see *far* and *much*, 9.27).

But *very* (not *too*) is usable with a few superlative forms:
> <the very best/worst; the very first/last; at the very least>.

Too and *very* are not, on the whole, used with attributive-only adjectives, many of which are themselves intensifiers (like the actual word *very*.) Nor on the whole are they used with the predicative-only *a*-series of adjectives, which are mostly too 'verbal'. Some *a*-words have their own special intensifiers — eg <*wide* awake> <*fast/sound* asleep> — while others use *very much*:
> <I am *very much* afraid that . . .>

Both *too* and *very* are possible with adjective-like participles, but not with verbal participles:
> <He is *too/very* tired/worried.> etc [adjectival]

But <*Conditions have been *too/very* changed.> Instead:
> <Conditions have been *much/greatly* changed.> [verbal]

or: <Conditions have been changed *very much/a lot/(far) too much*.>
Opinions vary as to where the borderlines come: <? He is *too* fatigued.>   <? She is *very* weakened.>

Very . . . indeed   *Very* + adj/adv can be followed by *indeed*:
> <It was *very good indeed*.>
> <Thank you *very much indeed*.>

Too can itself be premodified by various adverbials as shown in the first column, but *very* cannot. Notice that the 'determiner type' modifiers (*much* etc) are not used with countable nouns: <*Much too many people . . .>

(b) Both *too* and *very* can precede determiners/pronouns — *much/many, little, few* (2 & 3).

9.24 *Too* and *enough* — with adjectives and adverbs (positive degree)

+ adjective	:	The cake is *too soft* inside (to cut properly.)
		It isn't *firm enough* (to cut easily.)
+ adverb	:	You've cooked this *too quickly*. You didn't read the recipe *carefully enough* (to cook it properly.)
+ verb	:	You were rushing *too much*. The cake hasn't been cooked *enough*.

(a) Semantically, *too* and *enough* are often contrasted. *Too* indicates an excess; *enough* means sufficient. Both can be followed by *to*-infinitive clauses as shown. As with other structures involving a post-modifying *to*-infinitive (8.16), there may be ambiguity:
    <They were too far away to see.>
Are *they* subject or object of *see*? (? They were too far away to see something, or ? they were too far away for someone to see them.)
(b) *Enough* as an adverb always follows any adverb or adjective it modifies. (Contrast determiner *enough* 3.17.)
(c) *Enough* can modify a verb, but *too* never does. Instead we use *too much*. After a transitive verb with no expressed object or complement, *enough* is normally interpreted as a pronoun:
    <You've eaten enough.>
But after an intransitive verb, it is an adverb:
    <You look tired. You've worked enough for today.>

9.25 *Much/very much* — with gradable verbs

Subject	Mid position	Verb	
		admire	what you have done.
I	much	*appreciate*	that sort of activity.
		regret	your action.
They	*don't much*	*care*	about it.
		mind	what happens.
We	very much	*agree/doubt/enjoy/fear/hope/ (dis)like/object to/want . . .* (*love)	

Much/very much As an adverb (roughly meaning 'greatly'), *much* can take mid-position, but only with a few gradable verbs as shown. Notice negative *don't much care/mind* — never <*I (very) much care/mind. . .>. *Very much* is possible in mid-position in a few more cases as shown

above. *Very much* (not *much*) can sometimes come between the verb and its object when the object is long:
<I admire very much what you've done.>
But <*I admire very much Tom.>
In almost all cases *very much* in end-position is a good alternative.

9.26 *Much/very much* — intensifying or quantifying?

Intensifying (a few gradable verbs)	I *very much* want to see you. I love you *very much*. I *don't much* mind about the weather.
Quantifying (ungradable verbs)	I drive (my father's car) a *lot*. I don't drive (it) *(very) much*. *I *(very) much* drive the car. *I drive (it) *very much*. *I don't *much* drive it.

The limited use of *much* and *very much* as intensifiers with a few gradable verbs (9.25) must be distinguished from the much wider use of *much/very much* to talk about quantity. With this quantifying meaning, although the function is perhaps partly adverbial, mid-position is quite impossible. In fact *much* and *very much* in this second usage are like quantifying determiners or pronouns (3.17). They are therefore non-assertive, and positive statements use *a lot*.

9.27 *Far* and *much* + *more/most/less/least*

A	With preference verbs					
I	(*would*)	far	prefer			coffee.
	would 'd	much	rather sooner	have drink		wine. whisky.

B	With comparative and superlative adjectives and adverbs			
far	nicer/the nicest better/the best worse/the worst quicker/the quickest			*far the nicest* holiday a *much quicker* train *far better* advice *much the nicest* book(s)
much	more less	attractive(-ly) expensive(-ly) interesting(-ly) surprising(-ly)		a *much less* expensive place *far more* interestingly *far more* interesting people *much more* beautiful places
much the	most least			*far the most* boring idea *much the least* interesting

With quantifying determiners/pronouns			
far much	more the most less	money wine	[mass nouns]
much	the least		
far many	more	people books	[count nouns — plural]
far	fewer (less) the fewest		

D | ***more/most/least* with verbs** |
|---|
| That was what I *most feared.*
It happened when we *least expected* it.
I *more thought* you would accept their terms. |

Far and *much* are associated with comparative and superlative (not positive degree). They are used with:

A The 'preference' verbs. Note: *very much* cannot follow these verbs. *Far* is also used with a few verbs like *exceed, outshine:*

<It far exceeded my wildest dreams.>

B Comparative and superlative (not positive degree) of adjectives and adverbs. With superlatives, *by far* can be used before or after adjectives or nouns:

<By far the nicest hotel, the nicest by far, by far the most expensive>. Notice that although we can say either *far less* or *much less*, we prefer *much the least* (*far the least) for superlative.

C Quantifying determiners/pronouns. When *much* is used to intensify a comparative or superlative adjective (as in B) it is obviously possible for a countable noun, singular or plural, to follow:

<a much less expensive place>. But if *much* precedes *more* or *less* when they are quantifying determiners, then strictly speaking only mass nouns can follow:

<much less money> <*much less people>. Countable-plural nouns need <*far more/many more* people> <*much more people>, or <*far fewer* books>, but not <*much fewer> <*many fewer>. Compare *much + too* (9.23).

D *More/most/least* are used as intensifiers with verbs.

9.28 Other intensifiers of comparative adjectives and adverbs

a lot lots any no	That disco is *a lot noisier.* And *lots more expensive.* Is it *any better?* It's certainly *no less crowded.*

A lot/lots are informal (just as they are as determiners), and *any* is non-assertive.

Other intensifiers used with comparative forms — and also with positive-degree adjectives and adverbs — are: *kind of* [infml], *sort of* [infml], *somewhat, a bit* [infml], *(a) little, hardly, scarcely, almost, nearly.*

9.29 *How* and *so*

| How { | *pretty* she is!
beautifully she dances.
I love her. | She is
She dances } so {
I | *pretty.*
beautifully.
want to see her again. |

How and *so* can intensify adjectives, adverbs and verbs. Note position. They can also intensify the *much*-series of determiners in exclamations:

<*How much wine* there is! And *so little time* to drink it!>
<*So many girls!* And *how few opportunities!*>

Compare determiners *what/such* + *noun* (3.36) where the determiners act as intensifiers.

For *so/such . . . that* — see 11.19.
For *so do I/I hope so* — see 12.3.

9.30 *Just* and *well*

| He's *just* perfect!
I *can well* believe that. | I *just* adore him!
I *can well* understand your problem. |

Just in mid-position or before an adjective or adverb, and *well* in mid-position (often after (*can/could*) can intensify. Contrast *just* as a focusing adverb:

<I *just* asked — that's all.>

Notice that *simply* also has both meanings. See also *just* (time), *well* (manner).

9.31 *Barely/hardly/little/scarcely* *almost/nearly*

They *barely/hardly/scarcely* survived the ordeal. [But they *did*.]
We *barely/hardly/scarcely* know anybody here. [But we know some.]
I *could hardly* accuse him to his face. [So I did *not*/will not.]
I *could hardly* walk the last hundred yards — I was so tired. [But I did.]
You *can hardly/scarcely* call her a girl — she's fifty! [Don't.]
He *little realised* the danger he was in. [He didn't.]
I *almost/nearly/practically* died. [But didn't.]
It costs *almost/nearly/practically/virtually* nothing. [But it costs something.]
They *almost/nearly* survived. [But they didn't.]

(a) *Barely/hardly/little/scarcely* The general meaning of these words is negative or near-negative. They do not take *not, never* etc and they require non-assertive determiners/pronouns (*anybody* etc). When *can/could* precede *hardly* or *scarcely* the meaning may be total negation. Context usually makes the meaning clear. *Little* usually implies total negation. It is used with mental state verbs (eg *expect/imagine/realise/ think*). *Hardly/little/scarcely*, like other adverbs of near negative meaning, can take front-position for emphasis, with inversion. (See 9.39).

(b) *Almost/nearly*, when modifying a verb differ from *barely*, etc in that they always totally deny the truth value of their statement. Contrast the first and last sentence in the box above.

9.32 *Fairly/quite/rather*

1	*fairly/quite* [moderately] *rather* [considerably] + 'sliding-scale' words	*cheap, cold, dark, early, expensive, fast, good, heavy, hot, kind, late, light, likely, lucky, miserable, old, poor, probable, similar, slow, surprising, well, etc*
2	*quite* [completely] *rather* [considerably] + 'extreme' words	*absurd, alike, appalling, blissful, delicious, devastated, different, disgusting, exhausted, extraordinary, huge, incredible, marvellous, outrageous, superb, unexpected, unspeakable, etc*
3	*quite* [completely] + complete 'limit' words	*alone, boiling, finished, freezing, mistaken, perfect, ready, right, unique, untrue, worn out, wrong, etc*

A With adjectives and adverbs

Fairly, quite and *rather* are all intensifying adverbs with meanings somewhere below *too* and *very*.

(a) *Rather* is near the upper end of the scale, meaning 'considerably', and it can sometimes have 'bad' implications: <It's rather expensive> = [It's almost too expensive.]

It is the only one of these three words ending in -er and the only one used with comparatives. Because of its essentially comparative meaning, it is not normally used with adjectives that have a complete 'reached the limit' meaning <*rather alone, rather untrue>. But it can be used to intensify words of extreme meaning (2).

(b) *Fairly* is farthest from *too* or *very*, and means 'moderately'. It sometimes suggests 'not quite good/desirable enough':

<It's fairly warm — but perhaps not warm enough for swimming.>

On the whole this means that *fairly* is used with desirable qualities, but it can be used with undesirable ones too — <fairly boring/dull> etc.

(c) *Quite* has two meanings:
- like *fairly, quite* tones down to 'moderately' — words of 'sliding-scale' meaning (1); but
- it intensifies upwards to mean *completely/absolutely* words with extreme (2) or complete 'limit' meaning (3).

The table shows adjectives, but usage is the same with related adverbs:

<fairly cheaply, rather absurdly, quite perfectly>.

Actually, the table oversimplifies, since many adjectives and adverbs have shades of meaning that do not fall neatly into watertight categories. For example, *sure/certain* are perhaps limit words (see 3 above), and <I'm quite sure/certain> means 'completely'. But we can also say <fairly sure/certain> [moderately], though perhaps not <*rather sure/certain>.

Quite may be ambiguous with some adjectives — unless context or intonation makes the meaning clear. Contrast:

<It *was quite beautiful* — I've never seen such marvellous scenery.>

<It *was quite nice* — but we were a bit disappointed.>

B Fairly/quite/rather + nouns and verbs

(a) Both *quite* and *rather* can intensify a singular noun without an adjective, and all three words can intensify [adjective + noun] combinations. See 9.33 Note the position of *a/the*. Only *rather* can precede *too*.

(b) *Quite* and *rather* can intensify a few verbs. *Quite* has the meaning of 'moderately' if the verb is on a scale (*enjoy/hope/like/want/wish*) and 'complete' if it is not (*agree/think/ understand*). Do not confuse this use of [*rather* + verb] (meaning 'considerably') with *would rather* (4.16 and 9.27). *Fairly* can be used to intensify verbs but this is informal:

<He fairly screamed at her.>

Fairly and *unfairly* are of course regular manner adverbs.

9.33 Summary of usage

	fairly	quite 1 *moderate* 2 *complete*	rather
+ positive-degree adj and adv	*fairly* cheap(-ly)	**1** *quite* cheap(-ly) **2** *quite* absurd(-ly)	*rather* cheap(-ly) *rather* absurd(-ly)
+ comparative adj/adv		only *better* as 'health' adj <quite better, thanks>	*rather* cheaper *rather* more cheaply
+ superlative adj		*quite* the cheapest *quite* the most absurd	
+ singular noun (without adj)		*quite* a bargain/an expert/a problem/a success	*rather* a bargain/an expert/a problem/a success
+ adj + noun	a *fairly* cheap watch some *fairly* cheap watches	*quite* a cheap watch (or a *quite* cheap watch) (some) *quite* cheap watches	*rather* a cheap watch (or a *rather* cheap watch) (some) *rather* cheap watches
+ too			*rather* too cheap
+ verbs	[very rare] (but *fairly/unfairly* as manner adverbs)	**1** I *quite* liked it. **2** I *quite* understand.	I *rather* like it.

9.34 Sentence adverbs

> A   *frankly, honestly, personally, seriously*, etc
> B   *actually, arguably, certainly, clearly, definitely, doubtless, evidently, indeed, maybe, obviously, perhaps, possibly, presumably, probably, really, surely; in fact, of course*
> C   *annoyingly, hopefully, luckily, naturally, oddly, rightly, surprisingly, understandably, wrongly*

Form Many of these adverbs have the *-ly* ending and function as manner adverbs in different contexts.

Function Sentence adverbs (disjuncts) do not modify the verb or some other part of the sentence, but reflect the speaker/writer's attitude to what he is saying:

A He explains how he is speaking:
  <*Frankly*, it's a pity sport is mixed up with politics.>
B He comments on the likelihood of some action/event:
  <*Obviously*, the Minister is going to interfere.>
C He explains his reaction to some action/event:
  <*Annoyingly*, nobody thinks of letting the players decide.>
  Position Front-position is normal for most of these, except *definitely*, *possibly*, *probably* which favour mid-position (9.13).
  See also comment clauses (11.51).

9.35 Connecters

A	**Listing and adding**	first, second . . . , firstly, secondly . . . finally, last, lastly for a start, to begin with anyhow, anyway again, also, besides, further, furthermore moreover, next, then, too in addition, in any case, above all, what is more equally, likewise, similarly
B	**Summing up**	altogether, thus, therefore, in conclusion, to sum up
C	**Explaining**	for example, for instance, eg, namely, in other words, that is, ie, that is to say
D	**Changing the subject**	by the way, incidentally, now, well, meanwhile (time)
E	**Result**	accordingly, consequently, hence [fml], now, so, therefore, thus, as a result
F	**Negative condition**	else, otherwise
G	**Concession/ contrast**	*Concession:* however, nevertheless, only, still, though, yet; in any case, in any event, at any rate, at all events, after all, all the same, on the other hand *Contrast:* alternatively, conversely, instead, then; on the contrary [*contradicts* statement], in/by contrast, in/by comparison [*points out* comparison or contrast]

Form Connecters include some *-ly* forms, some closed class adverbs and some phrases.
Function Connecters signal a meaning connection between sentences (and sometimes clauses). Usually they point back to a previous sentence — so they do not normally stand at the very beginning of an utterance. Explaining connecters (C above) sometimes explicitly mark apposition: <the UK, that is to say Great Britain and Northern Ireland>.
Position Front-position in a sentence is the commonest position, and is probably essential for some (eg *again, altogether, besides, further, hence, only, so, still, yet*). Mid-position is possible, particularly for explaining connecters (C). End-position is unusual except for *anyhow, anyway, though*.

Meaning The seven categories (A - G) given here are only one way of classifying by meaning. Connecters are not an exclusive class and some connecters also function as ordinary adverbs, eg time (*now*, *then*), focusing (*also*, *only*), intensifying (*so*). Some sentence adverbs (9.34) may also link the sentence back to the previous one, so at times they act as connecters (eg *indeed*, *in fact*, *of course*). Formally, however, we can distinguish sentence adverbs from connecters in various ways. One difference is that a sentence adverb can stand alone — or just with *yes/no* — as a reply:

<'Do you understand me?' 'Yes, *indeed. Certainly.*'>
Connecters do not do this. So *not* <*Yes, moreover.>

A few connecters overlap with conjunctions. *Though* can be both conjunction and connecter (adverb); *although* is a conjunction only. Contrast:

<He eats a lot. He is very thin, *though.*> [connecter].

<*Although/though* he eats a lot, he is very thin.> [conjunctions]
So and *yet* are probably on the borderline between connecters and conjunctions (11.11).

9.36

Connecters: examples in context
The town's traffic problems are appalling. *For a start/First/To begin with* the town lies on a major commercial route. *Second/Next/In addition*, it generates its own rush-hour traffic. *Moreover/Furthermore* it is near enough to London to be caught by the capital's weekend traffic. *Anyway/Besides/In any case* the narrow streets were not built for today's cars and lorries. *Thus/Altogether* action is urgently needed. There is a simple solution — *namely/in other words*, a by-pass. *Incidentally*, travellers were complaining of this road in the nineteenth century.

The local Road Action Group says a by-pass was promised forty years ago. *Meanwhile* the problem gets worse. There are bitter differences of opinion. *Accordingly/As a result/So* a public inquiry is to be held. The Department of Transport must decide. *Otherwise* nothing will be done.

New roads, *however/though*, devour land. The road lobby say a by-pass would benefit the town. The conservationists, *on the other hand*, say the cost to the countryside and villages is too great.

Not all the conservationists are country dwellers whose peace would be shattered by the by-pass. *On the contrary*, some of the greatest critics of the by-pass scheme actually live in the town.

Effect of position on meaning

9.37

It is clear from sections 9.14-36 that the different types of adverbs favour different positions. So what exactly is the relationship between position and meaning? And why can the same word take on a different meaning by changing its position?

Obviously several factors interact here — the intrinsic semantic possibilities of the word, the other constituents of the sentence, questions of information-focus and so on. But there are some general trends.

A	**End**	
	Manner: She wrote the letter *illegibly. Not* *She illegibly wrote . . .*	
	She *dances* the tango *beautifully. not* *She beautifully dances . . .*	

B	**Mid**	
	Comment on whole predicate	*Contrast — manner*
	She primly *said no.*	She *said* no *primly.* [tone of voice only]
	He carelessly *spilt coffee on the carpet.*	He *spilt* coffee . . . *carelessly* [How else would you spill coffee?]
	She sensibly *advised him to stop complaining.*	*She advised him *to stop complaining* sensibly. [!]
	Focus	
	I just merely simply } *want you to be happy.*	*I want you to live simply/quietly/frugally.*
	Intensifying	
	We badly *need a new house.*	The move *has turned out badly.*

C	**Front**	
	Sentence comment	*Contrast — manner*
	Clearly, there's been a mistake.	You should *write* your name *clearly.*
	Or There's *clearly* been a mistake.	
	Rightly or *wrongly,* he decided to leave her.	You've *added* your figures *wrongly.*
	Seriously, why don't you get married?	I have never *seriously* thought about it.

D	**Adverbs with words other than verbs**	
	Only Susan eats meat.	Susan *only* eats *meat.*
	[The rest of us are vegetarians.]	[Nothing else! — Purists of course want <She eats only meat> — *fml*]
	We come to this restaurant *fairly often.*	You are not *acting fairly.*
	Tom *alone* is coming.	Tom is *coming alone.*
	[absolutely nobody else]	[That is how he is coming.]

A End-position adverbs often modify the verb only (not the whole predicate). Hence this is the normal position for manner adverbs. Conversely, if the adverb is to modify the whole predicate, mid-position may be necessary. This explains why a manner adverb may be unsatisfactory in end-position if there are two verbs, as it will be understood as belonging to the second verb.

B Mid-position adverbs may often cover the whole predicate. This also explains why so many focusing and intensifying adverbials come here. These adverbs almost always immediately precede the words they are modifying — hence if they are modifying the verb (or the predicate) they must be mid-position. (In *end*-position some of them could be manner.)

C Front-position is an emphatic one for adverbials. It is particularly typical for sentence adverbials — especially adverbs which could otherwise be manner in another position.

D Position is particularly important with focusing and intensifying adverbs (left column in the table). Notice how *fairly* and *alone* can be manner adverbs after a verb.

9.38 Negation — with *not*

A			
Please	⟷ don't ever	⟷	stop loving me.
You	⟷ mustn't even	⟷	look at anyone else.
You	⟷ needn't always	⟷	laugh.
I	⟷ can't always	⟷	be serious.
We	⟷ don't often	⟷	quarrel.

B

	Compare:
I *haven't still got the keys.* [I had them once, but no longer.]	I *still haven't* got the keys. [no keys so far]
He *didn't actually win.* [He nearly did.]	He *actually didn't* win. [His not winning was a surprise.]
She *isn't naturally forgetful.* [not by nature]	She *naturally won't* forget. *Naturally she won't* forget. [Of course she won't.]
I *don't particularly want to go.* [But I don't mind.]	I *particularly don't* want to go. [I have strong reasons for not going.]
I *wouldn't merely refuse* — I'd explain. [not *only* . . . but also]	I *merely wouldn't* go. [I wouldn't do anything else.]
I *don't just think*, I know! [not *only* . . . but also]	I *just don't* think we should go. [That's all.]

A   Since contracted negative (*n't*) is attached to the operator, and mid-position by definition means 'after the operator', it follows that mid-position adverbs (eg adverbs of indefinite frequency) normally follow negation (A). The effect of this on the meaning is to include the adverb in what is negated, because negative meaning starts at the *not* and goes to the end of the clause. So <Don't ever stop> means 'Never stop', and <You don't always laugh.> means 'You sometimes laugh.'

A few mid-position adverbs can precede [operator + *n't*] with only a change of emphasis, not meaning:
<It *doesn't generally* rain very much. / It *generally doesn't* rain very much.>
But in most cases meaning is drastically different if the adverb precedes *not. Always not* for example means 'never', and is more normally so expressed:
<He *never* laughs.> and not <*He *always doesn't* laugh>.

B   Sentence adverbials, being comments on a whole sentence, are normally outside the *scope of negation,* and therefore must precede [operator + *n't*], even if they do not come at the very front of the sentence. (Compare the examples and meanings with *naturally.* Focusing and intensifying adverbs, with their ability to precede many different words can obviously precede [operator + *n't* + verb]. Here the meaning is usually a strong emphasis on the negative. (Notice the examples with *merely* and *just.*)

9.39 Inversion with negation

A			
Nowhere else in the world		can you	see such monuments.
Not since I was a child Not since 1975 Never/rarely/seldom/ Hardly ever/scarcely ever		*have I*	enjoyed a holiday so much.
Little		*did he*	realise the danger.

B	Hardly Scarcely	*had I arrived*	when	the fireworks started.
	No sooner		than	

C	Not only *was the holiday* marvellous, but it was (also) cheap.	

D	I *neither* listen to the radio,	*nor (do I) watch* TV.
	'I can't bear cold weather.'	'Nor/Neither can Peter.'
	He refuses to join a bookclub,	*nor will he use* a library.
	He denied letting off the fireworks.	Nor *would he admit* that he had seen them.

A Some negative and semi-negative adverbials that are normally mid-position can be fronted for emphasis. When they are, the subject and operator are inverted. It is rather formal.

B If *hardly/scarcely* are fronted in complex sentences followed by *when . . .*, and in similar sentences on the pattern *no sooner . . . than*, subject operator inversion is obligatory.

C The correlative pair *not only . . . but (also)* behaves similarly if *not only* is fronted and focuses on the verb. Contrast:
   <Not only the hotel, but the food too, was super.>

D With the correlative pair *neither . . . nor* in the same sentence, it is the second verb (following *nor*) that takes inversion. Sometimes a separate sentence beginning *neither/nor* follows a sentence containing a negative or a verb of negative meaning (eg *deny, refuse*). Again the verb in the second part is inverted. But when *not/never + either* is used as an equivalent of a *neither/nor* second clause or sentence, there is no inversion:
   <'I can't bear cold weather.' 'Peter can't either.'>
   (See also 11.11)

10. PREPOSITIONS

What are prepositions?

10.1 Prepositions are a minor word class. They serve to connect major words (usually nouns) to other parts of the sentence. Some prepositions also belong to other classes (eg adverbs, conjunctions, even adjectives). But prepositions are 'closed class' in the sense that we do not invent new single-word prepositions.

10.2 Form

Prepositions are not distinguished from other word classes by any characteristic form and they are not inflected.

There is a group of frequently used and mainly short words (eg *up/down*), that can be both prepositions and adverbs. Some grammarians label these words, however they are functioning, as particles. Or the term 'adverb particle' (or prepositional adverb) is used when the words are functioning as adverbs. Other grammarians use the term 'particle' to cover a bigger range of short words stretching from conjunctions (eg *and*) to interjections (eg *oh*). Here we mainly stick to the traditional labels of adverb and preposition, but also use the term particle to indicate words that are both.

A number of two- and three-word phrases behave like simple prepositions. They are marginally 'open-class', because new combinations could perhaps be formed. The term 'complex preposition' is given to such phrases (eg *in spite of*). This must be distinguished from the term 'prepositional phrase' which means a preposition + complement, usually a noun phrase — eg <in the garden>.

10.3 Position/function

The name 'preposition' (= 'place before') obviously indicates a word preceding another word (or words), usually a noun or noun phrases.

There are important exceptions to this position rule, but prepositions are always closely linked syntactically to another word — and this is one way in which they differ from adverbs. For example the word *in* is a preposition in (a) and an adverb in (b):

(a) <Why are you standing *in the garden*?>
(b) <Please come *in*.>

10.4 Prepositions, particles and problems of class membership

Mainly prepositions only († = also conjunction)
after†, *against*, *among*, *as*†, *at*, *bar*, *barring*, *beside*, *but*†, *despite*, *during*, *except*, *following*, *for*†, *from*, *including*, *into*, *like/unlike*, *minus*, *of*, *per*, *plus*, *than*†, *to*, *toward* (Am Eng), *towards* (Brit Eng), *till/until*†, *upon*, *via*, *with*, *worth*

Particles (prepositions and adverbs) († = also conjunction)
aboard, *about*, *above*, *across*, *along*, *alongside*, *around*, *before*†, *behind*, *below*, *beneath*, *besides*, *between*, *beyond*, *by*, *down*, *in*, *inside*, *less*, *near*, *off*, *on*, *opposite*, *over*, *outside*, *past*, *round*, *since*†, *through*, *throughout*, *under*, *underneath*, *up*, *within*, *without*

There is considerable overlap between prepositions and adverbs, and to a lesser extent between prepositions or particles and conjunctions. There are also some problem words.

(a) *After* is normally a preposition only. The corresponding adverb is *afterwards*. (*after* as adv = rare)

(b) *Beside/besides*. *Beside* is a preposition of place [at the side of]. *Besides* is a preposition [in addition to] and an adverb [also, anyway]:
    <Come and sit *beside* me.> [prep]
    <What shall we have *besides* steak and chips?> [prep]
    <I don't really like steak: *besides*, it is expensive.> [adv]

(c) *Like* (and *unlike*) is partly like an adjective — it can be preceded by *more/most*. It is also like a preposition — it can be followed by a noun phrase:
    <She gets *more like her mother* every day.>

(d) *As/like* are both used to compare, but the meaning is different. *As* can mean 'in the role of' and it may or may not imply there is only one person/thing — it depends on the context, whereas *like* specifically implies that the two things being compared are two separate things/people:
    <*As your father* I advise you to think again.> [I am your father.]
    <*Like your father*, I advise you to think again.> [Your father and I both agree.]
    <She's working *as a waitress*.> [She is a waitress at present.]
    <That man is dressed *as/like a woman*.> [But he isn't one!]

As is also used in the pattern [V + O + *as* + NP/adj]:
    <I think of him *as an unreliable person*.>
    <We don't see this *as (being) necessary*.>

(For *as/like/than* as conjunctions — see 11.22 and 11.23.)

(e) *Worth* resembles a predicative adjective in that it can only follow a linking verb (usually BE), but it resembles a preposition (and the word *like*) in that it must be followed by a noun phrase or *-ing*:
    <This watch is *worth £200*.>
    <What's *worth doing* is *worth doing* well.>

(f) *But/except* are also on the borderline between prepositions and conjunctions. In some prepositional uses there is no problem:
    <There is nobody here *but/except me*.>

But a problem arises when the word following *but* or *except* is felt to be the logical (though not the grammatical) subject of the action, and in such cases *but/except* may be treated as conjunctions (like *as/than*):
    <Nobody *but me* (?I) knew the inside story.>

Compare true conjunctions joining clauses:
    <Nobody knew, *but* I had a fair idea.>
    <Nobody knew, *except* that one could imagine.>

(g) Notice that although the list of particles contains various pairs of words like *off/on, up/down*, the word *out* is missing. In standard British English *out* is an adverb only, and the preposition is *out of*. But informally — as in standard American English — *out* can be a preposition:

    <The cat jumped *out* the window.>

10.5 Complex prepositions

according to, apart from, as for, as to, away from, because of, but for, due to, except for, further to, instead of, next to, on to, out of, owing to, regardless of, up to; as well as, by means of, in addition to, in case of, in face of, in favour of, in front of, in spite of, in view of, on account of, on behalf of, on top of, with reference to, with regard to

Complex prepositions consist of two or more words that function like a single-word preposition. But the boundary between simple and complex prepositions is not absolutely clear. Compare *into* (one word and therefore considered simple) and *on to* (usually written as two words).

The distinction of meaning that is made by writing *into* for a preposition and *in to* for an adverb followed by a separate preposition occurs of course with *on to*:

    <The dog jumped *on to* the seat.> [complex prep]

    <Let's walk *on to* the next bus-stop.> [adv + prep]

(a) There is no very clear dividing line between complex prepositions that are unalterable (*because of*) and those like *in front of* or *on behalf of*, which have variants that are not prepositional — such as *in the front of, in front* or *on John's behalf*.

Notice that in the complex prepositions containing nouns listed above, the noun is used in a general sense without an article. If the first noun in a sequence of [prep + n + prep + n] has an article or adjective, <in the front of the car> <in full view of everyone>, we would normally not analyse as a [complex prep + n] — like for example <in *front of* + *the car*> but as [prep + NP] <in + *the front of* the car>. Notice that the different analysis usually reflects a difference of meaning.

(b) Some complex prepositions can become other parts of speech by dropping their final preposition. Eg *instead, out* [adverbs]; *because, except, in case* [conjunctions]; *in front, on top* [adverbials].

(c) *Due to* presents problems of class membership. *Due* is clearly an adjective in:

    <We must give credit where credit is *due*.>

Prescriptive grammarians condemn the use of [*due to* + noun] as an adverbial, saying it should only be used as [adjective + PP] but the wrong usage is very common:

    <He *became* ill *due to* overwork.> [adverbial — 'wrong']

    <His illness *was due to* overwork.> [adjective — correct]

10.6 Prepositions at the end?

The name preposition and the traditions of Latin-based grammar have wrongly led some people to state that prepositions must always precede their complement (or object — the two terms are used interchangeably in this context). But this mistaken rule only leads to some very unnatural English <*For what are you looking?> and is sometimes actually impossible to obey (eg c below).

In the following cases, prepositions normally come at the end of their clause:

(a) *wh*-clauses and questions: <Where are you *from*?> <What I'm looking *for* is an interesting job.> <What a lot of things you complain *about*.> <What is your new job *like*?>

(b) Relative clause: <The girl he's in love *with* is only seventeen.> or <The girl *that/who(m)* he's in love *with* is . . .>. <The girl *with whom* he's in love> is formal.

(c) Passive of prepositional verbs etc: <The children were looked *after* by their aunt.>

(d) Infinitive complementation: <There's *nobody* to talk *to*.> <You're nice to be *with*.>

But not all prepositions like final position. At any rate, some marginal prepositions usually precede their complement (*concerning, during, but, except*). Most complex prepositions also must precede:

<the years during which he was in prison> but *not* <*the years he was in prison during>

<a person I stood in front of> but *not* <*the difficulties I came in spite of>.

Prepositional phrases

10.7 Form

1 Prepositions can be followed by various word classes to form prepositional phrases. Eg (a) nouns <at night> <in the shop>;
(b) pronouns <for us> <to me>;
(c) *wh*-clauses <I can't live on what they pay me.> <They argued about how to do it.>;
(d) -*ing* clauses <by working hard>; and (e), unusually, by adverbs <before now> and adjectives <in short>.

But the typical prepositional phrase consists of [preposition + noun].

2 Pronouns after a preposition must be in object case in standard English <between you and me> <*between you and I>.

But there is some vacillation with marginal prepositions that function partly as conjunctions (10.4 and 11.23).

3 Prepositions are not followed by *that*-clauses. (An apparent exception is [*in that* + clause], but *in that* seems to be functioning as a complex conjunction, meaning 'for the following reason':

<She has a problem, *in that* she's deaf.>

4 Some prepositions on the borderline with conjunctions (*but, except, than, as well as*) can be followed by infinitives:

<He did nothing *but/except complain*.>

<It would be better to telephone *than (to) write*.>

<You should write *as well as telephone/ telephoning*.>

Otherwise the only part of a verb that can follow a preposition is a verbal noun (gerund):

<I did it *without thinking*.>

<*Instead of walking*, he took a taxi.>

10.8 *To* preposition and *to* + infinitive

It is important to distinguish between the preposition *to*, which can be followed by -*ing* clauses, but never by an infinitive, and the infinitive-particle *to*, which is followed by an infinitive (7.30). See over.

Verb + prepositional phrase	Verb + *to*-infinitive
I *object to* paying twice.	I would like *to go.*
(*What* do you object *to?*)	(*What* would you like *to* DO?)
We *look forward to* seeing you soon.	We are longing *to see* you.
The English *are used to* driving on the left.	She used *to live* in Cambridge.
(*What* are they used to DOING?)	

10.9 Prepositional phrases: function

Prepositional phrases are not grammatically parallel to noun phrases or verb phrases. Long noun phrases or verb phrases function as simple nouns or verbs do, but prepositions are a minor part of speech and have to be attached to something else. A prepositional phrase therefore has quite different functions from a simple preposition. Prepositional phrases can function as:

(a) *adjectival* (usually post-modifying in a noun phrase): <a girl *with red hair*> <the cupboard *under the stairs*> <visitors *from Mars*>;

(b) *adverbial:* place <I like sitting *by the window.*>, time <Meet me *at six o'clock.*>, manner <We shall tell them *in no uncertain terms.*>, other <He was killed *with a blunt instrument.*>;

(c) *complement to a verb:* <This consists *of rubbish.*>;

(d) *complement to an adjective:* <aware *of the problem*> <keen *on tennis*>.

(*Note:* Not everyone would analyse (c) and (d) in this way. Since verbs and adjectives of this type may require particular prepositions, an alternative analysis is to say, not that the prepositional phrase is a complement, but that the verb or adjective plus preposition forms a phrase, and what follows is the 'object' of the preposition. Whichever solution you prefer, the fact is that a prepositional phrase can follow many verbs and adjectives.)

(e) [*for* + NP + *to*-infinitive]: *for* plus a noun phrase can give a logical subject to a *to*-infinitive:

<*For him to go* is foolish.>

<I have arranged *for the bank to send* you the money.> (7.42);

(f) *object of another preposition:* <I'll be there *in under an hour.*>

10.10 Prepositional phrases: position

As shown above, prepositional phrases usually come immediately after what they are attached to. But when they are adverbial, they can occupy various positions — just as simple adverbs can. End-position is usual (10.9b), particularly for prepositional phrase adverbials of manner, place and time. Front- and mid-position are possible if the phrase is a sentence adverbial or a connecter:

<He spoke *in a great hurry.*> [manner adverbial]

<*With the greatest respect,* I think you're wrong.> [sentence adverbial, disjunct]

<He admitted, *to my amazement,* that he didn't know.> [sentence adverbial, disjunct]

<*In other words,* we couldn't understand him.> [connecter]

The versatility of prepositional phrases and their ability to occupy so many positions in a sentence is a potential source of ambiguity for careless writers. For example:

<Ministry officials received complaints of mosquito attacks by residents.> [Which noun phrase does *by residents* belong to? — complaints or mosquito attacks?]

<England almost certainly failed to qualify for the World Cup final in Spain next summer, *for the third successive time*, following their defeat last night. . .> [? they failed for the third time or, having qualified twice they won't now qualify for a third time?]

Meaning

10.11   (a) A major use of prepositions is to relate things or people in various ways in place and time. Many common prepositions apply to both place and time, with very similar meanings. 10.12-15 show some of these place and time prepositions. 10.16 shows prepositions mainly of place only. 10.17 shows prepositions mainly of time only.
(b) Some of these place/time prepositions carry over much of their meaning into figurative uses, though some have other meanings as well. There are also some common prepositions (eg *with, of*) that do not have place or time meanings. 10.18 deals with all these.

These tables do not attempt to list all the various usages of prepositions — which can be found in a good dictionary. Rather, the tables attempt to indicate the basic meaning of each preposition, from which the other (apparently different) meanings derive. This is not to claim that the 'correct' preposition in a particular context is always obvious, but at least in many cases usage may be understandable.

10.12 Place and time: nine common prepositions

Prepositions		Adverbs
A Place & time	**B** Place	**C**
1 at / to	(away) from	— / (to) ——— away
2 on / on (to)	off	on ——— off
3 in / in (to)	out of	in ——— out

	Examples (place only)
1	Is Mrs Smith *at* home?
	No. She's gone *away*. [adv]
	I saw her drive *away from* here this morning.
	She's gone *to* London.
2	My watch was *on* the table. But it fell *off*. [adv]
	It fell *off* the table, and *on to* the floor.
3	My money was *in* my bag. Who's taken it out? [adv]
	Has anyone taken it *out of* my bag and put it *in(to)* their pocket?

Here we have nine closely related prepositions:

A Three pairs of words all used for both place and time: *at/to; on/on(to); in/in(to)*. In each pair, the first word (*at, on, in*) on the whole represents static location or time, and the second word represents direction (whether in space or time). *On to* (or *onto*) is mainly place.

B Three related prepositions of contrary direction (*away from, off, out of*). These mainly refer to place, except *from* which has both place and time uses.

C Related adverbs. *At* is never an adverb, and *to* only exceptionally (see phrasal verbs). More detailed meanings of these words as prepositions are given in 10.13.

10.13 Meanings of these nine prepositions

	at, on, in (mainly static)	
at — *Points*	*Place* at home, at school, at the cinema at the Hilton, at the Red Lion, at Tom's at the front, at the back We live at the sea, at the seaside. The train doesn't stop at Glynde. I'll meet you at Victoria Station. at the North Pole	*Time* at one o'clock, at 5.15pm. at dawn, at sunset, at midnight, at night at the weekend (Brit Eng) at Christmas, at the New Year [periods seen as *points* on calendar] at the beginning, at the end, at first, at last at this point, at that time, at times, at any moment at a glance love at first sight He wrote his first novel at the age of 60.
on — *Lines, surfaces,* *areas* (Place); *Time similarly* *seen as having* *surface but not* *interior*	on the floor/the table/the wall, on a stool, on a hard chair on the cover, on page 10 on a main road, on the river on the South Coast on the M.1. (motorway) Henley-on-Thames, Leigh-on-Sea on an island on Earth, on the Equator a spot on my chin	on Sunday, on 23rd April on that date, on that occasion on the weekend (Am Eng) on the morning of 23rd April on Sunday afternoon on Christmas Day Please be on time. [exactly] *On* opening the letter, he found a cheque inside. [Action seen as whole, with no 'interior']

in — 3-dimensional enclosing spaces. Time also seen as having *interior*	in the cupboard/the garden/the forest in the North of England in London, in Cambridgeshire, in America in heaven, hell, the sky in the world, in the Tropics They live in a little village called Glynde. in this book, in an armchair in the front/back row a pain in my throat	in April, in 1980, in the winter in Easter Week in the 19th century in the morning, the afternoon, the evening Five minutes in every hour He went round the world in 80 days. I'll be back in ten minutes. Please be in time. [early enough — before the end of some implied period] in the end [eventually] never in all my life In opening the letter, he unfortunately tore the stamps I wanted. [Action with 'interior' time dimension — in the middle of opening the letter]

to, from, on to, off, into, out of (mainly direction)

	Place	Time
to — Goal	We're going to Scotland.	The exhibition is open (from Monday) to Saturday. Only 300 more shopping days to Christmas! It's five to four. [opposite = past in Brit Eng and after in Am Eng]
from — Source, starting point	We've already driven from Land's End. We're going from Land's End to John O'Groats. I bought these souvenirs back from Spain.	She lived abroad from the age of 7. The exhibition is open from Monday (to Saturday). I'll be here from midday.
on to — Surface & goal	The cup fell on to the floor. I can't fix this shelf on to the wall. He walked on to the platform.	
off — Separation from surface	It fell off the wall. Keep off the grass.	
into — Interior & goal	I went into the library. The child climbed into the (branches of the) tree. He came/hurried/ran/rushed/walked/went into the room.	This will take us into the nineteen-nineties. Will the railways survive into the 21st century?

out of — Separation from interior	The dog jumped out of its basket. My purse must have fallen out of my handbag. Take your cigarette out of your mouth.	

(a) *at, on, in* We use:

at for points of place and time (seen as having no dimension);

on for lines and surfaces of place, and similarly for time — having as it were area but no interior (ie two-dimensional);

in for three-dimensional *spaces* and for time having 'interior'.

In general terms this means that we tend to use *in* for large places (eg *America*) and *at* for places seen as points (*the North Pole*). Sometimes we have a choice depending on our viewpoint: They live *at* Glynde [a point on a map] or *in* Glynde [a village of some dimension]. We can stay *at* or *in* the Hilton Hotel. We can park a car *in* or *on* the road. But often there is no choice: We live *on* a river [a line], but swim *in* it [three-dimensional water]. We live *at* the seaside [the point where land and sea meet], but *on* the South Coast [a line]. With time, choice of preposition is more limited than with place.

(b) *To* and *from*; *on to* and *off*; *into* and *out of* are often pairs with contrasting meanings.

(c) *In/into* and *on/onto* As a rough rule, *into* and *on to* have a meaning of goal like *to* that *on* and *in* lack. So directional movements prefer *into* and *on to*. But with some verbs of movement *in* or *on* are possible:

<Go and jump in the lake!>

(d) *From* (and *since*). Both *from* [prep] and *since* [prep, adv & conj] give a time for the beginning of an activity, but *from* gives no indication of the end of the activity, whereas *since* links the action to the moment of speaking or to some specified past time. *Since* therefore normally needs a (present or past) perfect tense. Contrast:

<He { had studied / studied / (?has studied) } English from the age of 10.>

<He { has studied English since 1970.> [and still does] / had studied English since 1970.> [The situation at some past time] }

<* He studied since . . .>

10.14 Omission of prepositions with some time expressions

At/on/in are not normally used before the following types of time expression:

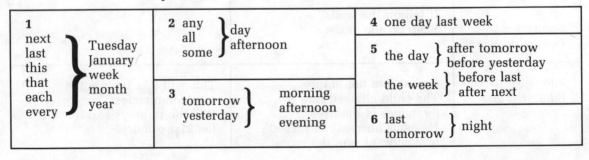

1 next last this that each every } Tuesday January week month year	2 any all some } day afternoon	4 one day last week
		5 the day } after tomorrow before yesterday
	3 tomorrow yesterday } morning afternoon evening	the week } before last after next
		6 last tomorrow } night

10.15 More prepositions of place and time

	Place	Time
about [*approximate, direction*]	He kept pacing about the room.	about six o'clock about a week
(a)round [*surrounding, curved, circle*] (*around is more usual in Am Eng, round in Brit Eng*)	They live (a)round the corner. We have a hedge (a)round the garden, and fields all (a)round us. Let's sit (a)round the fire/wander (a)round the town/look (a)round the museum. She put her arms round his shoulders.	We'll be there around 6 o'clock. around the turn of the century
beyond [*direction, but no proximity*]	Beyond the beach we could see oil tankers out in the Channel. The train doesn't go beyond Hastings.	I can't stay beyond midnight. You can't extend this ticket beyond 31st December.
by [*proximity, but probably not touching*]	She sat by the window. We walked by the river. There's an old mill by the river.	I'll have finished by the 30th. If the plane leaves at 7, we must be at the airport by 6.
for [*extent, — also intended destination*] *see* 10.18	for six miles for miles and miles They've just left for Brighton.	I lived in Hong Kong for three years. We'll wait for another hour.
past [*proximity — probably not touching, plus path from one side to another*]	The bridge is past the mill. We walked past the mill. The train runs past the beach.	It's past midnight. Quarter-past five [Br Eng; Am Eng = Quarter *after* five]
through [*path/direction plus inside something three-dimensio- nal*]	Once we're through Brighton, we'll be able to drive faster. It'll take ages to get through Customs. There's no water coming through this pipe.	*all through* the day/night/my life Monday through Friday [Am Eng] May through October [Am Eng; Br Eng = *from . . . to . . .*]
throughout [*through + complete extent*]	There are troubles throughout the world.	throughout the day/the night/the summer/1984/my life
toward(s) [*direction/goal but incomplete*]	We walked towards the bridge, but it was too far.	towards six o'clock/dawn/midnight

The table above gives some more prepositions of place and time with related meanings.

1 All these prepositions are also adverbs except *for* (which can be a conjunction — see 11.11) and *toward(s)*.

2 Meanings of the corresponding adverbs are similar to their prepositional meanings of place. Compare:

<They were standing/rushing *around/about*.> [adv]

<The police were standing *by*.> [adv]

<Several girls walked *by/past*.> [adv]

3 *For* is often used to refer to periods of time extending to a particular point (whether past, present or future) and in these cases perfect tenses are used (see also chapter 5):

(a) <We had known each other *for* three months *when we got married*.>

<We have been married for five years *now*.>

<*By A.D. 2000* we will have been married for 25 years.>

But any tense can be used when the length of time is not related to a fixed point in time:

(b) <We were/will be away *for six weeks*.>

In sentences like (a) and (b), the *for* can often be omitted. It cannot be omitted when the meaning is more like 'until after'.

(c) <He won't reach Acapulco *for another two days*.> Compare: <He will reach Acapulco in another two days.>

10.16 More prepositions of place

across [*direction, path crossways*]	They live across the road from us. Don't run across the road. There's a footbridge across the river. A tree has fallen across the path. It's too muddy to walk across the fields.
along [*direction, path lengthways*]	There are trees along the road, and a path along the river. We walked along the river bank for three miles. Where's the lavatory? Along the corridor.
among + *more than two things/people seen as an undivided surrounding group*	I don't like living among strangers. a little village among the mountains. Silver is highly prized among the tribesmen.
between + *two or more surrounding (or partly surrounding) things/people, all seen separately*	between you and me and the gatepost! Bexhill is between Eastbourne and Hastings. Air New Zealand fly between New Zealand, the Pacific Islands, Singapore and the U.S.A.
Time:	between 3.15 and 4 pm between May and September.
up [*movement, direction; sometimes higher*]	You're driving me up the wall! The train wound slowly up the mountainside. There's a fish and chip shop up the road.
Time:	up until 1939/up to 1939 (But not * up 1939/up the centuries etc)
down [*movement, direction; sometimes lower*]	It's easier walking down the hill. [than walking up it.] There's a fish and chip shop down the road.
Time:	down the ages/the centuries

above [*higher, no intrinsic* *contact or* *movement*]	500 feet above sea level Windsor is on the River Thames above London. The mountains tower above the town. We were flying above the clouds. They live three floors above us. He's got a plaster above his eye. [on his forehead]
below [*lower, no intrinsic* *contact or* *movement*] *Compare* *metaphorical use*	The Dead Sea is below sea level. Greenwich is on the Thames below London. The post office is up the hill below the church. The people below us are very noisy. [*under, underneath* possible] His leg was amputated below the knee. She's *above/below* him in class/in the firm/in ability. Ten degrees *above/below* freezing point. I can't go *above/below* £50. [raise/drop my price] *above/below* average
over [*superior +* *path/movement;* *contact possible*] **Time:**	We flew over France (to Italy). Alfriston is over the hill. [You have to take a path from here to the other side.] They are building a new bridge over the river. [*across* possible] They live over the road. [on the other side] They live over a shop. [*above* possible] The dog's run all over the flowerbeds. Put your coat over the chair. He had a plaster over his eye. [covering it] over Easter/over the weekend/over the years
under [*inferior +* *path/movement;* *contact possible*] *Compare* *metaphorical use*	The police station is under the bridge. [perhaps actually beneath the arches, or perhaps via a path through to the other side] They're building a tunnel under the Channel. The people in the flat under us are noisy. [*below, underneath,* possible] The dog ran under the chair. I've got a scar under my chin. He's *over* them. (= He's the boss.) He's got twenty people *under* him. *over/under* £20, *over/under* 40 [years old] *over/under* 30 degrees *over* age/*over* ripe [= too old etc] *under* age/*underdone*/*underdeveloped* [= not enough]
beneath **underneath** [*lower,* *contact possible,* *vertical relationship*] *Compare* *metaphorical use of* *beneath:*	There's a huge cellar beneath/underneath the house. [*under* possible] Put a pillow underneath/beneath his head. [*under* possible] The chair broke beneath his weight. [*under* possible] *beneath* contempt/*beneath* one's dignity
on top of [*higher, with contact*]	Why are your shoes on top of the cupboard? The castle is on top of the hill.

against [*proximity, contact*] Also metaphorical use [*opposed*]	Put your bicycle against the wall. You're banging your head against a brick wall! It was a war *against* a ruthless enemy. They were all *against* him. [Contrast *for* 10.18]
behind [*rear of something three-dimensional*] Also metaphorical use [*supporting*]	The child ran and hid behind a tree. I hate driving behind a bus. There's a big garden behind the house. His family were right *behind* him.
in front of [*antonym of behind and related to 3-D object*] **opposite** [*facing*]	The people in front of us at the cinema were eating peanuts. Please don't park in front of the entrance. There's a block of flats opposite our house. If you sit opposite me, it's easier to talk than if we sit next to each other.
beside [*at the side of 3-D object*] **inside** [*interior of 3-D object*] **outside** [*exterior of 3-D object*]	Come and sit beside me. There's a noisy disco right beside our house. She was standing just inside the door. [ie inside the doorway/room/house etc] It was very dark inside the cave. What's life like inside a prison? There are always a lot of jeans on rails outside the shop. Outside the hotel, the temperature was below freezing.

The prepositions above mainly refer to place, but a few have limited reference to time, and most of them, of course, have metaphorical uses. (Notice the common figurative uses of *against* and *behind*.)

The prepositions are arranged in this table mainly in pairs, which are either opposites (*up/down*) or closely related but different (*among/between*). Notice how *above/below* are intrinsically different from *over/under*, even though they may sometimes be interchangeable.

All these prepositions are also adverbs — except *against, among, beside* (adv *besides*), *on top of* and *in front of* (adverbials *on top, in front*).

10.17 More prepositions of time

after [*subsequent to, later than*] **before** [*prior to, earlier than*] **Place** (in lists)	after breakfast the day after tomorrow ten after six [Am Eng; Br Eng = *ten past six*] before dinner the week before last before now/before then P is *before* Q. My name comes *after* yours.

since [*in the period* *beginning; links to a* *later point — but* *neutral about ending* *of activity*]	since the war since 1975 since the age of 10 since the beginning of time
till/until [*extended period* *with end but without* *mention of* *beginning*]	The good weather lasted till/until the end of October. He lived in Wales till/until his death. I'll wait till/until 5 o'clock. I didn't see them till/until yesterday.
during [*located in time, but* *not extent*]	I've only seen them once during the past year. [*in* also possible] Where do the birds go during the winter? [or *in*] I must wash the car (some time) during the weekend. Contrast: I'll be busy throughout the weekend. [extent]

Several common prepositions have time reference only, not place:
(a) *Before* and *after* can be used with meanings of place, but this is rare, except in lists as shown. Place equivalents are *in front of* and *behind* (10.16). Notice that *till/until* are similarly time only (contrast *to*).
(b) *Before* and *since* are also adverbs.
(c) All these words are also conjunctions except *during*.

10.18 Extended meanings + *with, of*

Most prepositions of place and time have figurative meanings, often closely related to their literal meanings. A few examples are given in 10.16.

Here we give some further examples to distinguish sets of words that cause confusion. Notice *with* and *of* — two important prepositions, that do not have either time or place meanings.

A *at/to/for*

At/to Both have a sense of goal, but *at* sometimes has an additional sense of 'target', often combined with a feeling of aggression. If you throw something *at* someone, you hope to hit them; if you throw it *to* them, you hope they will catch it. (For verbs taking *to* or *for* as an alternative to indirect object pattern, see 7.8).	
at [*goal/target*]	Don't aim your gun at me. Don't laugh at me. Don't throw stones at the dog. Stop talking at me. [lecturing me unpleasantly] Please look at me.
to [*goal/destination*]	Please pass that book to me. Throw the ball to the dog. Please talk to me/listen to me. You ought to give some money to charity.

To/for Both have a sense of destination, but with *for* the destination is sometimes intended rather than achieved. Compare *place*: <go to Brighton> <set out for Brighton>.

for	I bought a book for Tom. [but possibly forgot to give it to him]
[*intended destination/ purpose; in favour of*]	I have been listening for the postman. [but I haven't heard him]
	Let's go for a walk/prepare for an exam/pray for peace/hope for the best.
	Too much sugar is bad for you.
	I'm saving for a car.
	We're all for it. [Contrast *against*]

B by/with/from

The main meaning of *by* (other than place and time) is means/agent. It is the main preposition for the agent in passive structures.

by	Gravity was discovered by Newton.
[*agent*]	The climbers were struck by lightning.
	The President was shot by an assassin.
	These photographs were taken by a child.
[*means*]	She keeps healthy by jogging every day.
	It happened by accident/chance.
	We came by car/train.

with	a girl with red hair
[*having, accompanying*]	Come with us!
	She lives with her mother.
	We're with you. [on your side. Compare *for*]
	This pudding is made with eggs [and other ingredients]
	My coat is covered with mud.
[*instrument*]	He was shot with an automatic. [Contrast <by a gunman>]
	These photographs were taken with (or on) a cheap camera. [Contrast <by a child>]

from	The best sugar comes from cane.
[*source, origin*]	The table was made from a single tree trunk.
	Here's a letter from my sister.
	I've just bought a second-hand car from a friend.
[*cause*]	He's suffering from exhaustion.
[*separation*]	I was prevented from coming.
	It's different from the others.

C about/on

In their place/time meanings, *about* has somewhat vague connotations, while *on* relates to a definite line or surface. This difference carries over into other subject matter.

about	Can we talk about something cheerful for a change?
[*vague, in general*]	He told me about his illness.
	I'm writing a popular book about birds and bees.
on	I hope to write the definitive book on the subject.
[*more definite/ serious*]	She wrote a thesis on the chemistry of molecules.

Of is the commonest of all prepositions, and sometimes seems to have little meaning beyond grammatical linking (eg h). However a variety of meanings can be seen. (Compare also *'s* genitive 2.32)

(a) possession/have	the wealth of these people!
	the end of the road, the key of the cupboard
(b) subjective genitive	the arrival of the plane [The plane arrived.]
	the novels of Graham Greene [G.G. writes novels]
	the cost of a new roof [A new roof costs . . .]
(c) objective genitive	this waste of good food. [Someone is wasting . . .]
	the pursuit of happiness [People pursue . . .]
(d) being (and apposition)	The Isle of Skye [Skye = an island], the City of Bath
	the sense of taste
	It is kind of you to . . . [You are kind]
(e) cause, source, origin	to die of cancer/old age
	the cause of . . ./the result of . . .
	This necklace is made of solid gold. [It *is* solid gold]
	Contrast: The table is made *from* a tree trunk. [virtually nothing else, but is *not* a tree trunk now]
	and contrast:
	The cake is made *with* brandy. [and a lot of other ingredients]
(f) containing	a cup of tea, a bag of peanuts, a bottle of milk, a book of short stories, the Gang of Four
(g) quantities	a pint of milk, a kilo of sugar, a piece of paper
(h) some determiner structures	*some* of the people [compare g], *both* of the books etc

Adjectives and prepositions

10.19
ADV
Complementation of adjectives by prepositions is only one kind of adjective complementation (8.16-17). Here a few more examples are given of common adjective and preposition combinations.

about [concerning]	I am *curious about* his motives. Also: *angry, annoyed, anxious, certain* (or with *of*), *careful, careless, enthusiastic, happy, pleased, sure* (or with *of*), *worried*.
at [emotional reaction to (a cause)]	I was *angry at* their not telling me. Also: *amazed, annoyed, delighted, disappointed, excited, frightened, hurt, pleased, shocked, worried*, etc [Verbal past participles can also use *by* + agent]
[ability at (a skill)]	She's *good at* languages and *bad at* tennis. Also: *adept, brilliant, clever, expert, hopeless, quick, slow, useless*

for [goal, purpose]	We are *eager for* news. Also: *adequate, appropriate* (or with *to*), *bound, eligible, essential* (or with *to*), *famous, fit, necessary* (or with *to*), *ready, responsible, sorry, sufficient, suitable*
from [separation]	He was *absent from* the meeting. [Contrast *present at*] Also: *different, distinct, free, immune* (or with *against, to*), *safe, separate*
in [within three- dimensional area]	He's *successful in* everything he does. Also: *efficient, experienced, interested, lacking, (un-)lucky, successful*
of [having relation, or objective genitive]	Some children are *afraid of* the dark. Also: *ashamed, aware, capable, certain, confident, conscious, convinced, critical, envious, fearful, fond, full, glad, guilty, hopeful, ignorant, independent, innocent, jealous, proud, tired, (in-)tolerant*
on	She is too *dependent on* her parents. [Contrast *independent of*] Also: *based, intent, keen, reliant, set*
to [goal, target]	Your arguments are *contrary to* reason. Also: *(un-)acceptable, adjacent, answerable, applicable, attentive, contrary, distasteful, equal, essential, fatal, generous, hateful, inferior, kind, loyal, natural, painful, peculiar, pleasant, polite, preferable, (ir-)relevant, rude, sensitive, similar, strange, superior*
with [accompanying]	(a) Your arguments are not *consistent with* your previous remarks. Also: *comparable, (in-)compatible, complete* (but — *incomplete without*), *content, (in-)consistent, discontented,* etc. [Notice *con* — which suggests 'with', from a Latin root] (b) Other adjectives: *angry, busy, familiar, furious, happy, impatient* (c) Participle-type adjectives: *bored, delighted, disappointed, excited, horrified, pleased, upset.* [Past participles also use *by* + agent]

Prepositional and phrasal verbs

10.20   First, a question of names. [Verb + particle] combinations (eg *come across, give up, look at, put up with*) are a common feature of English. They function in many ways like single verbs, and they often have idiomatic meanings. Some textbooks refer to all verbs of this kind as 'phrasal verbs'. Others also use the term 'prepositional verb'. Sometimes the distinction made between the two is semantic, sometimes it is formal.

In *Current English Grammar* we distinguish on formal grounds between prepositional verbs (10.22-23); phrasal verbs with objects (10.24); phrasal-prepositional verbs (10.25) and phrasal verbs (intransitive) (10.26).

Meaning is not ignored in this analysis — in fact, tests of possible
transformations are used that rely on meaning (see below). But degrees
of literalness or idiom are not satisfactory as the main basis of
classification, because [verb + particle] combinations cover a wide
range, from straightforward meaning:

<Take your coat off.> [remove]

to combinations where both words are opaque:

<He took us in.> [deceived].

Often, too, the same verbs are used with different meanings.

10.21 Difference between prepositional or phrasal verb plus 'object' and ordinary verb plus prepositional phrase

A			B		
prepositional or phrasal verb	+	'object' (*What? Who?*)	ordinary verb	+	adverbial PP (*Where? When?*)
He ran up		huge telephone bills.	He ran		up the hill.
He turned down		my offer.	They turned		down the lane.
We joined in		the celebrations.	We joined		in April 1980.
She waited for		her boyfriend.	She waited		for a long time.
He looked at		his watch.	I looked		at six o'clock.

(a) In spoken English these two patterns are usually distinguished by
potential pause, as indicated in the table: He ran up — *pause* — huge
telephone bills. but He ran — *pause* — up the hill. They are also
distinguished by stress. With 'ordinary' verbs, it is the verb, not the
preposition, that is stressed. With prepositional or phrasal verbs, there
is usually a stress on the particle.
(b) The unity of a prepositional phrase as an adverbial (B) is also
shown by its possible mobility and by the possible insertion of an
adverb between the verb and the prepositional phrase. With phrasal or
prepositional verbs, by contrast, the particle belongs more closely with
the verb:

<*Up the hill* he ran.> but <*Up huge bills he ran.>
<He ran hurriedly *up the hill*.> but <*He ran stupidly up a bill.>

(c) Passive transformation is not likely with the noun of an adverbial
phrase, but is possible with a noun following a prepositional or
phrasal verb where the noun is felt to be the object of the verb
combination:

<My offer was turned down.> but <*The lane was turned down.>

(d) The transitive nature of the prepositional and phrasal verbs in A
and the intransitive nature of those in B is also shown by the
difference between the questions that might reasonably be asked:

<'What/who [object] did he look at?' 'His watch.'/ 'His girlfriend.'>
<'Where/when [adverbial] did he look?' 'At six o'clock.'/'In the
street.'>

10.22 Prepositional verbs

	Verb	Object
(a) He	looked (briefly) at	the timetable.
(b) He	looked at	it.

Patterns: 'Objects' — whether noun phrases or pronouns — follow the preposition. (They never come between the verb and the preposition.)
   Adverbs are sometimes possible between verb and particle.

Other examples:

I	←→ ran	into ←→ Peter yesterday.
I'll never	←→ get	over ←→ this tragedy.
A.A.	←→ stands	for ←→ Automobile Association.
Peter	←→ takes	after ←→ his father.
The animal	←→ turned	on ←→ me.

Prepositional verbs are so called because the particle behaves like a preposition — that is, it must normally precede its object, whether noun or pronoun (a and b above). In effect this means that (except occasionally when an intervening adverb is possible, as in a above) the verb and particle cannot be separated as they can in phrasal verbs (10.24).
   <I ran into Peter yesterday.> <*I ran Peter into.>
Combinations containing a word that can only be a preposition and never an adverb (10.4) therefore come into this category. So combinations with *at/for/into/to/with* are usually prepositional verbs (or occasionally phrasal-prepositional).
Some particles, of course, feature in both prepositional and phrasal verbs. Compare:
Prepositional verb: <I *came across* some old 78 records the other day.> or <I *came across* them.> *not* <*I came them across.> or <*I came 78s across.>
Phrasal verb: <He put his message/it *across* well.> or <He put *across* his message well.> *not* <*He put across it.>

10.23 Three types of prepositional verbs

Prepositional verbs can be divided into three categories.
1 There are a few verbs that must be followed by a preposition. These verbs are not intransitive (ie without an object, like *come*, *go*) but equally they cannot be immediately followed by a direct object as many verbs are (eg *bring*, *take*). Compare adjectives with obligatory complementation (8.16-17).

Verbs with an obligatory preposition include: *account for, amount to, connive at, consist of, long for, rely on.*

2 Some other verbs can stand on their own as intransitives, but need a preposition if a noun is to follow. Eg
   <Look!> but <Look *after/at/for* (etc) that child/those books.>
   <Listen.> but <Listen *to* me.>
   <I don't belong.> but <I don't belong *to* any clubs.>

> Verbs needing a preposition before a following noun or pronoun include:
> *abstain (from)*, *adhere (to)*, *assent (to)*, *beware (of)*, *care (about/for)*, *come (across/by/into/off)*, *comment (on)*, *complain (about/of)*, *comply (with)*, *conform (to/with)*, *cope (with)*, *depend (on)*, *go (for/into)*, *insist (on)*, *interfere (in/with)*, *laugh (about/at)*, *look (after/at/for/into/to)*, *object (to)*, *occur (to)*, *part (from/with)*, *quarrel (about/over)*, *react (to)*, *talk (about/of)*.

3 Many other verbs have alternative structures when a noun follows. With some meanings they can be followed immediately by a noun-object. With others they need a preposition and then the noun. Some of these verbs can also be intransitive:

      <You attend meetings.> *but* <You attend *to* your business affairs.>
      <The government imposes taxes.> *but* <You mustn't impose *on* other people.>
      <Do smell these roses.> *but* <Your breath smells *of* alcohol!>

> Verbs requiring a preposition in some meanings include:
> *approve (of)*, *argue (about/over)*, *ask (about/for)*, *believe (in)*, *break (into)*, *call (for)*, *do (with/without)*, *count (on)*, *dream (about/of)*, *feed (on)*, *recover (from)*, *refer (to)*, *see (about/to)*, *succeed (in)*, *take (after/to)*, *think (about/of)*, *wait (for)*.

10.24 Phrasal verbs with objects

	Verb	Particle	Object	Particle	
(a)	I looked	up	'egregious'	[*not possible . . .*]	in the dictionary.
(b)	*I looked	*up	*it.		
(c)	I looked	—	'egregious'	up	
(d)	I looked	—	it	up.	

Patterns: Particles can follow 'object' — (c) and (d), but
            cannot precede pronoun object — (b).
            Adverbs cannot separate verb and particle:
            Not <*I looked eagerly up the word.>

Other examples:
      I want to *get* my money/it *back*.
      You shouldn't *run* your friends/them *down*.
      Take your boots/them *off*.
      Don't *turn* my offer/it *down*.

      Many phrasal verbs have both transitive and intransitive (with and without object) usages — with different meanings. Compare the following with the same verbs used transitively above:

      <Things are *looking up*.> [improving]
      <When does the plane *take off*?>

> Phrasal verbs plus object include:
> *back up, bear out, break down/in/off/up, bring about/in/off/out/round/up, call off/in/up, carry off/on/out, clear away/out/up, cut down/off/out/up, do up, find out, get back/over†, give away/back/in/up, lay in/out/up, leave out, let down/off/out, make out/up, pay back, pull down/up, put across/down/off, ring up, run down/in/over/up, see off/out, take in/off/on/over/up, try on/out, turn down/off/on/out/up.*
> For *bring to* — see 10.26

†Distinguish two different verbs *get over*:

        <I'll never *get over* it.> [recover from it, ie recover from illness/shock — prepositional verb]

        <Why don't you *get* it *over*?> [cause something unpleasant to be done and finished with — phrasal verb]

10.25 Phrasal-prepositional verbs

	Verb + particles	'Object'
(a) You should	look up to	your father!
(b) You should	look up to	him.
(c) *not possible*		
(d) *not possible*		

Patterns: Whole combinations must precede 'objects' (a and b).
        Adverbs can occasionally come after the first or second word, eg:
            <We have *run* completely *out of* oil.>
        or <I'll *catch up* eventually *with* them.>
        But they are 'safer' not interrupting the verb:
            <We have completely *run out of* oil.>
            <I'll *catch up with* them eventually.>

Other examples:
        Some people *get away with* murder!
        Don't *run away with* that idea.
        My time is fully *taken up with* housework.

Combinations in this category contain some totally cohesive groups (eg *put up with*) that have no meaning if divided. But others are less merged, so that one can see, as it were, a phrasal verb plus a preposition (eg *drop out + of*).

> Verbs in this pattern include:
> *be fed up with, catch up with, drop out of, face up to, fall back on, fall out with, get away with, get out of, go back on, go in for, keep up with, look down on, look forward to, look out for, make up for, put up with, stick up for.*

10.26 Phrasal verbs (intransitive)

Look out! You'll hurt someone with that stick.

Pattern: The whole combination must come together.
        Adverbs can never separate verb and particle.

> *Other examples:*
>> Get up. It's late.
>> Don't *ring off* — I've something else to say.
>> The plane's just *taken off.*
>> Perhaps something will *turn up.*

Many of these verbs have corresponding transitive verbs, with related meanings — see 10.24.

> Intransitive phrasal verbs include:
> *bear up, break down/out/in/up, carry on, clear off/out, come about/off/on/out/to†/round/up, do without, drop in/off/out, fall off/out/through, find out, get off/on/out/up, give in/out/up, go off/out/round, grow up, hold on/out, keep on/up, let on, look back/in/round/out, make up, pull in/out, ring off/up, set off/out, show off, take off, turn out/up, wake up, wear off/out.*

Note: †*come to* [return to consciousness] and *bring to* [with object]. These two verbs are unusual because *to* is normally a preposition, not an adverb as here, and therefore combinations with *to* are normally prepositional verbs. *Bring to* is always in the pattern <bring someone to> not <*bring to someone>, eg:
<She was a long time *coming to* after the operation.>
<They *brought* Henry/him *to* eventually.>

10.27 Meanings of phrasal verbs

The meanings of many phrasal verbs are often not deducible from an understanding of their separate parts, and a dictionary must be consulted. However, some regularity of underlying meaning can be seen in some of the particles.

in [enter (or cause to enter), or (cause to) remain inside]	Burglars *broke in* while we were on holiday. Please *fill* this form *in.* Also: *call, drop, get, hold, join, keep, let, lock, look, move, send, show, shut, stay -in*
out [going to, or remaining on the outside]	My new book is *coming out* soon. [being published] Also: *break, bring, carry, go, get, keep, look, pass, put, set, slip, start, tear, turn -out*
[sudden emergence]	A typhoid epidemic *broke out.* Also: *burst, cry, shout -out*
[extending]	The teacher *gave out* the examination paper. Also: *hand, hang, hold, point, stick -out*
[clearness, loudness]	I can't *make out* what he means. Also: *find, read, shout, speak, spread, write -out*
[absence, disappearance]	You have to *blow* all the candles *out* at once. Also: *cross, die, knock, leave, rub, switch, throw, turn, wash, wear -out*

off	
[detached, separated]	They've broken off their engagement.
	Production has fallen off.
	The meeting has been put off. [postponed]
	The plane takes off from Heathrow.
	Turn/switch off the lights/heater etc.
	Also: call, clear, come, cut, die, get, keep, let, pass, pay, push, set, shut, wear -off
(and with BE)	The meeting/engagement etc is off. [cancelled]
	The milk/meat is off. [bad]
	They're off! [They have left their starting point.]

on	
[progress towards destination, continuity]	We shall carry on for another year. [continue]
	How are you getting on?
	Also: come, go, keep, move, pass, read -on
[joining, connection]	Hold on a minute — don't go. [stay]
	Turn/switch/put the lights/TV etc on.
	Also: hang, put, stay, stick, tie -on

up	
[higher/superior position]	The children were brought up by their aunt.
	It's time to get up. You can't stay in bed all day.
	Things are looking up. [improving]
	Also: come, go, grow, keep, put, set, sit, stand, stay -up
[direction towards]	A stranger came up and asked for money.
	He's taken up squash. [ie to himself]
	Also: drive, hurry, walk -up
[intensifying — completion or destruction]	I don't know the answer. I give up.
	Also: blow, break, clean, clear, cover, drink, dry, eat, finish, give, hurry, lock, pull, tear, use, wash, wipe -up

down	
[lower/inferior position — often with a sense of destruction]	The car's broken down again.
	Unfortunately I was turned down for that job.
	He's always running other people down.
	Don't try and shout me down.
	Also (lower): bend, climb, fall, get, keep, move, pass, pull, put, sit, take -down. Also (destruction): burn, cut, die, knock, pull, shut, tear -down.

11. CONJUNCTIONS, SUBORDINATORS AND CLAUSES

What are conjunctions?

11.1 The word-class conjunction is a traditional one, meaning words that join. Also traditional is the division of conjunctions into:
(a) *co-ordinating conjunctions* — which join elements that are grammatically equal.
(b) *subordinating conjunctions* — which join a subordinate 'dependent' clause to a main clause.

11.2 Form

Conjunctions include: (a) single words (including some words that are adverbs (eg *once, so*);
(b) compound conjunctions — some are like participles and many end with *as* or *that* (eg *as long as, in order that, so that, supposing that, provided that*);
(c) correlative conjunctions that split around an adjective or adverb (eg *so . . . that*).

11.3 Function/position

In general: **co-ordinating conjunctions** (a) can join single words (eg adjectives, adverbs and nouns as well as clauses); (b) must come at the beginning of a clause; (c) must come between the words or clauses they join. Hence, when two clauses are co-ordinated, the conjunction must start the second clause. A misunderstanding of this fact has led to the prescriptive rule that sentences must never start with *and/or/but*. Of course they can — but the conjunction then relates the sentence back to the preceding one.

Subordinating conjunctions (a) do not join single words (exceptions: *if* and *though*, as in *kind though silly*); (b) usually come at the beginning of the subordinate clause; (c) can start the first clause of the sentence.

11.4 Usage

The table below shows how co-ordinating and subordinating conjunctions differ in usage, and compares them with connecters (9.5).

Function and position	Co-ordinating conjunctions	Subordinating conjunctions	Connecters (adverbs — chapter 9)
between clauses	It was snowing, *but* I went out.	I went out, *although* it was snowing.	It was snowing; *however*, I went out. [really = 2 sentences]
initial in sentence	(It was snowing.) *But* I went out.	*Although* it was snowing, I went out.	(It was snowing.) *However*, I went out.
non-initial in clause			I went out, *however*. I, *however*, went out.
joining single words	cold *and* wet cheap *yet* good	(only *if/though*) cold *though* fine	
before ellipsis of 2nd subject	(only *and/or/but*) I went out, *but* — didn't walk far.		

Co-ordination and subordination

11.5   There are various ways in which co-ordinate and subordinate clauses can be combined. The standard labels for the resulting sentence types are:

(a) *compound* — for sentences containing two or more co-ordinate clauses:

    <It was snowing, *but I went out.*>

(b) *complex* — for sentences with one main and at least one subordinate clause:

    <*Although it was snowing,* I went out.>

(c) *compound-complex* — for sentence containing a mixture:

    <*Although it was snowing* I went out *and posted a letter.*>

Various factors favour the use of compound or complex sentences rather than a succession of simple ones. Quite apart from questions of style (a very big subject), a major factor is the possibility of explicitly showing relationships of meaning. In:

    <It was snowing. I went out.>

we have mere co-occurrence, and no explanation as to whether I went out although it was snowing, or perhaps because it was. The use of co-ordination (*but*) or subordination (*although*) or connection (*however*) all spell out clear explanations.

11.6 The meaning of co-ordination and subordination

ADV Are there differences other than style or semantic subtleties between the different possibilities in this case? The answer is, yes. Co-ordination, subordination, connection are grammatical devices with their own meaning. With co-ordination, both parts of the sentence are offered as new information. But with subordination, the content of the subordinate clause is simply presented as given. Contrast:

<Was it snowing and did you go out?>
<Is it true that it was snowing and you went out?>
— where both clauses are being questioned, with
<Did you go out, although it was snowing?>
<Is it true that you went out although it was snowing?>

where the fact that it was snowing is not in doubt. A subordinate clause, therefore, downgrades its information and helps to emphasise the main clause.

11.7 Clauses classified by verb structure

In older grammars, a clause is defined as a groups of words containing a subject and a finite clause. But it is convenient to widen the term 'clause' to cover not only
(a) finite clauses: <Although *it was snowing,* I went out.>
but also
(b) non-finite clauses: <When *feeling ill,* I don't go out.> and
(c) verbless clauses: <If *possible,* I don't go out in the snow.>.
In general, finite clauses can be both main and subordinate, but (b) non-finite and (c) verbless can only be subordinate.

11.8 Clauses without conjunctions

Although both non-finite and verbless clauses may be introduced by conjunctions, they do not always need to be, since the absence of a finite verb is often quite a sufficient signal of subordination:

<Running *down the road,* I tripped and fell.>
<Disliking *cold weather,* Susan stayed at home.>

All these non-finite and verbless clauses demonstrate how the information of a subordinate clause is considered of less importance than the main clause. Firstly, although the missing subject may be 'recoverable', the tense of the verb may be vague (because Susan *dislikes/disliked* cold weather?), and secondly the 'missing conjunction' may be unclear. (?*While* I was running down the road or ?*Because* I ran/I was running . . .)
Sometimes it is not even clear whether a clause is adverbial or adjectival — and probably it does not matter:

<Crispin, *delighted at the news,* rushed to the telephone.> Does this mean 'who was delighted', or 'because he was delighted'?
Co-ordinate clauses too may be related to each other without conjunctions — or perhaps, since they lack co-ordinators, we should call them equal-status clauses. For example we can interpret the following pairs as a kind of opposition:

<You don't like it: I don't like it.>
<It was bitterly cold: it was snowing.>
<She didn't go out: it was too cold.>

Notice also several clauses simply joined by commas:

<I came, I saw, I conquered.>
<I trembled, I quaked, I resolved.>

11.9 Subordination

Subordinate clauses are usually divided into three types by their function as elements of structure:
1 *adverbial* **2** *relative (or 'adjectival')* **3** *nominal (noun)*.
Modern grammar does not disagree with this, though it usually adds **(4)** *comment* clauses. And it sometimes separates comparison clauses from other types of adverbial clauses. However in traditional grammar, only adverb clauses and some noun clauses are introduced by conjunctions. The introducers of other clauses are relative pronouns and relative adverbs. Such an analysis obscures the considerable overlap that exists between all the words that can introduce finite subordinate clauses. Modern grammar therefore groups all such words together as subordinators.

11.10 Subordinators

Function	wh-words	that/as	Other
to introduce: adverbial clauses	*when, whenever, where, wherever, however, whatever, whoever, whichever* *No matter who/what/which* *whether . . . or while, whereas*	*so that* [purpose] *so . . . that* [result] *now that, seeing that, provided that, suppose that*, etc *as* [time, reason, manner, concession]	See 11.13-23 for a big group of conjs restricted to introducing adverbial clauses. Notice also: *if* [conditional] and ZERO with: (a) change of word order in conditionals (6.26) (b) non-finite and verbless clauses
nominal clauses	*when, where, why, how*; *what, who, which* (+ *ever*); *whose; whether . . .* (*or*)	*that*	ZERO is often possible (11.36) *if*
relative clauses	*when, where, why* [adverbs] *what, which, whose, who, whom*	*as* *that* [rel pro]	ZERO is possible with (i) 'contact' clauses (11.27-29) (ii) non-finite and verbless clauses

The table shows the extent of the overlap that exists among the subordinators introducing adverbial, nominal and relative clauses.

Wh-word subordinators include not only some true conjunctions (*while, whereas, whether*) but adverbs used as conjunctions (*why, how* etc) and some determiners and pronouns (*which* etc).

Many of these *wh*-words, and also *that* can introduce all three types of subordinate clause. *If* can introduce both nominal clauses and adverbial clauses (of condition); and ZERO is also general. (ZERO here means the optional omission of *that* or simply no conjunction). Notice that *as* is included here among relative pronouns because it is sometimes an alternative to *that* or *which*:

<He knew nothing about it, *as* soon became clear.>
See also 11.23.

It should be noticed that there is a difference between the ways true conjunctions and some other subordinators are used. Conjunctions join complete clauses, whereas some subordinators — particularly some *wh*-words — are an essential part of their clause, and the clause is incomplete without it. (See 11.29.)

11.11 Co-ordination

and, or, **but**	**A**	*My sister and I* are going to join a book club. This way you get the books *quickly but easily.* [Single words co-ordinated] If I'm not satisfied, I may return the books, __ *my membership* will be cancelled *and* I will owe nothing. [*and* understood] You could join a literary book club, __ a country book club or a history book club. [*or* understood] I'm going to join because I like books *and* (because) they are good value. [2 subordinate clauses] I enjoy thrillers *but* __ don't want to join a crime book club. [ellipsis of subject] I've sent off my cheque *and* __ am looking forward to receiving my first parcel. [order of clauses not reversible]
so, yet, **for**	**B**	I have just ordered four books, *so* I'll be busy. These books are cheap *yet* good. [single words co-ordinated] You have to take at least four books a year, *for* that's how the club works. [fml]
Correlatives	**C**	I *both* belong to a book club *and* borrow library books. You pay *either* now *or* later. (1) You can *either* pay now *or* later. [Note word order] (2) He refuses to join a book club, *nor* will he use a library. He has *neither* explained, *nor* (has he) apologised.

Co-ordinating conjunctions include:
    and, or, but
    so, yet, for, neither, nor
    both . . . and, either . . . or, neither . . . nor
    not only . . .(but also)

A *And/or/but* are the most central co-ordinators (according to the definitions in 11.3-4). *And* and *or* can join more than two clauses, and when this is done, *and* or *or* is only needed between the last two clauses and is understood between the others. Commas are necessary in writing. *But* cannot join more than two clauses, because we would understand an ellipted *and* or *or*. <You get three low-priced books now, __ you can buy as many bargain books as you like, *but* you must take at least four a year.> *And/or/but* can join two equal subordinate clauses.

When two clauses are joined by *and/or/but,* the subject of the second clause, if the same as the subject of the first, can be ellipted. (This cannot happen with subordinate conjunctions.) *And/or/but* can precede, but not follow, other conjunctions: <and so> <but yet> etc, not <*so and> <*yet but>.

In meaning, *and* is the most neutral conjunction. It may simply imply some sort of addition, or some similarity. In such cases the two clauses may be reversible. In other sentences the second clause may be the result of the first or later in time, in which case the order is important.

Or usually means an alternative. Sometimes both alternatives are possible, sometimes only one. (For *and* and *or* after imperatives — see 6.23.) *But* implies contrast.

B   *so* (meaning 'therefore', 'that's why') and *yet* (= 'but at the same time') are partly like co-ordinating conjunctions and partly like connecters (ie adverbs). Like *and/or/but* they can sometimes allow ellipsis of the subject, and *yet* can join single words: <cheap *yet* good>.

But *so* and *yet* are more like connecters or subordinators in allowing other conjunctions to precede them (*and so, but yet*). Notice that *so that* (meaning result) is like a co-ordinating conjunction in never introducing the first clause. But otherwise it is subordinating — see 11.19.

For is marginal. Like *and/or* it must come between two clauses, and it must always start a clause, without any other conjunction. Contrast *because:*

<'Why?' '*Because* I say so, *and because* it works like that.'>
But: <*'Why?' '*For* I say so, *and for* it works like that.'>
On the other hand *for* is like a subordinator or a connecter in not allowing subject ellipsis.

C   The correlative pairs (*both . . . and, either . . . or, neither . . . nor, not only . . . but also*) are used for emphasis. But the pairs are not merely emphatic versions of their second words, because the usage is slightly different. *Both . . . and* for example always needs some kind of ellipsis:

<*Both I have joined this book club and Tom's joined the library.>
When a pair joins single words, prescriptive grammar says that the two words of the pair must immediately precede the two units being joined (as in C1), but this does not in fact always happen (C2).

For *neither/nor* used separately to introduce a second clause or sentence — see 9.39.

11.12 Non-finite clauses with co-ordinating meaning

ADV   Non-finite clauses are usually analysed as subordinate (11.8-9), but sometimes *-ing* clauses seem to have more of a co-ordinating meaning:

<Mr Harold Evans finally resigned as editor of The Times last night, *ending days of confusion.*>
<The lenses compensate for the natural variations in intensity of daylight, *protecting your eyes from the strain of constant adjustment.*>
<A plane has crashed on an internal flight, *killing all 137 people on board.*>
Compare sentential relative clauses (11.30).

Subordinating conjunctions and adverbial clauses

11.13   **Form** Subordinating conjunctions introducing adverbial clauses can be single words (*as, because*), compounds (*as long as*), correlatives (*whether . . . or, so . . . that*). Some conjunctions are also adverbs (*where, since*) or prepositions (*since*).

Position

(a) Subordinating conjunctions themselves come at the beginning of their clause.

(b) Adverbial clauses — like adverbs — can appear in front-, mid- or end-position in a sentence (although mid is rare). In other words, adverbial clauses can precede or follow a main clause. But with correlatives, clause order is fixed.

Meaning Adverbial subordinators and their clauses are usually classified by the meaning relationship they bear (eg time, reason). Notice that some conjunctions appear under more than one heading — so that in some sentences the relationship may be ambiguous. Note especially : *as* (time, reason, manner, concession), *as long as* (time, condition), *if* (condition, concession), *in case* (purpose in British English, but condition in American English), *now that* (time, reason), *since* (time, reason), *so that* (purpose, result), *when* (time, concession), *while* (time, concession).

11.14 Reduced clauses

Some, but not all, subordinating conjunctions can be followed by non-finite or verbless clauses. Some grammarians call all such clauses 'abbreviated clauses' and reserve the name 'reduced clauses' for reduced relatives (8.31). *Current English Grammar* uses the term 'reduced clauses' for both.

11.15 Relationship to single adverbs

Finite and non-finite adverbial clauses broadly fulfil the same function in a sentence as some single adverbs or phrases. Sometimes all four possibilities exist. For example, time can be expressed:

    <I shall leave
$\begin{cases} \textit{soon.} > \text{[adverb]} \\ \textit{after dinner.} > \text{[prepositional phrase]} \\ \textit{when I've had dinner.} > \text{[finite clause]} \\ \textit{after dining.} > \text{[non-finite clause]} \end{cases}$

But adverbial clauses also express concepts (eg reason, result) that cannot be expressed by single adverbs. There are also concepts that can be expressed by non-finite or verbless clauses (eg *with/without* clauses) where there are no corresponding finite adverbial clauses.

11.16 Time

As I entered the room, I saw the great picture facing me. (1)
As he grew older, he feared death more. (2)
Once he had bought a house, he never sold it. (3)
Whenever he could afford to, he bought back his own paintings. (4)
When he died, many hitherto unknown paintings were discovered. (5)
He was still working on a painting when he died. (6)
While the war was raging, he was painting. (7)
Now (that) he is dead, we can see these new masterpieces. (8)
He had no sooner died than}
He had hardly died when } the family arguments began. (9)

Time conjunctions include: after, as, before, immediately, once, since, till, until, when, whenever, while, now (that), as/so long as, as soon as, no sooner . . . than, hardly/scarcely . . . when.
Also a few noun phrases: <The moment/Every time I entered . . .>

(a) As/when/while are not synonyms. When has the greatest range of meanings. As often means 'at that very moment' (1). It is also common in structures of parallel development — note comparative forms in (2). When often puts two events in sequence (5). (But not <*as he died> which would suggest 'while he was actually dying'.) Both when and whenever can be used for repeated habit (4). Normally a when-clause (being subordinate) contains 'given' or less important information, and the main clause contains the important new information — the focus. But sometimes the relationship is reversed and the new information comes in the when clause. Note clause order and tenses (6).
While suggests duration, and is not for brief single actions: <*While I entered the room, I saw. . .>. It is often used with a progressive tense. When/while can both suggest a background to some other event:

    <When/while he lived/was living in Provence, many people visited him.>

    <While the war was raging/raged, he . . .>
But <*When the war raged, he painted> (which would suggest cause — and effect.)
(b) No sooner . . . than/hardly . . . when usually take perfect tenses (9) (see 9.39 for inversion).
(c) Reduced clauses: Only some time subordinators can take reduced clauses, including:
when/whenever/while: <When (he was) a young man,/whenever possible,/while living in France, he . . .>
after/before/since + ing: <After achieving fame, he . . .>.
until + -en: <Until finished, a painting was shown to no one.>
Since (time) occurs in non-finite clauses: <Since inheriting the money, she has . . .> but not in verbless clauses <*Since young, she has . . .>. <Since his youth> is acceptable, but this is [preposition + noun], and does not form a separate clause.

11.17 Place

He lived *where he liked.*
He painted *wherever he happened to be.*

This is not a very important category. Use of *where* and *wherever* in clauses of place should be distinguished from
(a) their usage as interrogative adverbs:
    <*Where/Wherever* did you get that hat?> and
(b) *where* as a relative adverb:
    <The shop *where I got it* has closed down.>

11.18 Cause/reason

As/Since/Seeing that he left no will, there were bound to be lawsuits. (1)
He didn't sell all his paintings to private buyers, *because he wanted the public to enjoy them.* (2)
He was very rich, *because I read it in the paper.* (3)

As/since clauses tend to come before a main clause, because they provide a given circumstance for the new fact of the main clause, which receives the end-focus (1).
Because clauses tend to follow, because the emphasis is on the reason (2). A sentence with a negative in the main clause plus a *because* clause can be ambiguous (though intonation and context can make the meaning clear).
    <He didn't sell his paintings . . . because he wanted the public to enjoy them.>
can mean (a) 'He did *not* sell them [*fact*], *because* he wanted . . . [*reason*]'
or (b) 'He did not (sell them because he wanted . . .) [*not for this reason; he sold them for some other reason*]'.
As and *since* cannot be used in this second way.
    Because clauses (but not *as/since*) can be used alone in answer to *why* questions: <Because he was famous.>
They can also be used with a rather loose connection to the main clause (3).
    Reason clauses normally need a finite verb. *Because* is never used in reduced clauses. But *because of* and some other complex prepositions (*due to, owing to*) can express reason (10.5).

11.19 Purpose and result

A Purpose
So that he would/could have more space for painting, he bought a castle.
He sometimes painted realistic pictures, *in case the public would/should think* he couldn't.
Buy one of his paintings now, *in case they get more expensive.*

B Result

He bought a castle, *so* (that) he had more space to paint in.				(1)

He was	*so*	brilliant	(that) he became very wealthy. (2)
He painted		brilliantly	

This is	*such*	a marvellous picture	(that) I am lost in admiration. (3)
He showed		originality	
He painted		marvellous pictures	

His talent was	*such*	(that) he deserved to be famous. (4)

Purpose subordinators include *so that, in order that; in case* (Brit Eng = negative purpose); *for fear that, lest* (both *rare* and *fml*).

Result includes: *so that, so/such . . . that*.

Since successful purpose may lead to result, the overlap in conjunctions for these two meanings is understandable. But note the differences:

(a) *So that* clauses of result can normally only take end-position (with the main clause given first), but purpose clauses can come before or after the main clause.

(b) Result clauses usually contain ordinary tenses (denoting facts), but purpose clauses often contain modals, showing that the meaning is tentative.

Ambiguity sometimes occurs:

<Someone removed his brushes *so that* he couldn't paint.>

This could mean 'so that he wasn't able to' (result), or 'so that he wouldn't be able to' (purpose).

(c) In result clauses, *so* and *that* can be separated, with [*so* + adjective/adverb] in the main clause and *that* introducing the subordinate (2). For nouns, the pattern is [*such* + noun + *that* (3)]. *Such* can also function alone as a pronoun (4). *That* is sometimes omitted. For inversion with result clauses see 1.12.

Although result clauses normally follow the clause that explains the cause, it is possible to reverse the order with two independent sentences or clauses:

<I am lost in admiration — it is *such* a marvellous picture.>

This can sometimes lead to ambiguity, as to whether an intensifying *so* (of result — *so that*) or a connecter *so* is intended:

<He was an eccentric man. So many people went to see him.>

Does this mean 'He became eccentric because such a lot of people . . .' or 'He was eccentric. Therefore a lot of people . . .'?

For connecters of result — see 9.35.

11.20 Condition

If (they were) collected together, his paintings would fill a museum.
Unless (they are) looked after, they will deteriorate.
You could buy one, *provided you had the money*.
I'll lend you the money, *on condition/so long as you take my advice*.
Suppose they found a will now, what would happen?
Whether you like his work or not, you can't deny its power.
Why not go to Megao? *In case the Italian map was correct* we could go from there back to Goro. [Am Eng]

> Conjunctions of condition include: *if, unless, provided (that), providing (that), on condition (that), as/so long as, suppose (that), supposing (that), whether . . . or.* Note: *in case* (Am Eng with conditional meaning).

Unless introduces a negative condition, and is often glossed as *if . . . not*. This is usually true, but *unless* is odd or impossible in unreal conditions:

    <If he hadn't become a painter, perhaps he would have become a writer.>

But <*Unless he had become a painter, he would have become a writer.>

Suppose/supposing (as conjunctions) normally introduce questions. They are obviously verbal in form — which again shows the overlap of word classes.

Reduced clauses can be introduced by *if, unless* and *whether . . . not,* but not the other conjunctions listed.

For tenses with conditionals, and for conditional signalled by inversion, see 6.21-26.

11.21 Concession and contrast

> *Although/Though he was Spanish,* he spent most of his life in France.
> *While/Whilst I don't really like modern art,* I find his work impressive.
> He was famous and rich in his lifetime, *while/whereas many artists die in poverty and obscurity.*
> *Even if you don't like art,* you must have heard of him.
> *Old though he was,* he continued to paint.
> *Hard as I try,* my paintings are no good.
> *Much as I admire him,* I don't like all his work.
> *However many pictures he painted,* he went on painting more.
> *No matter what the subjects were,* his paintings sold.

> Conjunctions of concession and contrast include: *although, though, while, whilst, whereas, even if, even though,* adj/adv + *as/though, much as,* wh-compounds (*whoever, however etc*) and *no matter what/who etc*

There is an overlap in meaning with condition. Notice especially *whether . . . or,* which could be listed here, and *even if* which is obviously partly condition.

When *while* implies a sort of parallelism (perhaps a mixture of contrast and time) either clause can come first:

    <*While many artists die in poverty,* he was famous in his lifetime.> (Compare the example in the table).

But when *while* is strictly concession, the *while* clause comes first and the main clause with the new information second:

    <While I don't really like . . .>

Whilst is a less common variant of *while* with the same meaning and function. *Whereas* only means contrast, not concession: <*Whereas I don't really like modern art, I find . . .>.

As/though (but not: *although*) are sometimes used in the pattern
[adj/adv + *as/though* + subject + verb]
<Old though he was, he . . .>
No matter what/who etc function like *whatever/whoever* in these
clauses ie <Whatever the subjects were, his paintings sold.>
Reduced clauses can be introduced by *although, though, even if.*

11.22 Manner

He painted *as only he could.*			
As he had wished, his collection of 'old masters' went to the nation.			} (1)
His children contested the will, *as did his grandchildren.*			

It sounded		you liked his work.	
	as if		
You sound		you like(d) it.	} (2)
	as though		
He painted		he was/were inspired.	

I wish I could paint *like he did.* [infml]	
Do it *how you want.* (infml)	} (3)

There is always an element of comparison in manner clauses — they
bear little resemblance to manner adverbs — and for this reason some
grammarians do not make a separate category for them. But there are
differences:
Manner clauses (a) roughly answer the questions 'How?' 'In what
way?';
(b) are introduced by a simple (one-word or two-word) conjunction;
(c) can sometimes precede the main clause.
Clauses of comparison (11.23) (a) compare two or more people or things
for equality or inequality;
(b) need a comparison element in the main clause (ie they use
correlatives); and
(c) can only come after the main clause.
As (1) appears in many different subordinate clauses, with varying
meanings.
<*as did his grandchildren*> If rephrased without inversion <as his
grandchildren did>, this would clearly be manner or comparison. With
inversion, it is perhaps more like co-ordination (ie and his
grandchildren did too).
As if/as though (2) Tenses vary.
<You sound as if you like it.> [present — presumably fact]
<He painted as if he was/were inspired.> [more hypothetical]
Like and *how* (3) are sometimes acceptable in informal English, though
prescriptive grammar forbids them.
See also *as/like* as prepositions (10.4).
For *as you know* etc — see comment clauses (11.51).
Reduced clauses are possible with *as if/as though* (eg as if afraid to).

11.23 Comparison

He was *as* rich *as* he was famous.	
Some artists are *not so/as* lucky *as* he was.	(1)
He bought up *as* many of his early paintings *as* he could.	

He *was richer than* any of his fellow artists were. He became *more* famous *than* he had imagined possible. His wife loved the countryside *more than* he did/him/her husband.	(2)

ADV	That is *as* much *as*/is known about him/is necessary/seems relevant. There is always *more* work to do *than* can be afforded.	(3)

Comparison clauses are traditionally treated as a kind of adverbial clause. Modern grammar sometimes treats them separately, because the main clause is often incomplete — ie it must contain an element (*as, -er, more, less*) that points the need for the subordinate clause, introduced by *as* or *than*, which must come second. Prescriptive grammar likes *not so* (rather than *not as*) in the negative, but *not as . . . as* is common (1).

(2) In comparisons of comparative degree, the comparative element may be an adjective or an adverb, or [*more/less* + adverb/noun].
    <more quickly than/less money than>.

Than me or *than I?* Comparison clauses are frequently reduced very considerably by ellipsis. When the comparative clause contains a verb, if the subject is a pronoun, then subject (not object) pronoun is essential:
    <than he did.> <*than him did.>
The difficulty arises when the clause is reduced right down to the pronoun. The usual comment is that *than he/I* etc is more formal and somehow more correct, while *than him/me* etc is informal (and 'not good grammar'.) Modern grammarians prefer to view *than* as a subordinator when a clause (ie subject and verb) follows, but as a preposition when only a noun or pronoun follows. On this analysis *than me* is in fact more correct than *than I*. It is certainly much more usual. But the formality/informality distinction remains true for some people. The use of an object pronoun, as of a noun, can lead to ambiguity:
    <His wife loved the countryside more than him/her husband.>
Does this mean 'more than she loved him'? or 'more than he loved it'?

ADV (3) *As . . . as* and *more . . . than* can be used in a type of clause that seems to fall between a comparison and a relative clause. Very oddly for English, the second clause lacks an expressed subject (it has neither noun nor pronoun) though the subject is clearly deducible from the first clause. The verb is often a linking verb or in the passive. (Compare 3.36 and 11.10.)

11.24 Proportion

The *older* he got, *the more* rumours there were about hidden paintings. The *more* famous he became, *the higher* the prices his pictures fetched. The *sooner, the better*. The *brighter* the light, *the darker* the lens. The *more tickets* we sell, *the better* I'll be pleased. The *more* I try, *the less* I seem to achieve.

Comparative forms are essential in this structure, but the meaning is parallel change or proportion rather than comparative degree. Technically *the* in these structures is not the definite article, but an adverb, and [*the* + comparative adjective] must be followed by another *the* before a noun: <the higher the prices . . .>

11.25 Non-finite and verbless adverbial clauses

A	*On arriving home*, he took off his shoes. [time]
	Without his shoes on, he slipped on the polished floor. [circumstance]
	Despite having taken off his shoes, he made a noise. [concession]
	He disturbed everyone *by coming home late*. [manner]
B	*All being well*, he won't do that again. [condition]
	I couldn't sleep *with my front door not locked*. [circumstance]
C	*Taking off his shoes*, he crept up the stairs. [time = after]
	Carrying his shoes, he crept up the stairs. [at the same time]
	Afraid of the dark, he switched on all the lights. [reason]
	A foolish young man, he acts without thinking. [reason]
	Whether annoyed or not, they didn't complain.
D	He took off his shoes *(so as) to make less noise*. [purpose]
	He took them off *so as not to make a noise*. [neg. purpose]
	To see him, you'd never think he was 20. [condition]
	He was an idiot *not to have realised*. [reason]
	I got to the museum *(only) to find it was shut*. [consequence]
	He isn't so unworldly *as to despise money*. [result — fml]
	He isn't such an unworldly man *as to . . .* [result — fml]
	He lived long enough *to become a legend in his lifetime*. [result]
E	*Rather/Sooner than sell any of his homes*, he kept them all.

Reduced adverbial clauses may be introduced by conjunctions as shown in sections 11.12-23. But there are other possibilities for non-finite and verbless adverbial clauses, and a number of meanings are possible that do not exist with finite adverbial clauses.

A Clauses can be introduced by certain prepositions:
on [time], *by* [manner], *despite/in spite of* [concession], *besides* [adding], *instead of* [contrast], *with/without* [circumstance]. Verbs following prepositions are always in the -ing form (10.7)

B Participle clauses can have their own subjects, and no element shared with the main clause. Such clauses are called 'absolute' constructions. They usually have no subordinator, but they too can be introduced by *with/without*. (Compare the way a subject can be given to a *to*-infinitive clause with *for*.)

C In clauses with no subordinator (often participle clauses) the exact meaning relationship with the main clause may be uncertain. Time and reason are common meanings. Notice how — unusually — a noun phrase may have adverbial force <A foolish young man, he . . .>

D *To*-infinitives, sometimes expanded to *so as (not) to* or *in order (not) to*, often express purpose. Less often *to*-infinitives may mean consequence, condition, result.

E *bare infinitives* Non-finite clauses with *rather than/sooner than* are unusual in that they use a bare infinitive. The meaning is preference. Compare *would rather/would sooner* DO (4.16).

11.26 Unattached participles

When the subject of a participle clause is not expressed, it is normally understood to be the subject of the main clause. It is usually poor grammar, and sometimes absurd if this rule is broken: <*Trying to be quiet, a floorboard creaked.>

But the 'rule' is often broken when the subject is vaguely understood to be 'one', 'we', 'you', people in general:

<Looking ahead to the weekend, temperatures will be warmer.> [weather forecast]

<Talking to people who work in the NHS, a very different picture emerges.> [When one talks . . .]

The rule does not apply at all with comment clauses (11.51).

Relative clauses

11.27

A	**Defining** (no commas)	
(a)	*Personal —*	
	subject	The girl *that/who lives next door* is now in Scotland. (11.3 and 11.29)
	object	Is that the man __/*that/who(m) you met on holiday*?
	obj of prep	The girl __/*that/who I was telling you about* is in Scotland.
		The girl *of whom I was talking* is now in Scotland. [fml]
	possessive	The young man *whose car was stolen* went to the police.
(b)	*Non-personal —*	
	subject	A dog *that/which barks all night* is a nuisance.
		I would hate to have a car *that/which kept breaking down.*
	object	I'm enjoying this book __/*that/which I borrowed from the library.*
	obj of prep	That cat __/*that/which I am so fond of* belongs to an old lady.
		The cat *of which I am so fond* belongs to an old lady. [fml]
	possessive	Last year they stayed in some Welsh village { *whose name they have now forgotten.* / *that/which they've forgotten the name of.* / *of which they've forgotten the name.* / *the name of which they've forgotten.* }
B	**Non-defining** (with commas)	
(a)	*Personal —*	
	subject	Susan Grant, *who came on holiday with us*, is now in Scotland.
		My dog Fido, *who always sleeps on my bed*, enjoys holidays.
	object	My brother, *who(m) you met last year*, has got a new job.
	obj of prep	His fiancée Joan, *who(m) we were talking about/about whom we were talking*, is coming tonight.
	possessive	The Grants, *whose house has been burgled six times*, never go on holiday now.
(b)	*Non-personal —*	
	subject	I don't like the Grants' dog, *which barks all night*.
		Their car, *which is always breaking down*, is second-hand.
	object	I'm re-reading 'Heart of Darkness', *which I haven't read for years*.
	obj of prep	St Paul's Cathedral, *which the guide was referring to,/to which the guide was referring* [fml], was designed by Sir Christopher Wren.
	possessive	Canterbury, *whose cathedral is famous,/the cathedral of which is famous* [fml], is in Kent.

11.28 Function/position

Relative pronouns link a postmodifying clause to a preceding noun (or noun phrase). They are initial in their clause (though sometimes immediately preceded by a preposition.) This position may involve the clause itself in an unusual word order:

    <a village *whose name they have forgotten*> [They have forgotten its name.]

11.29 Form

Relative pronouns are listed in 3.35. The choice of the right pronoun depends on a combination of three factors: whether it
(a) stands for a personal or non-personal noun (or noun phrase);
(b) is subject or object in its clause;
(c) is defining or non-defining.

In form, only the pronouns for people (not things) distinguish between subject and object (*who/whom*), and even here modern English often uses *who* for object informally. But a much more important distinction between subject and object is the fact that ZERO __ (the omission of any pronoun) is frequent in object position in defining clauses. The resulting relative clause, lacking any surbordinator, is known as a 'contact clause'. In general, any finite English clause needs a subject. So if the person or thing signified by the noun that the relative clause refers to is to be the subject of that clause, a relative pronoun is essential to give the clause its own subject: <the girl *that/who lives next door*>. But if the preceding noun is in an object relationship to the verb of the relative clause, no object is needed in defining clauses: <the man __ *you met on holiday*>. No ordinary object pronouns (*him, it, them* etc) are added in relative clauses, defining or non-defining, since the relative pronoun or ZERO stands for the object: <*Is that the man __ you met *him* on holiday?*>

Except when *whose* is necessary, *that* is possible for people and things in all positions in defining clauses, unless a preposition is used before the pronoun, when *whom* or *which* is needed. *That* (never *which*) is used after
(a) *all* and other indefinite pronouns:
    <*All that glitters* is not gold.>
    <I'll do *anything (that) I can*.>
(b) superlatives:
    <That was the nicest/most extraordinary thing *that ever happened to me*.>

Whose Some people dislike using *whose* with non-personal possessors because of its link with *who*. But it is common in both formal and informal English:
    <. . . some village *whose name* they've now forgotten.>
    <The Way . . . turns up along a dismantled railway, *whose course* is now taken by a pipeline bringing water from Loch Lomond.>
    <The house *of whose park* this lake was the chief ornament has been demolished.>
Sometimes the alternative *of which* construction is possible and not too stilted, though it tends to be formal (see examples in the table). But it is difficult to rewrite the third example without an extremely odd result <? The house the park of which this lake was the chief ornament of . . .>.

11.30 Defining and non-defining

When they in some way define the preceding noun phrase, relative clauses are called 'defining' (or 'restrictive') relatives:

<'The girl is now in Scotland.' 'What girl?' 'The girl *that/who lives next door.*'>

There are no commas. But some relative clauses do not define — they merely add additional information about a person or thing that is already defined. These are 'non-defining' relative clauses. Note the commas:

<Susan Grant, *who lives next door,* is now in Scotland.>

Defining relative clauses clearly postmodify the preceding noun phrase and are part of it, and for this reason relative clauses are sometimes called 'adjectival clauses'. But non-defining clauses have a less clear function. Some are nearer to a co-ordinating clause:

<This is my brother, *who will tell you about his job.*>

Such a co-ordinating function is even more obvious with some *which*-clauses, where the pronoun does not refer back to a previous noun phrase, but to the whole main clause. *Which* in this use is called a 'sentential' relative and cannot be replaced by *that*:

<I met McEnroe, *which really thrilled me.*>

It is significant that *that,* a mark of subordination, is only possible with defining clauses. This strongly suggests that non-defining clauses are not really subordinate at all. So, once again, we notice an overlap of categories — the traditional relative clause includes subordinate clauses of adjectival function and also quasi-co-ordinate clauses. 'Relative' is therefore a better name than 'adjectival'. Defining relative clauses are common in both spoken and written English, but non-defining relatives tend to be more formal and are commoner in written English.

11.31 Relative adverbs

After a few words denoting time and place, it is possible to replace ordinary relative pronouns with other *wh*-words (namely *when* and *where*):

<the time of year *when* everyone goes on holiday>
<a place *where* I should hate to live>.

But this has limited usage and ordinary relative pronouns are possible:
<the time of year *that/at which* . . .> <a place *that* I should hate to live in / a place *in which* . . .>.

Words like *reason* or *explanation* are also sometimes followed by *why*-clauses, but the result is more like apposition than a relative clause. Contrast:

<The reason *why he refused* isn't clear.>
<The reason *that he gave* was feeble.>

In the first sentence we can analyse *why he refused* as a nominal clause in apposition. We can also say <The reason isn't clear. Why he refused isn't clear.> But we cannot do the same with the second: <*That he gave was feeble.> Nor can we say <*The reason why he gave . . .>. See also 2.38 and 11.36.

253

11.32 Non-finite and verbless relative clauses

Reduced relative clauses are discussed in chapter 8, where they are contrasted with the use of adjectives and participles in attributive position. Relative pronouns are not used in reduced clauses. Both defining and non-defining reduced relatives are possible:

<A dog *barking all night* is a nuisance.>
<The Grants' dog, *awakened by the noise,* started barking.>

11.33 As

As can introduce relative clauses, mainly after *the same* and *such:*

<We're going to *the same* place *as* we went to last year.>
<I'll give you *such* information *as* I have.>

Nominal clauses

11.34 Form

Finite nominal clauses are introduced by:
(a) *that* (conjunction, not relative pronoun) or ZERO
(b) *wh*-words and *if*. (*To*-infinitive clauses following *wh*-words may be thought of as non-finite noun clauses.)
The relationship of a nominal clause to its main clause is different from that of other subordinate clauses. Most adverbial or relative clauses could be omitted and still leave a complete grammatical sentence, just as the omission of single adverbs or adjectives would:

[After he died — *adverbial*] <his heirs argued about his fortune.>
<The girl [who lives next door — *relative*] is now in Scotland.>

But the omission of a nominal clause — like the omission of a noun (except in apposition) leaves an incomplete main clause:

(That she has achieved such fame) <* surprises her.>
<* From (what you say) she's brilliant.>
<* It's a question of> [which to choose.]

11.35 Nominal relative clauses

Some grammarians make a distinction between *wh*-word clauses derivable from interrogative sentences eg <I don't know who says so.>, and the so-called nominal relative, in which the *wh*-word acts as a sort of double pronoun:

<*Whoever* says that is a fool.> [any person who]
<I want *what* you want.> [the things that]

Most nominal clauses have a fairly abstract meaning, but nominal relative clauses can refer to people and things. Nominal relative clauses therefore (but not other nominal clauses) can function as indirect object:

<I'll give *whoever wants one* a copy.>

and as complement of object (11.37).

11.36 Functions of nominal clauses (See table: 11.37)

Both *that*-clauses and *wh*-clauses (including *if*-clauses) fulfil most of the functions in a sentence that an ordinary noun or noun phrase can do. *Wh*-clauses have more usages, and in particular can follow prepositions.

Nominal clauses in sentences with introductory *it* are analysed as subject. (But see 'cleft' sentences 11.49).

A nominal clause as subject usually takes singular verb, but nominal relative clauses can take a plural verb. Contrast:

        <*How she finds so many recipes* amazes me.> [ordinary noun clause]

        <*What we need* are some oranges.> [nominal relative]

Some verbs (eg *ignore*) cannot be immediately followed by a *that*-clause, but they can be followed by *the fact that* etc. In such cases the *that*-clause is analysed as being in apposition to the preceding noun (see also 2.38).

That can be omitted before a direct object clause, and sometimes in other predicative uses. Compare the possible omission of relative *that* in object position. *That* is never omitted when the nominal clause comes first in a sentence, even if this is a direct object clause:

        <*That there are other first-class cookery writers* she would not dispute.>

11.37 Functions of nominal clauses: summary

Function	*that*- clauses	wh-word clauses (including non-finite)
Subject	*That she has achieved such fame* surprises her. Is it true *(that) she's never had cookery lessons*?	*How she wrote her first book* is a story in itself. *Where to start* was a problem. It's not *what you know* but *who you know*!
DO	She believes *(that) vegetables are best eaten in season.*	You can see *why her kitchen was once compared to an old photograph.* Do you know *whether she's writing another book*? She's wondering *what to do.*
C of BE (ie SC)	Her belief is *that preparing good food is a labour of love.*	The problem was *which would be better/which to choose.*
Appo	The idea *that she collects her recipes all over the world* is probably correct. You can't deny the fact *that she's brilliant.*	The question, *where she gets her recipes*, is now solved. The question *where to start* is a worry.
C of adj	She's glad *(that) people like her books.*	I am not sure *who gave me this copy.* I am uncertain *how to cook this.*
C of prep		From *what you say*, she's brilliant. It's a question of *which to choose.*
C of obj (rare) nominal relative only		They said she could call her new book *whatever she wished.*

IO (rare) nominal relative only		I'll give *whoever* *wants* *one* a copy.

11.38 Nominal clauses and reported speech

When we report what someone says, whether we quote the words directly or indirectly, their words can be analysed as the object of the saying verb:

<She says: '*Fruit is best eaten in season*'.> [direct speech]

<'*Fruit is best eaten in season*', she says.> [direct speech]

<She says/said *that fruit is best eaten in season*.> [reported speech]

With reported speech, the quoted words are grammatically a nominal clause. Details about tenses are given in 11.45-48. Nominal clauses may similarly follow verbs of mental processes (eg *realise*, *regret*). But notice the possible semantic differences:

<Tim said that the food was terrible.> [where the nominal clause is a report that may or may not be true], and

<Tim realised/regretted that the food was terrible.> [where the nominal clause represents fact].

11.39 Transferred negation

With some verbs of mental processes — particularly *believe*, *consider*, *imagine*, *suppose*, *think*, a *not* that belongs, as far as meaning is concerned, in the subordinate clause is often transferred to the main clause:

<I *don't think* (*that*) Adrian will telephone now.> rather than

<* I think Adrian won't telephone now.>

11.40 'Reduced' nominal clauses

ADV   Some grammarians analyse the use of *to*-infinitive and *-ing* phrases when functioning as subject or following catenative verbs, and in various other positions, as non-finite clauses. Such clauses are not so obviously reduced clauses as reduced adverbial and adjectival clauses are, and there are technical difficulties about this kind of analysis. For practical purposes we can ignore the problem, and usage is dealt with separately in 7.20-22.

Clauses with a [*wh*-word + *to*-infinitive] are, however, fairly obviously reduced finite *wh*-clauses:

<We are wondering where we should go/where to go.>

Indirect speech

11.41   As explained in 11.38, reported speech uses nominal clauses for the quoted words.

(a) *that*- clauses (sometimes with *that* omitted — see 11.36) are used to report statements:

<She says that vegetables are best eaten in season.>

(b) *wh*-clauses (including *if/whether* clauses) indicate reported questions:

<I asked how much it cost.>

Notice that <I asked how much . . .> reports 'How much . . .?' but <I told them how much . . .> does not report the actual words (eg 'It's £10').

The *wh*-words cannot be omitted from these clauses.

It should be noticed that, whereas some people use the tems 'indirect speech' and 'reported speech' interchangeably, others make a distinction. Reported speech in its narrower sense means reporting what people have said (although not in the completely unaltered form of direct speech). Indirect speech is a wider term and therefore a more accurate one to cover such items as questions-within-questions (which are indirect questions with no reporting involved):

<Can you tell me if they are English recipes?>

In a still wider sense the term 'indirect speech' can usefully if loosely be used to cover sentences involving verbs of mental processes with nominal clauses as object (11.37-39), because such verbs follow the same 'rules' for tense changes and so on, as real reported speech:

<She thinks/believes that vegetables are best eaten in season.>

11.42 Direct, reported — or hybrid

A	Direct	'You are welcome to come. Would you like to bring Mary?', he said.
B	Reported	He said (that) I was welcome to come/go, and asked me if I would like to bring/take Mary.
C	Hybrid	He said (that) I was welcome to come/go, and *would I like to bring/take Mary.* [Note word order of question and absence of subordinator.]

There are two main ways of accurately reporting what people say:

A **Direct speech** — quoting the actual words. In writing, this is shown by quotation marks and other marks of punctuation.

B **Reported speech** The term 'reported speech' in course books means almost the exact words, subject to 'rules' about changes of verb tenses, pronouns, adverbs etc.

C **Hybrid** A sort of mixture of direct and reported is sometimes found.

In actuality there are, of course, many ways of reporting what people say, ranging from direct quotation or close reporting to freer summary and paraphrase. Grammatically, such reporting may include many structures in addition to nominal clauses.

Eg '*Why don't you . . .*' could be reported <They advised me to . . .>

'*I'm terribly sorry*' could be reported <He apologised for . . .>

'*No*' could be reported as <He denied it.> or <He refused.>

Commands in reported speech generally become infinitives:

'*Please (don't) go*' becomes <They asked/told us (not) to go.>

11.43 Indirect questions: *if/whether*

If-clauses and *whether*-clauses are both used in indirect questions, but usage is slightly different as shown over. *Whether*-clauses, but not normally *if*-clauses, can also function as the subject of a sentence:

<Whether these are easy recipes doesn't worry her.>

	if	*whether*
Indirect questions	I asked *if/whether* they were English recipes — or not. Do you know *if/whether* they are English or Scottish recipes.	
directly followed by *or not*	*if or not . . .	I wonder *whether or not* they are Scottish.
+ infin clause	*if to	She is wondering *whether to* illustrate the book herself.

11.44 *say/tell*

Direct speech	*Statements & Commands*	'I'm frightened. Listen! Don't move,'	{ Tom said (to us). said Tom. Tom told us/them.
		Tom said, 'I'm frightened. Listen! Don't move.'	
	Questions	'What's that noise?'	{ Tom said (to us). said Tom. asked Tom. Tom asked (us).
Reported speech	*Statements*	Tom said } Tom told us } (that) he was frightened.	
	Commands	Tom told us } to listen. Tom asked us } not to move.	
	Questions	Tom asked (us) what the noise was.	

The commonest verbs used when reporting speech, both directly and indirectly, are *say* and *tell*. There are important differences of grammatical usage.

Say — can precede its subject (ie inversion is possible) when both verb and subject follow direct speech.
— can be used with direct questions.

Tell — normally needs an indirect object (*us, them* etc).
— it can be used with direct and indirect commands.
Say is not used in the pattern <*say someone to DO>.

Ask — (or a similar verb) is needed with reported questions.
Indirect object is optional when *ask* is used to report real questions, but is needed if used like *tell* to report a command.

11.45 Changes of tense, pronouns, adverbs etc

Indirect speech often entails using different verb tenses, pronouns and adverbs from those in the original direct speech. But the changes are not made according to some rigid 'rules' unique to indirect speech. They simply follow from the fact that we write or speak with the tenses, pronouns etc natural to *our* viewpoint *here* and *now* (5.19).
Tenses changes are therefore only made when there is a time shift between our *reporting* viewpoint and the viewpoint of the original words. Tables 11.46-48 should be taken as guidelines only.
Pronouns, adverbs etc Pronouns, adverbs (of time and place) and some determiners may also change according to the same basic principle, that is, if there is a shift between the viewpoint of the original speaker and the new (reporting) speaker/writer.

Examples:	Direct	Indirect
	here	there
	now	then
	today	that day
	last night	the night before
	yesterday	the day before/the previous day
	two days ago	two days before/two days earlier
	this evening	that evening
	this (book)	the book/it etc
	come	go
	bring	take

11.46 Tense changes : essential

Present tenses in *direct speech*		*Past reporting verb and changed time context* + *indirect speech (past tenses)*
A *Pres simple*	'I *feel* ill today.'	He said (that) he *felt* ill that day. or Last Wednesday he said (that) he *felt* ill.
Pres prog	'I *am not staying* any longer.'	He said he *wasn't staying* any longer (and he left).
Pres perf simple	'I *have had* enough.' 'Oh dear, I've *forgotten* my key.'	He told me he *had had* enough. I realised I *had forgotten* my key.
Pres perf prog	'I *have been waiting* ages.'	He said he *had been waiting* ages.
B *Modals*	'I *can't stay*.' 'I'*ll telephone* soon.' 'Anything *may happen*.'	He said he *couldn't stay*. He said he *would telephone* soon. He maintained that anything *might happen*.
(shall/will)	'Shall I/we call the doctor for you, Joan? (1)	I/He/They asked if I/he/they *should* call the doctor for her. (1)
	'Shall/Will I/we be seeing you at the meeting?' (2)	I/We asked her if I/we *would/(should) be seeing* her at the meeting. You/He/They asked me (etc) if you (etc) *would be seeing* me at the meeting. (2)
	'I/We shall/will be all right.' (3)	I/We said I/we *should/would be* all right. You/He/She/They said you (etc) *would be* all right. (3)

In general, tense changes are only essential when:
(a) the reporting verb is *past* (*said, asked,* etc) and additionally (b) there is a change of time context (ie our reporting *now* is different from the original speaker's *now*).
This commonly happens when the reported verbs are present (A), including present perfect tense and also (B) *can, may, shall, will.*

shall: should or would?
Shall I/we . . .? questions (B1), when the meaning is a suggestion, an offer or a request for advice, are normally reported as *should*, even when the pronoun is changed to 2nd or 3rd person. Other uses of *shall* where *will* is also possible (B2 and 3) — including questions about the future — are normally reported as *would. Would* is essential for 2nd and 3rd person — although *should* is possible after *I/we*.

11.47 Tense changes: usually optional

Direct speech	Past reporting verb + indirect speech
A 'I *feel* ill today.' 'It *will* happen by the year 2000 AD.' 'What *are* you *doing*?' Honesty *is* the best policy. Water *boils* at 100°C.	*TIME CONTEXT UNCHANGED* He told me (that) he *feels/felt* ill today. She said it *will/would* happen by the year 2000 AD. I asked you what you *are/were doing*. *TIMELESS TRUTHS* I was told years ago that honesty *is/was* the best policy. I was amazed he didn't know that water *boils/boiled* at 100°C.
B 'I *loved* her dearly.' 'I *forgot* it.' 'I *loved* her once/in those days.' 'I *was* just *going* to telephone him when he *arrived*.	*TIME CONTEXT CHANGED, BUT REPORTED VERBS ALREADY PAST* He said he *had loved* (? loved) her dearly. He said he *had forgotten/forgot* it. He said he *loved*/(? had loved) her once/in those days. She told me she *was* just *going* to . . ./ (? *had* just *been going* to . . .) when he *arrived.*/(? *had arrived.*)

Tense changes are possible, but usually optional, when only some of the conditions in 11.46 apply — in particular, if the reporting verb is past, but:

A the time context is unchanged. This includes reported verbs in present tenses referring to timeless truths. *Or*

B the reported verb is already in a past tense.

Past simple and past progressive sometimes change to past perfect simple or progressive if the need is felt to state clearly that the action was 'perfected' before the original speaker spoke (compare 5.13). But whereas we are always aware that present time and past time are different, the distinction between past and some earlier past is usually far less important — they are both past! This helps to explain why present perfect must be reported as past perfect (there is 'perfection' and a change from present to past time) (11.46) but past simple often remains unchanged, in writing as in speech, though past perfect is possible.

To put this another way, past perfect tenses in reported speech may represent past perfect, present perfect or past tenses in direct speech, while past simple may report past simple or present simple:

Direct speech	Reported speech
I had (always) loved her. ———————	He said (that) he had (always) loved her. [past perfect]
I have (always) loved her	
I loved her.	
I love her. ———————	He said (that) he loved her. [past simple]

In the absence of other information <He said he loved her.> could imply that his actual words were 'I love her.' (or 'I love you.'). Hence the bogus rule that *I loved . . .* must be reported in the past perfect. But this is often unnecessary — there is no ambiguity about the tense implied in <He said he loved her once.>

11.48 No tense changes

A	Direct speech	Present reporting verb + indirect speech
	'It *was* difficult.'	He will tell you (that) it *was* difficult.
	'My mother *doesn't like* cats.'	She says her mother *doesn't like* cats.
	'I'm *leaving* next month.'	I have told you dozens of times that I'm *leaving* next month.

B	Direct speech *Reported verbs are 'distant'*	Past reporting verb + indirect speech
(a)	'He *had been waiting* for ages.'	I told you he *had been waiting* for ages.
(b)	'I *could/might* (etc)/*would like to/would sooner not/ought to* (etc) get a new car.'	At that time she thought she *could/might*(etc) *would like to/would sooner not/ought to* (etc)/ get a new car.
	'He *used to* ride a bicycle.'	She told me her husband *used to* ride a bicycle.
(c)	'I wish I *knew* what to do.'	She told me she wished *she knew* what to do.
	'I wish I *had said* nothing.'	He wished he *had said* nothing.
(d)	'I *would go* if Amanda *wanted* me to.'	Julian said *he would go* if Amanda *wanted* him to.
	'I *would be* happy if *she were* here.'	He said he *would* be happy if *she were* there.
	'I wish she *hadn't gone*.'	He said he wished she *hadn't gone*.
(e)	'He *must* be ill.'	She thought he *must* be ill.
	'He *must have forgotten*.'	They said he *must have forgotten*.
	'He *must* repay the money.'	She said he *must* repay the money.
	'You *must* have dinner with us.'	They said we *must* have dinner with them.
	'I *must* get some new clothes.'	She said she *must* get some new clothes.
	'*Must* you really sell your car?'	I asked (him) if he really *had to* sell his car.
(f)	'You *needn't* repay me.'	She said he *needn't* repay her.
	'*Need* I make a speech?'	He asked if he *need* make a speech.

Tenses are not normally changed when:

A the report*ing* verb is present (or 'future'), because in this case the time context is more or less the same for the original speaker and the reporter.

B the report*ed* verbs are 'distant' in some way; this category includes
(a) past perfect, both simple or progressive.
(b) the 'past' modals (*could, might, would, should*) including *would rather, would sooner*; also *used to, ought to, had better*;
(c) verbs after *wish* (which are never present tense);
(d) both parts of sentences of *imaginary or past conditions*. The indirect
     <Julian said he would go if Amanda wanted him to go.> may
report either 'I'll go if she wants me to.' or 'I'd go if she wanted me to.'
But the indirect
     <Julian said he would have gone if she had wanted him to.>
strictly represents only 'I'd have gone if she wanted me to.'
However, since the reporter *now*, with hindsight, may know that
Julian in fact did not go, this could represent the reporter's gloss on
the more open, but at the time not impossible 'I'd go if she wanted me
to.';

(e) *must* (and *must have*) as *deduction* remain unchanged. *Must* as *obligation* usually relates to obligation imposed by the speaker, and therefore when we report what the speaker says *must* can usually remain unchanged. We merely report that 'X said that Y (or X himself) must do something.' However if we feel that there was some sort of external obligation in the original circumstances, or we wish to report that the obligation was actually fulfilled, then we can use *had to* — though *must* is still possible. Questions with *must*, on the other hand, ask about the addressee's (not the speaker's) imposing of obligation. When this is reported in statement form the obligation becomes external to the original speaker, and *had to* is likely. *Mustn't* — the obligation not to do something — normally remains unchanged;
(f) modal *needn't* and questions with *need* can remain unchanged. Of course, in a looser kind of reporting, variants of regular *need to* (*we didn't need to/if we needed to*) and variants of *had to* (*didn't have to*, *had got to* etc) are possible.

Cleft sentences

11.49
ADV

The so-called cleft structure is used to emphasise a particular part of a sentence. The sentence often begins with an introductory [*It* + BE], and the result is a complex (two finite verb) sentence.
For example, the simple sentence:
<Her husband used to ride a bicycle to the shops on Saturdays.>
can produce the following cleft sentences:

It was *her husband* that/who used to ride a bicycle to the shops on Saturdays.	
It was *a bicycle* that her husband used to ride to the shops on Saturdays.	
It was *to the shops* that her husband used to ride a bicycle on Saturdays.	(1)
It was *on Saturdays* that her husband used to ride a bicycle to the shops.	(2)
It was *because he wanted exercise* that her husband . . .	(3)

The second clauses of such sentences are difficult to classify. In their use of *that* and some *wh*-words they resemble nominal or relative clauses, and structurally they appear superficially like relative clauses. But in fact they are not, as is clear from (1) and (2) above, where the antecedent is a prepositional phrase, or from (3) where it is an adverbial clause.

11.50 Pseudo-cleft

ADV

What	he wanted you need	was is	exercise. a bicycle.	(1)
Exercise		is	what he needed.	(2)
What	he did ←→ I'm doing ←→	was ←→ is ←→	(to) ride a bicycle. [Note infinitive] buying a bicycle.	(3)

The term pseudo-cleft is used for a similar structure that also divides a simple sentence and puts emphasis on a particular part. The typical sentence begins with a *what*- clause followed by BE (1), but the *wh*-clause can also follow BE (2). If DO is used in the *wh*-clause (3), then the focus can be on the verb or predicate. The verb is usually an infinitive, though the *-ing* form is possible, to balance *doing*. These *wh*-clauses are straightforward nominal relative clauses.

Notice that DO stands for dynamic, rather than stative verbs in this kind of structure: <*What she did was know>.

Comment clauses

11.51

A	He's had a lot of difficulties, *you see*.
B	He's done very well, *considering all the difficulties*. *To put it another way*, he's really persevered. *All things considered*, he's done very well. *Speaking from memory*, hasn't he got a rich aunt?

Comment clauses are clauses which, like sentence adverbials, are not an integral part of the sentence, but indicate the speaker's/writer's attitude to the action or event, or add a comment upon its truth.

A Typical finite comment clauses include: *you know, you see, I'm afraid, as I said, as you know*.

B Non-finite comment clauses include participle and *to*-infinitive clauses. Notice how they break the 'rule' about not allowing unattached participles (11.26).

Comment clauses are sometimes classified as a sub-division of adverbial clauses — but finite comment clauses (with no introductory conjunction) are similar to main clauses followed by a *that*-clause. Compare:

<He's done very well, *I think*.> [comment clause]
<*I think* (that) he's done very well.> [main clause]

The term 'verbless comment clause' is not normally used for a single commenting adverb: <*Frankly*, he's done well.>

(See 9.34 — sentence adverbs.)

12. SUBSTITUTION AND ELLIPSIS

12.1 What is substitution? What is ellipsis?

ADV   In complex sentences — and in more extended language across sentences — we may wish to mention parts of the utterance, without repeating all the words. Substitution and ellipsis are formal grammatical devices which help to avoid such repetition.

Substitution entails the use of *pro-forms*, (pronouns and so on) that stand for other words.

Ellipsis means omission.

The two processes are closely connected, and ellipsis has been described as 'substitution by ZERO'. According to strict definition, the omission of words is only to be considered ellipsis when the words omitted are 'uniquely recoverable'. That is, there is no uncertainty about which words have been omitted. This means that, for example, subordinate non-finite clauses with no conjunction, eg <*Sitting in the garden,* Tom fell asleep.>, do not illustrate ellipsis, or at any rate only weak ellipsis, since one could 'recover' several possible conjunctions (*when? while?. . .*). But missing words that are clearly recoverable from the text, even though a different inflection may be required, are classified as ellipsis:

> <Tom often *sits* in the garden and Susan may __ tomorrow.> [ie sit in the garden]

Ellipsis and substitution operate in:

(a) the noun phrase (12.2), (b) the verb phrase and (c) clauses. Within the verb phrase, there are two different types of ellipsis:

1 Ellipsis of the *lexical verb*. Since this ellipsis starts from the right of the verb phrase, the ellipsis may extend to all or part of the *predicate* (12.3-4).

2 Ellipsis of *auxiliary or modals*. This is ellipsis starting from the left, so the *subject* may also be ellipted (12.6).

Some combinations of both types of verbal ellipsis are possible in compound sentences with co-ordinate clauses.

Noun phrase

12.2

A   Tom has bought some garden chairs.
Now *he/Tom* doesn't like *them/the chairs.*
I like *them/the chairs* — do *you?* [reference only]
Tom says *he* (*Tom) doesn't like the chairs.
Although *Tom* chose the chairs, *he* (*Tom) doesn't like *them.*
Although *he* chose them, *he/Tom* doesn't like them.
He/Tom doesn't like the chairs, although *he* (*Tom) chose them.

B   'Have you any red garden chairs?'
No, sorry. We've sold *the last one(s)./the ones we had.*
We've got *a nice green one/ (some) blue ones with arms/these yellow ones.*

C	'Steak and chips, please.' '(The) same again for me.' I thought the steak was bad, and Tom thought the same.
D	If these are your garden chairs, where are my two?/the two I bought/those you told me about? I like these chairs. Have you any more? I need six. I'll take the blue (ones)/the cheapest (ones).

Pronouns, as the name implies, are often used in place of nouns or noun phrases, and most of the pronouns in chapter 3 can be so used. But there is a distinction between *reference*, which is a semantic phenomenon, and *substitution*, which is strictly a grammatical device — the substitution of words for other words. Contrast:
<He's bought some chairs, but he doesn't like *them*.> [reference to the same actual chairs in the 'real world']
<We've sold our last *ones*.> [substitution for the word *chairs*]

A **Personal pronouns** 3rd person pronouns (*he, him, she, it,* etc) are common substitutes for the noun phrase, but 1st and 2nd person pronouns usually refer directly to people outside the text.

With co-ordinate clauses, or where there is a reference back across a sentence to the previous sentence, there is usually the choice of using a pro-form or repeating the noun phrase. But with subordination, substitution is necessary and repetition of the NP is unacceptable.

B **one/ones** As a strict word substitute, *one* has plural *ones*. *One/ones* substitute for the head of the noun phrase (eg *garden chairs*) but not for the entire phrase. In fact *one/ones* in this usage must have some new specification:
<We have green ones.> but not <*We have ones.>
Contrast *one* and *some* as indefinite pronouns, implying complete identity with the whole noun phrase:
<'Have you any red garden chairs?' 'I think we have *one/some*.'>

C **the same** can be substituted for a whole NP, including a nominal clause as reported speech.

D **Part of noun phrase** When ellipsis occurs inside the noun phrase, it is typically the head that is omitted, leaving various determiners: <my two> <any more> etc.
However, only certain determiners can function as the head — in fact only those that double as pronouns — eg demonstratives (*those*) and numerals (*six*), but not articles, not plain *my, your,* etc, so perhaps these are cases of substitution rather than ellipsis. Adjectives also do not usually end an elliptic NP, though superlatives and adjectives of colour and nationality sometimes can: <the cheapest> <the blue>. But <*I want some cheap modern garden chairs and I can only find old-fashioned expensive.>

Total ellipsis of a subject NP (not substitution) can occur in the second of two co-ordinate clauses, with or without other ellipsis — see 12.6. For total object ellipsis — see 12.5.
For *the former/the latter* — see 8.13.

265

Verb phrase (and predicate)

12.3

A	'Has Tom arrived?' 'No, he *hasn't.*'	(1)
	I'll wait if you *will.*	(2)
	'He could have been delayed, *couldn't* he?' 'Yes, he *could have been.*/he *could have.*/he *could.*'	(3)
B	I thought he wouldn't telephone, but he *did.*	(4)
	Tom's bought some new garden chairs, and we *have (done)* too.	(5)
	Oh, *have you?* [*Have you done?]	(6)
	Tom *works in the garden at the weekends,* and Susan *does* too.	(7)
	Tom *works in the garden* at the weekends, but Susan only *does* on Sundays.	(8)
C	He advised me to work in the garden and I *shall*/I *shall do*/I *shall do so.*	(9)
	Tom sits in the garden more than Susan *does.*	(10)
	He's going to build a swimming pool. I wish we *could (do so).*	(11)
	Susan helped him, because she felt it her duty *to (do so).*	(12)
	While *doing so,* she hurt her back.	(13)
D	Tom works in the garden. So *does* Susan.	(14)
	He's bought some garden chairs. So *have* we.	
E	Tom's bought some new chairs. So he *has!*	
	He looks very like Susan. So he *does!*	(15)

A Ellipsis of the lexical verb means that the auxiliaries, or even the first of them only, can stand for the whole verb group. (1-3)

B In the case of simple past or present verbs in affirmative statements, nothing would remain if the lexical verb were ellipted, so instead of ellipsis we have DO-substitution (4). Where there are auxiliaries, there are two possibilities: either ellipsis of the lexical verb (ie leaving the auxiliaries alone) or DO-substitution [auxiliaries + DO]. The addition of DO is commoner in British English than in American English (5) but it is not always possible (6).

All or only part of the predicate may be represented by the ellipsis or DO-substitution (7 and 8).

C DO *so* is a variant of DO. Usually it is a free variant (9), but DO *so* cannot appear in comparative clauses after *as/than* (10). In some cases only DO *so* (not *do*) is possible. (11, 12, 13). One explanation offered for this puzzling fact is that DO *so* is essential where the substitution contains 'no element of contrast'. DO *so* is often more acceptable than plain *do* as a substitute for non-finite verbs (12 and 13).

D [*So* + operator + subject] Substitution or ellipsis is common in responses which add a new subject (ie new information). *So* comes first and operator and subject are inverted (14). Notice that the corresponding negative response — after a negative sentence — is: *Neither/Nor* does Susan. (See (9.39))

E [*So* + subject + operator] A different response, without inversion, roughly means — 'Now you say so, I see that that is true.' There is no negative equivalent.

12.4 Summary

To sum up, this type of ellipsis and substitution (often involving ellipsis of all or part of the predicate) is seen in:

co-ordinate clauses — 4, 5, 7, 8 <I thought he wouldn't telephone, but he *did*>.

subordinate adverbial clauses (finite) — 2 <if you *will*>

question-tags — 3 <*couldn't* he?>

answers to *yes/no* questions — 1 <he *hasn't*>

response questions — 6 <*Have you?*>

additions (with inversion) — 14 <So *does* Susan>

agreement (without inversion) — 15 <So he *has*>.

12.5 Other elements of the predicate: ellipsis

Tom is fond of gardening, but she isn't __	(1)
He looks __, but she really *is*, friendly.	(2)
She enjoys sitting in __, and looking at, the garden.	(3)
Tom has made __, but his wife has vetoed, some more plans for the garden.	(4)
'Has Tom made any more plans?' 'Yes, he has __./He has made some __.' (*He has made.)	(5)

Ellipsis of other elements of the predicate can occur without ellipsis in the verb itself (as in 12.4). The results are usually rather formal, except with the ellipsis of adjectival complements after BE and other linking verbs, which is common in either the first or second clause. (1 and 2).

Complete noun phrases can be ellipted after prepositions, but only in the first clause (3).

Ellipsis of an NP functioning as an object shared by two clauses is also possible. Again, it is the first clause that shows the ellipsis, thus preserving the total [S + V + O] pattern of sentences containing transitive verbs (4).

The object alone can never be ellipted across sentences (5).

Verb phrase (and subject)

12.6

A	Tom has cleaned and __ polished the car. [S and Op]	
	He is 65, so __ (is) eligible. [S and optionally BE]	
	He often works in the garden, but __ probably won't be home in time this evening. [S only]	
B	'What are you doing?' '*Thinking*.'	(1)
	'What do you want?' '*Garden chairs*.'	(2)
	'Where's Susan?' '*In the garden*.'	(3)
	'Who's cleaned the car?' '*Tom* (has).'	(4)

A Ellipsis of the auxiliary or modal is often accompanied by ellipsis of the subject in the second clause of a co-ordinate sentence. The subject may also be ellipted alone. This kind of ellipsis does not happen when two clauses are in main-subordinate relation <*Tom likes working in the garden, although __ prefers sitting in it.>

B Across sentences, ellipsis of both subject and verb (or operator) is common in answer to *wh*-questions, except of course when the *wh*-word is subject and a subject is needed in the answer. (4)

Clauses: substitution

12.7

A 'We're going to have a very cold winter.'	
Oh I hope *not*. Who says *so*?	(1)
How do you know __? How can they tell __? Somebody ought to ask __.	(2)
'Did they keep weather records in 1800?' 'I *don't* think *so*. I think *not*.'	(3)
It appears *so*. It appears *not*.	(4)
B 'The forecast says it's going to be hot tomorrow.'	
If so, I shall go swimming.	(5)
If not, I shall stay home and write letters.	(6)
C *It's* lovely weather for ducks.	
Perhaps *so*, but I'm not a duck.	(7)
'Oh you don't like rain?' 'Certainly *not*.'	(8)
D Somebody telephoned you, but I'm not sure *who*.	(9)
E 'It's a good idea to ask for the name and address.'	
I always used *to*.	(10)
I always forget *to*.	(11)

Although DO and DO *so* are often substituted for a whole predicate, they never stand for a whole clause (ie they do not include the subject). But *so* can be a pro-form for a whole clause, and this is the only case where *so* has a negative equivalent — *not*.

So and *not* are used as pro-forms in:

A **Reported statement clauses** (ie noun clauses as direct object) after:
- *assume, believe, expect, fear, guess, hope, imagine, presume, say, suppose, think, trust, understand; be afraid.* (1)

   They are not used after *ask, know, tell* which can often in fact ellipt a clause altogether. (2)
- *believe, expect, imagine, suppose, think* have alternative structures in the negative. They can use transferred negation (11.39): <I don't believe so.> or <I believe not.> (3)
- It *appears, seems* (4). But <*It looks so/not.>

B **Conditional** In conditional clauses, mainly beginning with *if, so* or *not* can stand for a whole preceding clause. (5 & 6).

C **Clauses of possibility/certainty** Short comments, expressing the speaker's attitude to the previous speaker's remark, can take *so* or *not* as shown:

   maybe, perhaps, possibly + *so* (7)
   apparently, certainly, obviously, perhaps, probably, surely, of course + *not* (8).

D **Wh-words** In reporting a *wh*-clause, the whole clause after the *wh*-word can be ellipted (9). Compare an ellipted *wh*-question as response: <'Somebody telephoned you.' 'Who?'> <'I've just received a cable.' 'Who from?'>

E **To** In complex verbal groups *to* can stand for the rest of the clause.

   For *this/that* with clausal reference — see 3.11.
   For *it* with clausal reference — see 3.30.

Ellipsis in informal speech

12.8

Oh well, can't be helped. [*it*]
Nothing the matter, I hope. [*There is*]
Sorry about that. [*I am*]
Think so. [*I*]
Coming? [*Are you* . . .]
Need any help? [*Do you* . . .]
Think of us, won't you? [*You will* . . .]

Most ellipsis and substitution, whether within complex sentences, or across sentences, is related to context. Words can be ellipted or pro-forms used because the words are somewhere in the context. There is also a minor type of ellipsis in simple sentences, where the missing words are 'recoverable' from the situation. Such ellipsis is mainly ellipsis of subject and auxiliary/modal. The missing subject is sometimes impersonal *it* or *there*. Otherwise, in statements and offers, ellipsis of the speaker is understood, while in questions (compare imperatives) we understand the person spoken to.

Headline English

12.9

Teachers to call half-day strikes	(1)
Six hurt in youth club stabbing	(2)
Print Kit Bingo Gang hit jackpot	(3)
Volcano Alert	(4)
Family of Four Die in Crash	(5)

The language of newspaper headlines often involves the ellipsis of auxiliary verbs (or BE); and in addition omission of articles: 'Teachers *are going* to call . . .' (1), 'There is/has been an alert . . .' (4).

Notice also the omission of a general noun 'six *people* hurt' (2). But this kind of language also involves grammatical features unrelated to ellipsis as such, though concerned with compressing the information. For example:

- *long strings of nouns* — A gang of people who went around playing *bingo* and had their own *printing kit (3)*.
- *simple present tenses* for past or present perfect — A family *has* died (5).
- *special vocabulary* Headlines often also use special vocabulary — usually short words that are not used much in other contexts eg *bid* [attempt] as in <Cliff Drama Rescue Bid>, *probe* [investigation] as in <Americans launch new space probe>, *quit* [resign, leave] as in <Three Top Directors Quit>.

Appendix 1
The sounds of English

The pronunciation of English is best shown by a phonetic alphabet, because there are more sounds than letters, and because the letters are far from consistent with the sounds.

Consonants are grouped according to the way in which they are made (stop, fricative, etc). They are also grouped into voiced sounds (made with the vocal cords vibrating) and voiceless sounds (made without the vocal cords vibrating).

Vowels are divided into (1) simple vowels and (2) diphthongs, in which one vowel sound glides into another. Some vowels tend to be longer than others and these are marked with /:/, but the distinction between long and short vowels is not absolute. All English vowels are voiced.

Consonants

Voiceless		**Voiced**	
stops			
p	pat, rope	b	bat, robe
t	two, bent	d	do, bend
k	came, back	g	game, bag
affricates			
tʃ	church	dʒ	judge
fricatives			
f	fine, safe	v	vine, save
ө	thanks, teeth	ð	they, teethe
s	sink, rice	z	zinc, rise
ʃ	show, wish	ʒ	measure, prestige
h	hat		
nasals			
		m	me, whim
		n	knee, win
		ŋ	wing
lateral			
		l	low, will
gliding			
		j	yes, __ unit
		w	why, wet
		r	road

The term 'sibilant' is used to describe the 'hissing' sounds: s, z, ʃ, ʒ, tʃ, dʒ.

Vowels

Simple vowels

i: beat, seen, complete, piece, receive, key, people, machine

ɪ bit, pretty, village, marriage, wicked, business, build, women

e bet, head, many, said, friend

æ bat, plait

ɑ: car, father, laugh, heart, half

ɒ hot, what, cough, because, knowledge

ɔ: cord, caught, all, saw, pour, thought

ʊ put, foot, good, could, woman

u: do, food, rude, through, true

ʌ cup, money, does, blood, young

ɜ: fern, turn, earth, world, bird, journey

ə mother, about, doctor

Diphthongs

eɪ day, take, wait, great, weight, they, atheist

aɪ high, height, hide, find, cry, buy, I, eye

ɔɪ boy, buoy, coin

əʊ oh, no, low, home, load, toe, sew

aʊ how, house, plough

ɪə ear, here, beer, pier, idea, really, weir

eə air, heir, fare, wear, rarely, there

ʊə tour, cure, who're

Appendix 2
Stress, rhythm and intonation

Stress

Every English word has its own stress pattern, ie, one of its syllables is more prominent than the other(s). For example:

house, hostel, hotel
complement, complete, complementary

In normal connected spoken English, words belonging to major word classes (nouns, verbs etc) tend to be stressed, while minor word classes (pronouns, articles etc) are usually unstressed. Note that some people prefer the term 'accent' to 'stress', and speak rather of accented and unaccented syllables.

Rhythm

The term 'rhythm' refers to the timing of the stressed syllables. In any typical stretch of spoken English, the stressed and unstressed syllables occur randomly:

When will you be having tea, Tom?

However there is a strong tendency to time the stressed syllables evenly — and to speed up the unstressed ones to fit this rhythm. This regular timing of stressed syllables is called stress-timed rhythm. Other languages like French, Spanish, Italian and many Indian and African languages have syllable-timed rhythm, in which the regular timing is based on the number of syllables, irrespective of stress. (Those who prefer the term 'accent' to 'stress' consequently call English 'accent-timed'.)

Intonation

Intonation is the meaningful use of pitch (the rises and falls in the level of the voice). In the so-called tone languages (eg Chinese, Thai, Hausa) pitch change is part of the intrinsic pronunciation of individual words. But in English, pitch changes belong to 'utterances' — possibly a whole sentence or a single word, but typically a group of words within a sentence. Each such utterance, with its own pitch change, is called a tone unit or a tone group. The example under rhythm would normally be spoken as a single tone unit, or possibly as two units with a separate unit for Tom. But the example below would probably be divided into six tone units:

/The cost of living is supposed to be coming down/ but look/bread's gone up/ and tea/oh/ at least coffee's still the same price/.

A tone unit (like the first one here) often contains several stressed syllables and is itself spoken on a gradually rising or falling tune, but by definition it only contains one significant pitch change or tone. (Do not confuse the terms 'tune' for the whole pattern of the tone unit, and 'tone', the significant pitch change.) The tone usually occurs on the last stressed syllable of the unit (called the tonic or nuclear syllable).

This is neutral intonation, but the intonation may be marked for contrast or emphasis etc:

/When will *you* be having tea, Tom?/ [contrasted with some other person]

/The cost of living is sup*posed* to be coming down./ [but it isn't really!]

The tones of English are variously analysed. The commonest tones are: *high fall* / ` /, characteristic of statements, commands and *wh*-questions (where only one item and not the whole proposition is in question); *high rise* / ´ /, commonly used for open (yes/no) questions; *low rise* / ˌ /, typical of unfinished utterances, or following a high fall for a subsidiary piece of information; *fall rise* / ˇ /, sometimes spoken on a single word or syllable, but often divided over an utterance, and used to express an implication not explicitly stated in the words; *rise fall* / ˆ /, often used for strong assertions. Less common is the *level tone* / ‾ /, which is ignored in some analyses.

In continuous texts, tone units are often indicated by obliques -/- and the tone symbol is placed immediately before the tonic syllable:

/When will you be having ˋtea, Tom?/ or

/When will you be having ˋtea/ ˌTom?/

/The cost of living is supposed to be coming ˋdown/ but ˋlook/ ˋbread's gone up/ and ˋtea/ ˋoh/ at least ˇcoffee's still the same price./

Functions of intonation

English intonation fulfils a variety of functions. The obvious use of intonation to indicate statements, commands, questions and so on is sometimes called the communicative function. Notice — as pointed out in 1.4 — that communicative function and grammatical form do not always correspond. At the same time intonation can express a wide range of emotional attitudes both to the hearer and to the message. This attitudinal function is popularly known as 'tone of voice' ('not what he said, but the way that he said it'). Thirdly, intonation allows the speaker to vary the emphasis or focus of his message. If he says

When will ˋyou be having tea, Tom?

then some previous reference to having tea at a certain time is assumed by the speaker, whose focus of attention is now on the hearer, ie *you*.

Occasionally intonation has a strictly grammatical (or syntactic) function, so that intonation is used to mark syntactic differences. Contrast:

He came to *hear* about it. [single clause with catenative verb phrase: 'He happened to hear about it.']

He *came/* to *hear* it./ [two clauses, the second an infinitive of purpose: 'He came in order to hear it.']

Over longer stretches of speech, intonation also has a 'discourse structure' — rather like paragraphing in the written language.

Appendix 3
Spelling rules

Many words change their spelling before adding endings (-ed, -en, -er, -est, -ing, -s). The rules are fairly regular.

Rule 1   Words ending in *y*

A   **Words ending in consonant + *y***

i *y* becomes *ie* when adding *s* (for noun plural and 3rd person singular present verb):

> *cry, cries; worry, worries; mystery, mysteries*

ii *y* does not change before *i*:

> *drying, worrying, hippyish, Toryism*

iii Proper nouns do not change their *y*:

> *the Kellys, the two Mollys*

iv Compounds ending with the word *by* do not change:

> *lay-bys, stand-bys*

v *y* becomes *i* before other endings:

> *duty, dutiful; deny, deniable; happy, happily, happiness; pity, pitiful, pitiless (but piteous); mystery, mysterious; dry, dried, drier, driest, drily (but shy, shyly; sly, slyly); fly, flier*

B   **Words ending in vowel + *y* do not change**

> *boys, buys, plays, lays, pays, says; grey, greyer, greyest; player, played, playful; employ, employment etc*

but *lay, laid; pay, paid; say, said; gay, gaily; day, daily*

Rule 2   Words ending in *e*

A   **Words ending in consonant + 'silent' *e***

i drop *e* when adding a vowel:

> *create, creating, creator; love, loved, loving, lover, lovable; nice, nicer, nicest; bone, bony; fame, famous; excite, excitable; response, responsible; but likeable, mileage, sizeable*

ii Rule 2Ai does not always apply to words ending with a 'soft' -*ce*/s/ or -*ge* /dʒ/, where dropping the *e*, particularly before *a* or *o*, could affect the pronunciation and turn the *c* or *g* into a 'hard' /k/ or /g/.

> *replace, replaceable; outrage, outrageous; manage, manageable; singe, singeing /sɪndʒɪŋ/ (Contrast sing, singing/sɪŋɪŋ/)*

but *age, ageing/aging (both /eɪdʒɪŋ/); wage, waging /weɪdʒɪŋ/;*

Note *space, spacious /speɪs, speɪʃəs/*

iii do not drop *e* when adding a consonant

> *lovely, nicely, hopeless, fateful*

B   **Words ending in *ie***

i change *ie* to *y* before *i*:

> *die, dying; lie, lying*

ii do not take another *e* when adding -*ed*, -*er* or -*est*

> *died, lied*

C   **Words ending in *ee***

i do not take a third *e* when adding an ending beginning with *e*:

> *free, freer, freest; agree, agreed; oversee, overseer*

ii but retain *ee* before other endings:

> *agreeing, agreeable; see, seeing*

D   Words ending in ue

Drop *e* before ending:

argue, argument; pursue, pursuing; true, truly.

Rule 3   Doubling of consonants

i If a word ends with a single vowel letter + consonant, and the last syllable is stressed, the consonant is doubled before *-ed, -en, -er, -est, -ing, -ish, -y:*

fat, fatter, fattest; pin, pinned, pinning; refer, referred, referring; begin, beginning; red, redden, reddish; mud, muddy

ii Do not double the consonant if

a the word ends with a silent *e:*

fate, fated; pine, pined, pining

b the vowel sound is written with two letters:

heat, heated, heating; mood, moody

c the last syllable is unstressed:

offer, offered, offering

iii In words ending with a vowel and final *l* or *p*, British English normally doubles the *l* or *p*, whether the last syllable is stressed or not. American English only doubles if stressed:

traveller (Br Eng)/*traveler* (Am Eng); *kidnapped* (Br Eng)/*kidnaped* (Am Eng)

Rule 4   Adding *s*

i When adding *-s* to nouns and verbs, add *-es*, not *-s*, to words ending with a sibilant sound (unless they are written with a silent *e*), that is, to words with a final *s, z, x, ch* or *sh:*

buses, buzzes, boxes, watches, wishes

ii For nouns ending in *-o* — see chapter 2.

Appendix 4
Irregular verbs

English irregular verbs may be divided into various categories, from those whose three principal parts (base, past simple, past participle) are the same, to those which have different forms for each part.

A All three parts the same (like *shut*), all ending in *t* or *d*:

bet, bid, broadcast, burst, cast, cost, cut, hit, hurt, let, put, quit, rid, (up)set, shed, shut, spit, split, spread

B First form — base, second form — past and past participle

1 Base ends with -*t*: internal vowel changes

get, got; light, lit; meet, met; shoot, shot; sit, sat; spit, spat

2 Base ends with -*d*: internal vowel changes

a vowel changes from /i:/ to /e/

bleed, bled; breed, bred; feed, fed; (mis)lead, (mis)led; read, read, (note spelling); speed, sped

b other internal vowel changes

abide, abode; (be)hold, (be)held; bind, bound; find, found; grind, ground; wind, wound; slide, slid; (under)stand, (under)stood

3 Base ends with -*d*: changes to -*t*

bend, bent; build, built; lend, lent; send, sent; spend, spent

4 Miscellaneous bases: ending changes to /ɔ:t/

beseech, besought; bring, brought; buy, bought; catch, caught; fight, fought (Note this is an internal vowel change only, as in B2 b); seek, sought; teach, taught; think, thought

5 Miscellaneous bases: add -*t*

a internal vowel changes from /i:/ to /e/

creep, crept; deal, dealt; feel, felt; keep, kept; kneel, knelt; leap, leapt; mean, meant; sleep, slept; sweep, swept; weep, wept. Note also *leave, left*

b other vowel changes

dwell, dwelt; lose, lost

6 Miscellaneous bases: add -*d*

a sometimes with vowel change

flee, fled; hear, heard; sell, sold; tell, told; say, said /sed/

b and sometimes without

lay, laid; pay, paid

Note also *make, made*, where /k/ changes to /d/.

7 Miscellaneous bases — alternative second forms (-*ed* regular or -*t* irregular)

burn, burnt/burned; dream, dreamt/dreamed

Also: lean, learn, smell, spell, spill, spoil

8 Miscellaneous bases with endings /k/ /g/ /n/ /ŋ/: internal vowel changes to /ʌ/

stick, stuck; strike, struck [But Am Eng strike, struck, stricken]

dig, dug

win, won

cling, clung; fling, flung; hang, hung; sling, slung; spin, spun; sting, stung; swing, swung; wring, wrung

Note also *shine, shone* /ʃɒn/.

C Other verbs with two parts the same

1 One form — base and past participle; other form — past
   (be)come, (be)came, (be)come; run, ran, run
2 One form — base and past; other form — past participle
   beat, beat, beaten

D All three parts different

1 Past participle ends with -en
a Miscellaneous bases: past forms take internal /əʊ/:
participle has -en
   break, broke, broken; choose, chose, chosen; freeze, froze, frozen;
   speak, spoke, spoken; steal, stole, stolen; (a)wake, (a)woke, (a)woken;
   weave, wove, woven
b base has internal /aɪ/: past simple takes internal /əʊ/: past participle
takes internal /ɪ/ with -en ending
   drive, drove, driven; ride, rode, ridden; rise, rose, risen; strive,
   strove, striven; write, wrote, written
c others
   bite, bit, bitten; eat, ate, eaten; fall, fell, fallen; forbid, forbade,
   forbidden; (for)get, (for)got, (for)gotten; (for)give, (for)gave, (for)given;
   hide, hid, hidden; shake, shook, shaken; take, took, taken
2 Past participle ends with -n
a base vowel /eə/ changes to /ɔ:/ in past forms
   bear, bore, born(e); swear, swore, sworn; tear, tore, torn; wear, wore,
   worn
b base vowel /əʊ/ changes to /u:/ and /əʊ/
   blow, blew, blown; grow, grew, grown; know, knew, known; throw,
   threw, thrown
Note also draw, drew, drawn; fly, flew, flown
c miscellaneous
   do, did, done; go went, gone; lie, lay, lain; see, saw, seen
3 Base has ending /m/ /n/ /ŋ/ or /ŋk/ with internal vowel /ɪ/: internal
vowel changes to /æ/ and /ʌ/
   begin, began, begun; drink, drank, drunk
Also ring, shrink, sing, sink, spring, stink, swim
4 Alternative past participles, with regular -ed, making the verb
completely regular, or with irregular -n/-en
   mow, mowed, mowed/mown
Also saw, sew, show, sow; swell, swelled, swelled/swollen
5 Some verbs that are regular in British English (with -ed for past
simple and past participle) are irregular in American English
   dive, dove, dived
   prove, proved, proven

Index

References are to chapter and section.

The main grammatical terms and general subjects are entered in CAPITALS (eg ABILITY, ADVERB), with subdivisions of these in ordinary type.

Individual words and phrases are printed in *italic* type (eg *a/an*).

Only words that are grammatically important or difficult are entered. Other words, eg many verbs, must be sought in the lists given in the appropriate chapter.

For abbreviations used see page 5.